Brother Bob's War

This book is a memoir of the service of Robert D. Ekwall

By

Ralph W. Ekwall

Copyright 2006
Second Edition

About the Cover Picture

The picture shown above is also the picture on the book cover. This plane was #238201 and the crew had given it a name, "Patches." The tail number and the markings identify it as a plane assigned to the 99th Bomb Group. It is possible that Brother Bob was on board this plane in the ball turret.

Also shown in this picture are some escorting fighter planes. This group of fighters were part of a group called the Checkertails. This group was unusual in that these fighters were manned by black pilots. Those black pilots were the first, or among the first, black soldiers to fly in support of combat missions. They had an excellent combat record.

Introduction

This book is a tribute to my brother, Robert D. Ekwall. But it is more than that; it is a tribute to all of those men and women who served our nation in the Great War.

For those readers who want to review the historical context of this book, they may wish to begin by reading: "A Brief History of World War II." This history is in the Appendix. It is a brief summary of the essential details of the Second World War

Some of the material is an actual reproduction of Bob's actual words that he wrote. Most are reproduced in a word for word fashion, but in some instances I have supplied a subject of a sentence where he did not. Or, I have changed the structure of his writing slightly to make his sometimes cryptic comments more understandable.

There is a moderate amount of material on the home life and background of Bob, but that adds a critical element of humanity. Wars are fought by humans; weapons are the tools they use.

I have always disliked long introductions to books and so this one is short.

Ralph Ekwall
Omaha, Nebraska
2006

Sgt. Robert D. Ekwall

Table of Contents

<u>Chapter 1 - Early Life</u>

Robert D. Ekwall, Brother Bob, began his life on 20 October 1920. Arthur and Bessie Ingels Ekwall were his parents. Arthur and Bessie had been married for nearly three years at that time and had an older daughter, Arlene.

We can better understand the character and background of Bob by learning some background information concerning his parents. His father, Arthur, did not marry until he was 30 years old. His mother was 21 years old at the time of their marriage. Although both were from farm families they were quite different from each other.

Arthur's parents had emigrated from Sweden to America in about 1868. The story of the Ekwall immigration from Sweden is interesting in its specifics, but in generalities it is much like that of other 19th century immigrants. The first Ekwall to come to America was Swan Ekwall. Swan had been a machinist and gunsmith in a large factory in Huskvarna, Sweden. Swan was an admirer of the famous Swedish inventor, John Ericsson. Swan came to America in 1865 and planned to work for John Ericsson. During the American Civil War John Ericsson had worked for the Union side and had an important role in the construction of the famous Union iron clad vessel, the Monitor of "Monitor and Merrimac" fame. Apparently Swan had some kind of connection to John Ericsson; it may have been a letter of introduction or perhaps someone in the factory where Swan worked may have known John Ericsson. At any rate that connection, however tenuous, was the basis of Swan's motivation to go to America. Swan arrived in America in the fall of 1865 just months after the end of the Civil War. Swan failed to obtain work because John Ericsson was not hiring any new help. The United States Government had terminated all such contracts at the conclusion of the war.

Swan, seeing no opportunities in the eastern states, struck out for points west. He went to Galesburg, IL where there were a number of factories including some railroad facilities. It appears that Swan got work at once. It probably helped that he had experience in working in factories. Galesburg had a large community of Swedish immigrants. It is likely that he wrote and told the rest of his family about American because they followed him to Galesburg, IL three years later. Swan's father, Magnus, and Swan's three brothers arrived in America in 1868. The three brothers were: Ernest, Peter and John. Ernest was the father of Arthur and the grandfather of Brother Bob.

Ernest worked in Galesburg for almost 20 years. At that time all of the four brothers had married and started families. Although they had good jobs they saw possibilities of better opportunities further to the west. They were attracted by the prospect of owning land and decided to go pioneering. The spot they selected was in Fillmore County, Nebraska. By that time all of the good homestead land in central Nebraska had already been claimed. However, the railroads had received grants of land to encourage them to construct railroads. The railroad companies had land for sale at a reasonable price. The entire Ekwall clan came to Fillmore County, bought land from the railroad and started farming.

Ernest Ekwall was moderately successful at farming. He probably knew little about farming considering his background However, he apparently learned and survived. Ernest had five sons and he made good use of that help to get farm work done. One of Ernest's sons was Arthur Ekwall the father of the subject of this memoir, Robert D. Ekwall. Arthur stayed on the family farm after several of his brothers had moved away to new opportunities. Ernest Ekwall died in 1916 and Arthur took over the operation of the family farm. The next year Arthur married the daughter of family who had recently moved to a farm less than a mile from the Ekwall home place. She was Bessie Ingels, the daughter of Anson F. Ingels. Arthur's mother, Tina Ekwall had moved to nearby Shickley, Nebraska before the marriage. So, Arthur and Bessie started married life on the family farm.

Bessie's family, the Ingels family, was much different from the Ekwalls. The Ingels (and related Hawkins and Bratchers) families had been in America since the earliest settlements in Massachusetts, New York and Virginia. As years went by they gradually moved west as new land opened up for settlement. They moved from eastern Virginia to Bedford County in western Virginia and then to Campbell County in Tennessee. They later moved to Nodaway County in the Maryville, Missouri vicinity where Bessie's father was born. Later Bessie's grandfather and father moved to Hamilton, County in Nebraska. They seemed to have had itchy feet and did not stay in one area and establish themselves as permanent, long time residents. They were hill country people who kept moving west until they got out of hill country. For the most part they were farmers with an occasional horse dealer, merchant, or informal veterinarian. The Ekwall family began farming in about 1889 when they moved to Fillmore County. The Ingels, Hawkins, and Bratchers had been farming in America for several hundred years.

Bessie's father was a farmer. However, Bessie's grandfather, Alexander S. Ingels was a man of many interests. During his lifetime made his living in many different ways. He was a horse dealer, veterinarian, debater, singing school teacher and a sometime farmer. Bessie had a great uncle who was killed in a gunfight in Doniphan, Kansas. The gunfight involved Northern and Southern sympathies just before the American Civil War. Bessie's great-uncle was a Union sympathizer. However, that was only an interesting footnote concerning her relatives and not typical of the family. The Ingels family were noted for a love of buying and selling. As a group they were expert at breaking and training horses. They sometimes went to western states and bought groups of unbroken horses and then broke them and trained them for use as riding horses or work horses.

The backgrounds of Arthur and Bessie were very different and their temperaments were likewise different. Arthur was an extrovert. He had a wide acquaintance of people and loved visiting with his wide circle of acquaintances. Bessie was more of an introvert and may have found it hard to adjust in a married life largely populated by a group of gregarious Swedish immigrants. The Ekwall families had great, extended Christmas celebrations where much of the conversation was in Swedish or a mixture of English and Swedish. Arthur spoke only a little Swedish but understood the language and when he talked to his mother at least half of the conversation was in Swedish. It must have been a difficult transition for Bessie Ekwall.

In Arthur and Bessie's family the Ekwall families were more often present than the Ingels families. There were several families of Arthur's relatives who lived within a short distance of the Ekwall home place and that made visiting easy. Bessie's relatives later moved to southeast Nebraska and were not in close proximity. Therefore, the Ekwall children had more exposure to the Ekwall relatives and much less exposure to the Ingels relatives.

Neither Bessie nor Arthur graduated from high school. Bessie had to cut her education short because of the death of her mother when she was 15 or 16 years old. She had to stay home and become a homemaker for her father.

Though she was poorly educated, she was a very intelligent person.

Brother Bob was born in 1920. Historians generally regard this period as a time of prosperity. Arthur Ekwall was, at this time, a moderately successful farmer. He lived on the farm owned by his mother and rented some additional land.

There was, however, a serious problem in the young family. Arlene, the older of the two children, was born deaf. Her deafness was not readily apparent to two young married people who were raising their first child. Since Arlene was their first child, they were not fully aware of times when babies were expected to walk and talk. When the second child, Robert, born in 1920, began to talk at shortly after age one, Arthur and Bessie began to be aware that Arlene was not normal in all respects. It took some time before they fully realized that Arlene was deaf.

This was a serious problem for a farm family that lived a long way from any city that offered schooling to deaf children. The local rural school, in Martland, Nebraska had no teacher trained to teach deaf children. It was a disturbing problem for Arthur and Bessie Ekwall.

There was a school for deaf children in Lincoln, Nebraska but it was 70 miles away. Commuting was out of the question in that time of slow and difficult transportation. They could conceive of no other choice but to move to Lincoln so that Arlene could attend school. Arthur and Bessie made the very serious decision to move to Lincoln, Nebraska so that Arlene could attend the school that taught deaf children. By the time the family moved to Lincoln, they had two more children - Norma and Richard. This was a major change for Arthur who had known only the farm and had only done farm work. However, he found employment in Lincoln. One of his jobs was with the Park Department. It was a job that had some similarities to the farm work that he had done before.

The Arthur Ekwall family lived in Lincoln for three years. Arthur was not happy or comfortable living in a city and wanted to go back to the farm. Arthur and Bessie learned that there was a resident school in Omaha for deaf children, The Nebraska School for the Deaf. In 1929 they moved back to the family farm in Fillmore County, Nebraska. During the school year, Arlene lived at and attended the School for the Deaf in Omaha and returned home during the summers.

Although Arthur Ekwall was more satisfied to be back on the farm, there were other problems that affected the Ekwall family. While the period of the 1920s had generally been a good period for everyone in America, the period of the 1930s was not a good period and it was a particularly bad period for the farmers of America. The 1930s were the years of the great drought in Middle America. Middle American farmers were hit with a double hardship: drought and depression. The Ekwalls, along with the rest of the Middle Western farmers, struggled to get by. The Ekwall family had grown and added two mouths to be fed. Now there were six children: Arlene, Robert, Norma, Richard, Ralph and Eldon Edward.

Robert attended a rural school in Martland, Nebraska. The Ekwall farm was less than a mile from the small village of Martland. Brother Bob and the rest of the Ekwall children got to school by walking the half mile across farm fields to the Martland School. At a later time the population declined to zero so that Martland disappeared from the map. At the time Brother Bob attended school in Martland there were several businesses in Martland: a train depot, a garage, a blacksmith shop, a grain elevator, a general store, a United Brethren Church, a community hall, and the Martland School.

The Ekwall family was very much centered on Martland. Arthur Ekwall sold his grain at the Martland elevator, bought groceries and got his mail at the Martland Store and his children went to Martland School. The family faithfully attended the United Brethren Church in Martland. This denomination later merged with the Methodist Church. The Ekwall family was very active in church affairs. They rarely failed to be in Sunday school and church on Sunday morning. Other members of the Ekwall family were prominent in church work. Arthur's cousin, John W. Ekwall was a prominent Methodist minister in Nebraska churches. In later years Brother Bob's sister, Norma Ekwall Harris and her husband Dr. George Harris were missionaries in West Africa. Brother Bob was strongly committed to the church and was active in church work. He especially liked to work with young people.

The Martland School was not like the ordinary one room eight grade country school. It was a two room ten grade school. There were two teachers. One teacher taught the elementary children from grades one to six. (There was no kindergarten.) The other teacher taught grades seven through ten. Total enrollment was about 40 students in the whole school. In earlier times the enrollment had been greater and the number gradually decreased.

The elementary teacher sometimes was a high school graduate who had a high school level course called "Normal Training." It was a high school course designed to train students to teach in rural schools. Sometimes the teacher of the first six grades had a few college hours - maybe 6 hours of college courses earned in a single summer session. The upper grades teacher usually had two years of college. The upper grade teacher had to teach algebra and geometry - a challenge for some of the teachers.

Brother Bob did well in the Martland School. He was especially good at mathematics; he excelled in algebra and geometry. One of his teachers relied on Brother Bob to do the difficult geometry problems that were beyond the mathematical skills of that particular teacher.

There were enough boys in the upper grades for playing both baseball and softball. Brother Bob, a left hander, did well at such sports. He had a considerable amount of athletic ability, but never became a top notch athlete because of his size. He never grew taller than five foot six inches.

Brother Bob was growing up on a working farm and he did farm work for his father. Arthur, at that time, was still farming with horses and Bob learned to work horses. He did all of the hard labor required on a farm. Each day he had to milk cows help feed cows, chickens, hogs, and horses. Caring for animals is a demanding task that had to be done every day regardless of the weather. In extremely cold weather much additional attention was required. Bob did farm chores before he went to school and he did farm chores after school. There was always farm work to do. There was value in the work that Bob had to do. He developed a work ethic that stayed with him throughout his life and served him well. As Bob got older and able to do a man's work, some of the neighbors hired him to do farm work.

Essential for an understanding of Bob's character was the fact that he grew up during the Great Depression in a poor farm family. Bob, because of the shortage of money, had to practice habits of thrift and foresight. These habits served him well throughout the rest of his life. Money and jobs were hard to come by for boy growing up in the 1930s.

Bob welcomed the opportunities to do work for pay. There were not many ways for a farm boy to make money. Farmers helped each other at harvest time and no pay was involved, but sometimes farmers hired help when they had a lot of work to do that needed to be done in a hurry. Bob also did some trapping and sold the skins of skunks, rabbits, weasels and other animals to a dealer in town. There were not many opportunities to make money.

For several summers Bob worked for his Uncle Emil who lived on a farm near Lincoln, Nebraska. Uncle Emil, in addition to his farming enterprise, raised purebred collies. Bob helped with the farm work and helped do dog chores. He received some pay, but times were tough and no one could afford to pay high wages.

Bob was the oldest son in the family and his parents expected him to assume a certain degree of responsibility. He acted as a sort of mentor to the younger children. He was the one who would help a sibling struggling with a math homework assignment. As the oldest child he assumed a role much like an adult. He knew more than the younger children and could tell the younger children what the world was like. Brother Bob would take the time to teach his younger brother about the parts of a gasoline engine and then explain the function of each of the parts. He could provide information on world affairs, advice on proper behavior and coaching for athletic skills.

Bob finished going to Martland School he still had two more years of high school to complete. At that time many rural students attended only 8 grades of school. Students who lived close to the Martland School usually took advantage of the extra two years offered by the Martland School. Many of the Martland school students left school after finishing 10 grades. Bob did well in school and liked school and wanted additional education. He decided to attend Geneva High School. Geneva was about 8 miles from the Ekwall farm. That meant he had to get to and from Geneva five days every week. That was no easy thing. The Ekwall family car was not sufficiently reliable to drive to Geneva each day. For his first year in Geneva High School Brother Bob rode with another rural student, Dale Otte, who drove into Geneva each day. Brother Bob had to walk about half a mile and wait for the ride. This was not especially difficult for him. His driver was a football player so Brother Bob went out for football. He played guard and got in some playing time as a junior in Geneva High School. In his last year of high school Bob could not get a ride to Geneva High School because the driver had graduated. He had to find another way to get to Geneva. He got there by various means. For part of the time he rode a horse three miles to the John Carl farm and then rode to school with several members of the Carl family who drove to Geneva each day.

In Geneva High School Brother Bob got interested in and participated in the debate team. He had found another area where he excelled. The Geneva debate team had a very capable instructor and the team was very successful. It won a number of honors. Bob developed a speaking capability as a result of his work in debate.

Brother Bob graduated from high school in 1939. The great depression was waning but jobs were still hard to find. Bob wanted to attend college but his prospects for getting a college education were not bright. His parents were not able to provide help. Their priority was feeding their children and there was no extra money left over to help pay for Bob's college.

By a combination of fortunate circumstances, Brother Bob was able to attend college. Bob had an Aunt Edna Nielsen and Uncle Chris Nielsen who lived in Wayne, Nebraska. Edna was a sister to Arthur. To make extra money to help her family survive Edna kept a boarding house for students who attended Wayne State College. She encouraged Bob to attend college and arranged for Bob to come to live with her and help with all of work involved in running a boarding house: washing dishes, cleaning, setting tables and whatever else needed to be done. Bob also had other part-time work. In addition he was enrolled a full-time student at Wayne State College. He took pre-engineering courses and math related courses. Bob did not have a car at this time and when he came home for Christmas Vacation, he would hitchhike home and then hitchhike back to the college again.

From what we now know, Bob had no serious lady friends during the time when he was in high school nor in his college years. It is likely that he had friends of the opposite sex, but conducting serious courtships without an automobile and with very little cash was difficult. At a later time, when he was in the service, he wrote a letter home and said he had gotten a letter from Bette. He identified her as a friend from his days in college. That is all he had to say about her.

Soon after Bob started his second year in college, in 1940, Congress had passed a Selective Service Act requiring eligible young men to take one year of military training. The world situation began to intrude on Brother Bob's life and affected his plans for his future life.   Bob, on finishing his second year of college, had a decision to make. He could stay in college or get a job. Throughout his entire life Bob and his family had been poor. They had always had enough to eat and clothing sufficient to keep them warm, but times had been hard. Bob was getting tired of being poor and wanted to make some real money. He was aware, in that spring of 1941, of the war already going on in Europe. By that time The United States was beginning to rearm; it was beginning to build up its armed forces. Factories were reopening to build materials for the rearmament. The Great Depression of the 1930s was almost over. Factory and construction jobs were beginning to be available. Bob had the opportunity to get a real job that paid reasonable wages. The temptation to escape from poverty was too great for Bob. He put off his education and began to work in defense related activities. One of the jobs that he worked on was building The Naval Ammunition Depot near Hastings, Nebraska.

Not long after Bob had left college, the Japanese attacked Pearl Harbor and the United States was at war. With the beginning of the war, Congress passed a new and much more comprehensive Selective Service Act. It required all men between the ages of 18 and 45 to register for the draft. It required those drafted to serve for the rest of the war and perhaps as much as 6 months after the end of the war. Bob knew that as a 21 year old single male he would certainly be among those selected for the draft.

Bob decided to enlist in Army Air Force as an Aviation Cadet. Aviation Cadets were to be trained to pilot airplanes, either fighter planes, bombers or transport planes. To Brother Bob it must have looked like a good way to do his service in the Armed Forces. He would certainly be drafted, and if he was drafted, he would not have his choice of the type of service. It is unlikely that Bob had ever ridden in a plane when he made the decision to enlist as an Aviation Cadet. He may have been influenced by a certain degree of glamour that attached to serving in the Army Air Force. Service as an Aviation Cadet required two years of college work and a high level of physical capability. Bob met the requirements without difficulty.

He did not immediately enter the Army Air Force. The Aviation Cadet program was very popular and had more enlistees than it could use. Bob had to wait until early in1943 before he was called to duty to take Aviation Cadet training.

Chapter 2 - Entering the AAF - Training

Bob was home for Christmas in December of 1942, but he had received his orders to report in January for active duty training as an Aviation Cadet. The requirements for acceptance into the program were very strict. Aviation Cadets had to have least two years of college training. In 1941-43 college attendance was not common and this requirement eliminated many who would have like to have been in this program. This apparently was not a hard and fast rule and at later date the AAF dropped the requirement. Scoring high on an intelligence test may have enabled some candidates to qualify. The physical standards were also high. Cadets had to have good vision and had to be free of any defects that would make it impossible for them to fly airplanes. In spite of the strict requirements, the Army Air Force had a backlog of qualified men who wanted to be trained as pilots. There were several reasons for the popularity of this program. Pilots who were aces got their pictures in newspapers often with some military or civilian celebrity. The pilots did not do their fighting in muddy foxholes; their uniforms were almost always clean. The men in the Army Air Forces ate their meals in mess halls and it was warm food and the quality was superior to the C rations that the infantrymen ate. The infantrymen ate C rations and looked dirty. There was little glamour attached to the Infantry, Field Artillery or Armor branches. The Army Air Force was perhaps the most glamorous of all the services - hence it great popularity.

Brother Bob reported to an Army intake center in Salt Lake City, Utah. From there he was sent to the San Antonio, Texas Aviation Cadet Training Center for additional physical, psychological, and mental testing before entering Aviation Cadet Training.

Bob wrote home and told of his early experiences in the AAF. He experienced several assignments to KP, guard duty and began to experience military discipline. He told of meeting men from Texas and other parts of the country. It was a new experience for him and new experience for all of the men newly arrived in a military setting.

For some reason, unknown to this writer, Brother Bob did not pass all of the tests to qualify for Aviation Cadet training. In a letter to his parents his disappointment was great and obvious. He wrote that the standards were very high and noted that many others who had entered the program for Aviation Cadet Training had also failed to pass all of the tests.

He told of some whose vision was not quite up to AAF standards; he said that several had fainted while getting shots. At this late date is difficult to identify the exact reason while he failed to get into the program. One family member remembers that Bob had a problem with recurrent nose bleeds. In letters home, Bob told of an interview with a Captain Brown at which they discussed the type of training that would best suit both Bob and the Army Air Force. Bob wrote that some specialties such as meteorology required additional college level training that he could not qualify for. Although it was not clear from Bob's letters, it appeared that after he was dropped from the Aviation Cadet program, his status was same as a new recruit entering the Army Air Force.

His next step was Hondo, Texas for basic training. This was a relatively short course. At that the Army Air Force was still considered a branch of the US Arm much like other Army branches. The basic training covered the things that all Army personnel needed to know. He learned the basics of Army discipline. He certainly would have learned how to handle and care for a rifle and perhaps some other weapons.

When he completed basic training in Hondo, Texas, the AAF sent Bob to Goldsboro, North Carolina for training as an aircraft mechanic. This course was an extensive and comprehensive training in aircraft mechanics. It was six months long. Later in his Air Force career, Bob did work as an aircraft mechanic. Bob, who was mechanically inclined, probably enjoyed the technical training in aircraft mechanics. It is not entirely clear what the Army Air Force had in mind, but it was common AAF practice to train men as aircraft mechanics and then send them to gunnery school for additional training.

Bob went to Goldsboro in the first part of May and he was in aircraft mechanics school until at least into the month of October. His next stop was Buckingham Field at Fort Meyers, Florida where the AAF sent him for gunnery training. Fort Meyers is located in southwest Florida close to the Gulf of Mexico. This course lasted three and one half months and was a very intensive course. At different times the length of the course differed.

Some material adapted from (2-1)

The initial part of the gunnery training was an intensive familiarization activity to teach the gunners everything there was to know about .30 and .50 caliber machine guns. Student gunners cleaned, disassembled, and assembled machine guns repeatedly. They had to be completely expert at handling, adjusting, firing, and making machine gun repairs. They were introduced to the sights and they learned about the sighting system. The system sounds simple, but in fact was very complex. There was a sight on the front end of the machine gun much like the sight on a .22 rifle, or even an air rifle. The rear sight was different. It was circular in shape. Gunners used that circle to learn how make "leads." This meant that they had to learn to fire ahead of the target - lead the target. They learned the skills of making different leads for different situations depending on the speed, distance, and the angle of attack of an enemy fighter.

Another, very important, element of the early training was familiarization with the different types of airplanes that they might be assigned to. They had many classes in aircraft recognition - both friends and foes.. They learned about the common enemy tactics and how to react to different types of attacks. Tactics for offense and defense changed constantly. Early in the war, before the B-17 had a nose gun, the Germans developed a tactic of attacking the B-17 frontally. This was a successful tactic until American reacted by adding another machine gun to the nose of the B-17. This countered the tactic that the Germans had developed, and they then developed new tactics. Tactics were in a state of constant change.

They had to acquire a general familiarity with the planes, but they also had to learn to operate certain pieces of equipment, other than the machine guns. For example, they had to learn to operate the turrets. They learned how to get into and how to get out of the different positions and they learned how to operate the turrets and became skilled in their operation. Gunners had to learn how to use and fire from every machine gun position on the B-17. They learned how to operate all the different systems and controlled the turrets. There were other types of equipment on the B-17 that they learned to operate - systems such as hydraulic systems, electrical systems and hydraulic and pneumatic systems. There was much to learn.

An important element in gunnery training was "skeet" shooting. Hunters who hunted quail, partridge, grouse and pheasants practiced and improved their hunting skills by skeet shooting. Brother Bob did not start this training with zero knowledge as he had hunted pheasants with a shotgun in civilian life. The student gunners used the same type of shotgun that hunters used in shooting game birds. Originally, when shooting was first practiced in European countries, a servant would release a real, live pheasant or other game bird and the hunter practiced on real, live birds. However this was expensive practice and real, live birds were difficult to obtain. So, they practiced with model of a pigeon made of clay. The developed a spring loaded device that would hurl the clay pigeon into the air in somewhat the same manner as a real bird might break from cover. The clay pigeon would make a noticeable explosion when hit. (The *term clay pigeon is still used in skeet shooting.)* This system was cheaper and allowed for more practice. The Army Air Force simplified the target still more by changing the shape of the target to a disc shape. There was no real need for a target to look like a game bird. The training was still further refined by launching the disc into the air from different positions: near the ground, at shoulder level, higher levels, from the front, side etc. The targets were released from unexpected places and at unexpected times.

A common mistake among novice gunners is to aim the gun at the object as it flies through the air. This always results in a miss. By the time the shooter reacts, pulls the trigger, and the shot flies through the air, the bird, or the target, will have advanced far out of range. The novice gunner will almost always shoot behind the intended target. The secret of the accurate gunner is firing in front of where the target is flying - firing at the spot where the target will be. This is called a "lead' or it is called leading the target. The gunner must learn how much to lead. Lead more if the target is far away; lead more if the target is moving rapidly. Shorten the lead on slow moving or closer targets. They learned to consider the effect of rapid speed when both gunner and target were moving together on a parallel course. They had to learn to fire in a really complex situation, when the gunner and the target were on a parallel course but going in at an angling course was still another problem. Most of the gunners enjoyed the skeet shooting and appreciated its value in learning a needed skill, but they left practice with sore shoulders. The recoil of a 12 gauge shotgun is significant!

The Army Air Force further refined the skeet shooting by posting student gunners on the back of moving trucks and firing at moving targets. The student gunner fired at a target while in motion. This was, to some extent, similar to what a B-17 gunner would actually do in a combat situation.

The Army Air Force learned that "Skeet shooting" was an excellent method of teaching aerial gunners some of the basic skills of reacting quickly, learning how much to "lead" targets, and develop confidence in their own skills.

Achieving skill in aerial gunnery was a demanding task, and the Army Air Force developed a number of methods to train gunners. Part of the training of gunners needed to be in actual bombers. Skeet shooting was good for developing basic gunnery skills, but a gunner had to get the actual feel of firing from a bomber. One of the practice activities was to have small plane pull some sort of a target for gunners to fire at. Sometimes it was a cylindrical sleeve towed by a small plane. One conjures up a mental picture of the pilot towing the target and being edgy and uncomfortable in regard to the skills of the novice gunners who, perhaps for the first time, were firing live ammo in a live fire exercise. After the live ammo exercise was complete, instructors would count the number of holes in the target to get a measure of the student gunner's aim. The Air Force conducted many of the training exercises over the Gulf of Mexico. Spent bullets would fall harmlessly into the Gulf.

In other training activities, gunners were at their stations, with no ammunition, and then the bombers were subjected to simulated attacks by

fighter planes. There was no live ammo in these exercises. The Air Force
made every effort to provide meaningful and useful training to student
gunners. The student gunners needed the best the Air Force could provide,
because combat was not far away.

Near the end of the war, the Air Force developed some bullets that
shattered on contact with metal. Bombers and fighters engaged in actual
battle simulations that were very close to the real thing. When gunners fired
at fighters, the fighter pilot could tell when the gunners made hits. The
bullets would shatter harmlessly. This got really close to a combat situation.
However, this simulation was not a great success. Sometimes the shattering
bullets caused some damage to fighter planes. Brother Bob was long gone
from Fort Meyers before this ammunition came into use. Actual
implementation of this project came too late to have an important effect on
training American aerial gunners.

Graduation from gunnery school was an important event. One thing that
made it special was the fact that every graduate became a sergeant. Trainees
entered gunnery training at different ranks, but all graduated as sergeants.
This was an unusual circumstance. In the old Army enlisted men might be
in the Army for years before attaining the rank of sergeant. In gunnery
school it took just a few months.

Some of the following material has been adapted from: (2-2)

The next stop on Brother Bob's training schedule was advanced training
conducted at Ardmore, Oklahoma. Training at Ardmore was "operational
training" and the units were called OTUs for Operational Training Units.
Later the designation was that of Replacement Unit. At this stage of training
the Army Air Force brought together a crew of 10 men who took training
together. Later they went overseas together and fought together. The
training developed an emotional bond that carried the men helped carry
them through the stress of combat. They learned each other's strengths and
weaknesses. They knew the home town of every member of the crew.

The specific purpose of the training was to prepare the crews for making
bombing raids over enemy territory. The AAF designed the training to be
as realistic as possible. The general plan of training was to divide the
training crews into two sets of crews. Each day one set of crews had
classroom work for half a day while the ser of crews was flying. On the
other half day the situation was reversed.

On the half day that crews trained by flying, they honed and improved
basic skills and improved skills of their particular specialty. Overall, it was
a training situation that was close to what they would encounter when they
entered combat.

Pilots and co-pilots learned the art of flying in tight formations that they need to know for bombing raids. Tight formations had been developed by Air Force tacticians to maximize the defensibility of the B-17. As long as the planes kept their place in the formation, they had a greater defensive capability. If the formation fell apart, they lost much of their defensive capability. Pilots and co-pilots practiced flying in all kinds of weather so as to hone their capability of flying in bad weather and unusual or bad light conditions. Oklahoma is a windy state and provided practice in flying in unfavorable wind conditions. Some of the flying was in total darkness. Pilots learned and practiced maneuvers that they later used in combat. Another training tactic was acclimating pilots and co-pilots, and crew, to long missions- long distances and long time periods.

The bombardiers got actual practice in the use of the Norden bomb sights. They practiced dropping bombs (non-exploding) and their accuracy was later measured as ground crew members provided feedback to the bombardiers. This enabled both bombardiers and navigators to improve on succeeding missions. Pilots flew over cities so that bombardiers could get the "feel' of flying over cities. They did not drop bombs on the cities.

The navigators practiced the arts of navigation. They practiced navigation in darkness, windy weather, stormy conditions and other adverse situations. Navigators had to learn to function on their own. If, in combat situations, their plane straggled, then it was up to the individual navigator to get the plane back to the base. In formation flying there was always a lead navigator, and the formation followed the lead navigator. However, the lead navigator often asked for checks from other navigators in the formation.

Gunners practiced aerial gunnery in all sorts of conditions: bad light, high winds and other adverse weather conditions. Gunners changed positions so the waist gunner might operate as the top turret gunner. The belly gunner and the tail gunner might exchange positions. All gunners were expected to be able to operate any gun position.

Radiomen practiced their skills under a set of realistic positions. It was, for most of the radiomen, their first experience in a real world situation.

On half days in the classroom, crew members did additional work on aircraft identification, a critical skill for every crew member. It is likely that some of the instructors were AF personnel who had served overseas and had completed 50 missions. This added an extra bit of motivation. The training crews tended to pay close attention to instructors who had actually been in combat situations.

Training at Ardmore was the ultimate training in preparation for combat. Each crew member began to appreciate the importance and the contribution of every single individual. Successful training and successful missions demanded optimum performance from every crew member.

Somewhere near the first of May in 1944 Brother Bob and his fellow crew members completed the training at Ardmore, Oklahoma. Their formal training for their assignment was complete. The Army Air Force had certified that they were ready to fly in a combat situation.

The pilot of Brother Bob's crew was named Jay Weese. His name started with a W and that turned out to be a matter of some importance.

The next stop for Brother Bob was Kearney, Nebraska. The general plan was that crews who had been trained at Ardmore would pick up a B-17 there and fly it overseas. Although all the details of what happened are unclear, it appears that assignment of crews to planes was by alphabetical sequence. By the time that assignments had got down to the W's all the available planes had crews assigned to them. There was no B-17 available for assignment to LT Weese.

Thus it happened that LT Weese's crew did not fly a plane to their assignment in Europe. They went on a Liberty Ship.

Chapter 3 – Going Overseas – North Africa and Italy

Brother Bob and his crew had gone to Kearney, Nebraska to be assigned to a plane that they would fly overseas. Since there were more crews than airplanes, at that particular time, his crew was sent to a harbor near Norfolk, Virginia for transport overseas. (*Most of the following information was taken from a diary that Bob kept during that time.*)

Brother Bob noted that it was the first of May 1944. They spent two days aboard the ship prior to leaving and they were told that it would take them 20 days to get to their destination. It was not an interesting trip. Bob wrote that the ship was 401 feet long. Bob mentions the name of the ship; it was the Caleb Strong. It was named for a governor of Massachusetts during the American Revolution. It was not a name that got into many history books. There was little for the men to do and they spent their time as best they could. There were lots of card games and that went on almost endlessly with varying and constantly changing casts of card players. Many of the card games were poker games. After a long voyage the money tended to get concentrated into fewer and fewer hands.

Bob tells of reading a large number of Ellery Queen detective books and said that by the end of the voyage, he felt like a detective.

Bob noted that on his third day out he was a little bit seasick, but that problem seems to have passed without causing him any great problems.

To pass the long hours the men got together and held long "bull" sessions where they told each other about their civilian lives and interesting experiences that had happened to them. Not all the stories were certifiable as the absolute truth. Bob told a story that a man named Schmidt. This man, Schmidt, had been in the regular Army prior to the war. Schmidt had gone AWOL and had been sentenced to the disciplinary barracks and had served all but 30 days of his time. Schmidt was trying to play it safe so he could finish up his time and get out of the Army. One day they were called out for a work formation. Some of the men, not including Schmidt, decided they would not go out on the work detail. The men who were willing to work went out on the work detail. Schmidt was one of the workers. The non-workers were lined up and the guards turned a full pressure fire hose on them. It did not take long for the whole group to decide that – Yes, they did indeed want to go out on the work detail. Schmidt said that the food in the disciplinary barracks was not good. It was mostly bread and water. The old Army between wars was not good duty.

Bob met other interesting people on this trip. One was a man who was 35 years old. He was considered ancient by the young soldiers. This man suffered greatly from seasickness. He did not get over it and was sick during the entire trip. He vowed that when he got to land, he would never, never, under any circumstances get on board a ship again. He said he would stay in North Africa or Italy all the rest of his life rather than get on board a ship again.

Bob noted that many of the men on the ship were seasick for the first few days, but got over it in a few days. Bob had already had some experience with airsickness and he thought this helped him and others who had experience with airsickness.

The Caleb Strong was one ship in a very large convoy, with perhaps as many as 100 ships in the convoy. As a convoy, they had the protection of navy surface ships and, in all likelihood, submarines.

Twenty days after leaving the United States the Caleb Strong arrived at the port of Oran. Oran is on the north coast of Algeria. Spain is straight north of Oran. Oran is a port city on the north coast of Algeria. Algeria, at that time, was a French possession. Earlier in the war it had been held by the Germans, but by May of 1944 the Germans had been chased out of North Africa.

Brother Bob said that when they landed at Oran the men were loaded onto trucks and taken to a nearby facility in or near the town of Canastel, Algeria. Bob reported that the food was good there, but he had no other positive comments concerning life at Canastel. On their 2nd day there they were taken on 16 mile hike. It was probably badly needed exercise after 20 idle days aboard ship. Bob was not enthused about the return of such a strenuous activity. The officers at Canastel were Infantry officers and ran the facility according to Infantry standards.

Bob said he visited Oran twice on pass. He noted the presence of numerous MP Officers of middle rank and he had to be on his toes to be certain to salute every officer he met. Bob heard threats, or rumors, that failure to salute an officer might result in reduction in rank or a fine. He, apparently, carefully saluted everyone entitled to a salute.

Since the base was controlled by Infantry branch officers, there was a high level of hostility between Infantry and Air Force personnel. From Bob's journal it appeared that the Infantry felt the Air Force needed "shaping up." The Air Force personnel felt they had a job to do and could do it with less military spit and polish required by the Infantry.

Bob noted the presence of Arabs in and around the compound. They wore red turbans and baggy pants. Since Algeria, at that time, was a French possession He heard lots of French spoken. Oran was a port city and as such there were many people of different nationalities there. Bob said that he heard many different languages spoken in Oran. Bob was distressed by the filth on the streets and said that it made him appreciate the work of sanitation departments in his own country.

Apparently, Bob was in Canastel for only a few days. In the first part of June they were put aboard a British liner by the name of Samaria. It took them three days to get to Naples, Italy. Bob did not like the rations supplied by the British. He noted that the British meat had no salt. He listed the ingredients on the breakfast menu: liver, bread and water. Bob said that he passed on the liver and got by on the bread and water. Before leaving, Bob had the foresight to get some extra K rations and that helped him survive the British rations.

The British liner docked at Naples. The AAF personnel got off and stayed the night in quarters near the docks. The next morning they boarded onto boxcars on what Bob called a "little" train that took them to Foggia. There Bob received his assignment to the 346th Squadron of the 99th Bombardment Group. Foggia was the headquarters town for the 15th AAF. When the Allies had invaded Italy, the area around Foggia was an important objective. The Germans had built airfields in and around Foggia and when the Allied armies moved through and past Foggia they found that they could use the Foggia facilities with a minimum amount of rebuilding. This area became the new headquarters of the 15th AAF. The headquarters of the 15th AAF was at Foggia and there were some satellite airfields near Foggia. The 346th along with several other groups were stationed at the Tortorella Airfield.

At this time in June of 1944 in the Mediterranean Theater of Operations in the 15th AAF, the different elements of the AAF were as follows. The smallest combat group was a squadron. Generally speaking there were 12 bombers in a B-24 or B-17 squadron. In actual practice, fighting a war, 8 or 10 planes were actually operational. Bob was assigned to the 346th squadron. It was one of four squadrons in the 99th Bombardment Group or B.G. The other squadrons were the 347th, the 348th and the 416th squadrons. All of the squadrons in the 99th Bomb Group were B-17 squadrons. The 99th Bombardment Group was one of six bombardment groups in the 5th Wing. There were five American Bomb wings in the 15th AAF and apparently four British (RAF) wings. In addition there was a XV Fighter Command with two fighter wings – one of which had P-38 fighters and the other had P-51s. Besides the bombers and fighters, there were support services. Some of the support services flew photographic missions to measure the effectiveness of bombing raids. There was a special group called the 154th Weather Recon Squadron whose duty was to collect meteorological data for use in pilot briefings and operations planning. Not shown on the 15th AAF chart were the staff officers in each organization. Following is an explanation of the duties of different staff officers. The S1 or G1 staff officers were responsible for assigning and managing personnel. The S2 or G2 were responsible for general security functions and collecting and distributing intelligence. The S3 or G3 staff officers were responsible for planning combat operations The S4 or G4 were responsible for feeding, housing and supplying troops.

On arrival Bob had to attend some schooling and orientation sessions. He noted that the discipline was not as strict as it had been on his recent posting. He like the intermediate level of discipline and found it easy to converse with high ranking NCOs and even officers.

Brother Bob had come a long way. He had entered the Army Air Force intending to be an Aviation Cadet, but had not gotten into that program. He had gone through basic training, aircraft mechanic training and aerial gunner training. He had processed into and out of a number of Army Air Force bases. In his own life he had progressed from a farm boy to college student to a construction worker to a member of the Army Air Force. In terms of distance he had traveled to assignments in Texas, North Carolina, Florida and Oklahoma. He made additional stops for reassignment and processing. He traveled much in the United States. Then the Army Air force had loaded him onto a Liberty ship and transported him to Africa and thence3 to Italy. At the culmination of a very long process, he was about to do what head been trained to do: participate in the defense of B-17 bombers that would undertake the dangerous missions of bombing targets of great strategic importance. Bob, like so many other Allied soldiers was about to undergo the baptism of fire.

(Look in the Appendix to find an Organizational Chart of the 15th AAF).

<u>**Chapter 4 - The B-17 Flying Fortress**</u>

The Flying Fortress is arguably the most famous bomber of World War II. Some say it was the best. Apparently, it was not the most numerous; the B-24 Liberator won the numbers game by a relatively small margin. The B-24 was also an effective heavy bomber. There have been numerous comparisons between the B-17 and the other prominent American bomber, the B-24.

The Flying Fortress in the later versions was a formidable machine capable of delivering large loads of bombs to an enemy target. It could carry as much as 6000 lb of high explosive bombs- a deadly cargo.

It was equipped with thirteen 50 caliber machine guns for defensive purposes. The B-17s flew in defensive formations so as to maximize their substantial defensive firepower. There were no safe directions from which to attack a B-17. It was a durable plane and could take many flak hits and still fly home with flak holes of various sizes in strategic sections of the plane.

It could fly high and far. It could fly as high as 35,000 ft. It could fly as far 2000 miles without refueling and carry a full load of bombs. In some instances some disposable fuel tanks called, "Tokyo Tanks," were added to increase its range. It was not an especially fast plane; it was not capable of running away from an attacking fighter plane, but if it kept in formation it presented a formidable opponent to an attacker.

The B-17 bomber was developed in the period between World War I and World War II. America was in the middle of the Great Depression. From a world geo-political view America was still of an "Isolationist" mindset. In the 1930s the American government was spending only a limited amount of money on the development of new and better weapons.

There was no Air Force as such in the period between wars. The US Army controlled the development of equipment for the Army Air Force. The Army treated the Air Force as another branch such as Infantry, Field Artillery, Signal Corps and Air Force. One can speculate that the thinking and development of airplanes may have been guided by a mindset that the Army developed in World War I: how can airplanes be of assistance in winning a trench war?

However, there were some forward thinking, creative, air pioneers who publicized and experimented with new concepts. They were able to do strategic thinking and tactical thinking. They had a concept of fast planes that flew high, carried lots of bombs capable of crippling and destroying an enemy's industrial structure. They knew that America had the capability of building better bombers and better fighter planes. They could see that a whole stable of planes would be needed in the next war. Some of these pioneers had traveled to European countries and were aware of developments in Germany, France, England and the Soviet Union. They knew that America must hurry to stay even or move ahead of competing countries. Some aviation pioneers that promoted and expanded the airpower concept: Eddie Rickenbacker, Billy Mitchell, Hap Arnold, Glenn Curtiss, and Charles Lindbergh.

In 1934 the concept that evolved into the B-17 bomber was issued by the US Army. It called for the development of a multi-engine bomber. At that time there was another bomber in existence, the Martin B-10 bomber. The engineers at Boeing developed the concept of a bigger, faster plane that flew higher and faster and could be used in strategic bombing.

The Boeing bomber was initially named, or numbered, Model 299. Work began on the bomber in June of 1934 and the Boeing Company completed and flew a prototype by the following summer in 1935. Unfortunately, the first plane crashed and was destroyed in a test flight in October of 1935. Subsequent investigation proved that pilot error had caused the crash rather than a design flaw.

The United States Army Air Corps, aware that the Model 299 had crashed because of pilot error, ordered 13 more planes. By this time the plane had a new designation, the YB-17. The "Y" part of the designation indicated that the plane was an experimental model. There were some changes from the Model 299 to the YB-17. The engine size of the each of the four engines increased and there were other design changes...

By 1937 at least one Army Air Force Unit was equipped with the new B-17s. They developed and experimented with high altitude techniques and long distance bombing. The Army Air Force ordered 39 additional B-17s. These newer models of the B-17s were designated as B-17Bs. Over a period of years there were numerous models of the B-17. The B-17G bomber was the most produced and used in W

Without going into a detailed exposition of the transition from B-17-B to the B-17G and some still later models, it is most practical to explain the general nature of the revisions made to the B-17.

One of the revisions, made early in the series, was a change from 30 caliber to 50 caliber machine guns. The 30 Caliber machine guns had been effective infantry weapons. However, the 30 caliber machine gun did not have enough range for the kind of defensive fighting required of a B-17. A second consideration was that the destructive power of a 50 caliber weapon compared to that of a 30 caliber weapon. The difference in destructive power was significant. Over the years the type of weapon evolved from a 30 caliber machine gun to a mix of 30 and 50 caliber weapons to exclusive use of 50 caliber weapons.

The engines used in later series of the B-17 also went through an evolutionary process. The first engines were capable of developing 750 hp each and the second engine used could develop 930 hp. On later models the horsepower went up to 1200 hp and still later to engines capable of producing as much as 1380 hp.

The type and armament of defensive gun positions improved on the later models of B-17s. When the first B-17s entered combat, some defensive problems appeared. For example, German fighter pilots found that a weak spot of the B-17 was its vulnerability to a frontal attack. German pilots made it a standard tactic to attack the B-17 from a head-on position. The solution was to add a pair of 50 caliber machine guns under the nose of the B-17. This was sometimes called the "chin" turret. The same kind of problem led to the addition of double machine guns on the tail and the addition of a ball turret equipped with two 50 caliber machine guns. Still another new armament was the addition of a rear firing machine gun on top of the B-17. The table following shows the location of the machine guns on a B-17.

Type and number	Location
Two 50 Caliber Browning Machine Guns	Chin turret
Two 50 Caliber Browning Machine Guns	Dorsal turret
Two 50 Caliber Browning Machine Guns	Ventral ball turret
Two 50 Caliber Browning Machine Guns	Tail turret
One 50 Caliber Browning Machine Gun	Waist
One 50 Caliber Browning Machine Gun	Waist
Two 50 Caliber Browning Machine Guns	Nose
One 50 Caliber Browning Machine Gun	Top of fuselage

Total = Thirteen 50 Caliber Browning Machine Guns

For its time, the B-17 was a large airplane. From wingtip to wingtip it had a wingspan of 103 feet. From nose to tail its length was 7I was slightly over 19 feet in height. It could fly as fast as 300 MPH, but its cruising speed was in the range of 170 to 180 MPH. Its ceiling, or maximum altitude, was about 35,000 feet. The weight of an empty B-17 was about 36,000 lbs. The maximum weight it could carry was about 65,000 lbs. However, it is not likely that the regular load of a B-17 was 65,000 lbs.

There were numerous models of the B-17. As already mentioned, it started out as the model 299 and the next iteration was the B-17. There were models such as the B-17B, B-17B etc. The B-17 G was produced in the greatest numbers and it was the bomber most used in the bombing raids on Europe. The foregoing statistics on armament, length, width, height, speed and ceiling refer to the B-17G.

The range of the B-17G was listed at 2000 miles. The definition of range is the distance that an airplane can go from the time it takes off until the time it must land to refuel. The concept of range is rather complex and worth some discussion. The range figure as generally given refers to the maximum distance that a plane can go without refueling. Remember that bombing raids go from home base to target and back. Therefore the absolute maximum distance that a B-17 could go to bomb a target is 1000 miles rather than 2000 miles. The maximum range can be flown if the bomber does not have a bomb load and is able to load the maximum amount of fuel and not carry any bombs. However such a trip would be useless and dangerous. If a target was only 100 miles away, the round trip would only be 200 miles. In that case the bombers could be loaded up with a very large bomb load since they would not use a great amount of fuel flying only 200 miles. If the selected targets were farther away, then the bomb load would be lessened. At a distance of 800 or 900 miles the bomb load would have to be small. Remember that a distance of 800 miles meant a round trip of 1600 miles. High ranking officers such a colonels or generals made the target decisions... Those high ranking officers got their instructions from still higher levels. When a squadron, or a bomb group, was assigned a target, then staff officers would begin to do calculations. How far away was the target? How much fuel must each bomber carry in order to be sure that they had enough fuel to get to the target, drop their bombs, and return home? They had to work with numbers like this: empty weight of a B-17 was 36,000lbs - if loaded to the maximum the weight could be as much as 65,000 lbs. That meant that at a maximum the load of fuel and bombs could only be 29,000 lbs. On long bombing raids, a big part of those 29,000 lbs would be used for the fuel load and a smaller part would be used for bombs. On shorter bombing raids the opposite would be true - they would carry a large bomb load and a smaller fuel load. However, the above calculations would only apply in a few situations. It is unlikely that the B-17 would routinely be loaded to its maximum capacity. As a practical matter, the combined fuel and bomb load would be much less than 29,000 lbs. About 20,000 lbs might be a reasonable estimate.

Bomb load information is variable. One source mentions 6000 lbs as a typical bomb load. In Brother Bob's description of missions, he says that on one trip they carried thirty eight 100 lb fragmentation bombs, therefore 3800 lbs of bombs. Other sources mention three 1000 lb bombs or six 500 lb bombs as typical bomb loads.

A B-17 with a full load of bombs consumed more fuel than a B-17 without a load of bombs. This meant that a B-17 probably had to drop its bombs or it might not have enough fuel to return home.

There were other considerations that made the mix of fuel and bombs difficult to calculate. The bomber always had to have little more than the absolute minimum of fuel. If one engine got knocked out, then the other three engines would have to work harder and use more fuel. They needed extra fuel in such a situation. It was common for planes to be hit by flak and if a plane was hit it might start leaking fuel, and therefore it needed extra fuel for emergency situations. There were still other considerations such as headwinds, altitude and other factors.

The bottom line was that the published range of 2000 miles for a B-17 bomber did not represent the distance from home base to target. Since a bombing mission was a round trip, the absolute farthest distance would be 1000 miles. The bomb load, the extra allowance of fuel and other factors would reduce the effective range to about 1200 miles, round trip, or a distance from the target of about 600 miles.

The B-17 was noted for its durability. It could take multiple flak hits and keep on going. Some investigators and authors claim it may have been the most durable of any plane that flew in World War II. The name, "Flying Fortress," was well-chosen. Martin Caiden, in his book, (4-1) B-17: The Flying Fortress, describes the Fortress as one of the most rugged bombers ever built. He ascribes its great strength to design features such as interlocking structural elements. On the Steniwachs website, (4-2) there are excerpts from the Collings Foundation about the B-17 known as "Nine-O-Nine." They praise the ability of the B-17 to fly high and its bombing effectiveness and ability to absorb tremendous punishment while delivering crews home safely. They cite one particular example of the B-17's durability. The "Nine-O-Nine" was assigned to combat duty from February 1944 to April of 1945. During that time it dropped 562,000 lbs of bombs. It flew 140 missions without losing a single crewman.

However, the most famous of all B-17 bombers was the "Memphis Belle." It was the first heavy bomber to complete 25 combat missions over Europe without losing a single crew member. This famous bomber flew with the 8th Air Force out of bases in England. The Memphis Belle flew her missions from November 1942 until May 1943. When a crew had flown 25 missions they were allowed to return home. During the early part of the war casualty rates were high and it was difficult and very dangerous to complete 25 missions.

The Memphis Belle was a good example of the durability of the B-17. On five occasions she had engines shot out, but was able to make it back to home base even though crippled. On one mission a large part of her tail assembly was shot off, but she survived that injury and brought the crew home safely. The Memphis Belle is credited with shooting down eight enemy fighters - an extraordinary event. Most heavy bombers did not shoot down even a single enemy fighter.

The Memphis Belle was named for Colonel Robert Morgan's wartime sweetheart, Margaret Polk. After completing the 25th mission, the Memphis Belle returned to the United States and went on a public relations tour in support of the war effort. They visited 32 cities.

During the war a famous movie director, William Wyler, made a documentary about the Memphis Belle that was very popular. In more recent times, in 1990, there was another movie about the Memphis Belle.

The Memphis Belle is now in a museum in Memphis. Most of the information about the Memphis Belle is from this site.(4-3)

Another example of the durability of the B-17 is supplied by Captain Robert E. Black. He tells of flying out of North Africa in a plane called Plutocrate. The plane was used in 65 combat missions and during the course of these missions the bomber lost 22 engines, two vertical fins, one horizontal stabilizer and required the installation of a new nose. Captain Black said that the Plutocrate, "never let us down." Captain Black was awarded the DFC, the Distinguished Flying Cross. (Information from (4-4)

Brother Bob had some experiences that illustrated the durability of the B-17. On his first trip, which was not counted as a mission, one engine failed and the ship came home on three engines. On his next mission he says," got four or five holes in the ship - one in nose Plexiglas and several in wing and tail. None were bigger than a silver dollar."

In another early flight he says, " We only got a couple of small holes." In another mission he says, " We got about 15 or 20 holes the size of a quarter." In still another mission," we had a big hole in the rudder; rudder wouldn't work on landing brake only worked and so left plane standing on the edge of the runway." The next day they could not fly because the plane was so seriously damaged. Brother Bob says his good buddy, McGee, was on a mission where two engines were shot out and the oil system was no longer functional. They were flying over the Adriatic Sea at the time and considered ditching in the Adriatic. However, the crew threw guns, radio equipment and everything possible overboard and the B-17 was able to limp into home base. On another mission the left wing was so full of flak holes that it had to be replaced. On a bombing mission to Vienna where the flak was intense, he tells of a B-17 that lost two engines and was able to limp home. On still another flight the No. 1 engine was hit and caught fire and there was a serious oil leak. Luckily, the fire died down and the ship limped home on three engines.

The previous excerpts are only a few of the examples that Brother Bob provides about the durability of the B-17. After every mission the crew would inspect the ship for damage. If there had been flak, it was likely that they would find holes in the plane.

All of the foregoing examples are evidence of the durability of the B-17, but perhaps the strongest and most convincing evidence of its durability can be found in this website. (4-5) This website has a picture of a B-17 which one can click on any part of the B-17. For example, you can click on the nose of a B-17. Then there are a set of pictures of B-17s that have managed to return to base even with great amounts of damage to the nose. There is one especially graphic and convincing picture of a B-17 with a badly shattered nose section. In fact much of the nose section had been shot away. Two of the crew members were killed, but the plane returned the remaining crew members safely. In like manner there are pictures of B-17s that survived great damage to other parts of the plane: fuselage, tail, wings, engines etc.

The B-17 was a study plane and there is a great body of evidence that supports the durability of the B-17.

The B-17 was designed to be a sturdy heavy bomber capable of delivering large loads of bombs to an enemy over a long distance. It did what it had been designed to do and probably exceeded the designers' expectations. It made a significant contribution toward winning the second World War.

Chapter 5 –Other Bombers

In addition to the B-17, there was another very important American made heavy bomber - the B-24. Insofar as speed, bomb load and range were concerned, they were similar. In wartime and post-war discussions each plane had its partisans. Generally speaking those who had flown as part of B-17 crews favored the B-17 and those who had flown in B-24s favored that plane.

From a statistical comparison of the two planes, they appear to be quite similar as shown in the chart below.

Statistical Comparison – B-17 and B-24

Quality or Characteristic	B-17	B-24
Crew Size	10	10
Empty Weight	36,000 lbs.	36,500 lbs.
Gross Weight	40,260 lbs	64,000 lbs
Max Speed	302 mph	290 mph
Cruise Speed	160 mph	215 mph
Service Ceiling	35,600 ft	28,000 ft
Range	3750 miles	2100 miles
Max Bomb Load	4-6000 lbs	5-8000 lbs
Armament MGs	11-13 50 cal. MGs	10 -50cal.
Number Built	12,800	18,000

A review of the qualities and statistics presented in the foregoing chart shows that the B-17 had more range than the B-24. The B-24 was the faster plane and could carry a somewhat heavier bomb load. Outwardly there was little to distinguish between the two.

The next table is a summary of the performance of the two planes. Data for both charts from (5-1)

Performance Summary of B-17 and B-24 in the European Theater

Bomber Type	Number of Sorties	Bomb Tonnage	US Aircraft Lost in Combat	Enemy Planes Claimed Destroyed
B-17	291,508	640,036	4688	6659
B-24	226,775	452,508	3626	2617

Per Plane Cost of Selected American Fighters and Bombers

Plane	Cost in 1944 Dollars	Cost in 2006 Dollars (est.)
Heavy Bombers		
B-17	$238; 329.00	$2,882,000.00
B-24	$297,627.00	$3,676,000.00
Medium Bombers		
B-25	$142,000.00	$1,920,000.00
B-26	$172,000.00	$2,120,000.00
Fighters		
P-38	$97,000.00	$1,270,000.00
P-51	$57,000.00	$870,000.00

A review of the performance of the two bombers show that B-17s flew more sorties, dropped a greater tonnage of bombs, lost more aircraft and destroyed more enemy aircraft than the B-24. America built more B-24s than B-17s but still the B-17s flew more sorties and delivered more tons of bombs. The fact that B-17s were cheaper to build is another factor in their favor.

An Air Force major at the Air Command and Staff College did a relevant study of the difference between the two bombers. Major Nanette Benitez did her study in 1997. The title of her study was, "*Why were the B-17 and B-24 produced in Parallel.*" *(5-2)*

She quotes from General Doolittle in 1944. He said that attempts to decrease the vulnerability of the B-24 to enemy fighters had reduced the capability of the B-24. He, apparently, considered a recommendation to stop production of the B-24.

As a result of his questions the AAF did a comparison study of the two planes. Here are some of the conclusions of that study group.

1. The B-17 was easier to maintain.
2. Less time was spent on modifying the B-17 than was spent on modifications of the B-24
3. When B-17s were used to fly sorties, it resulted in a 40% savings of personnel and material.
4. The number of man hours needed to produce a B-17 was less than the number of man hours needed to produce a B-24.
5. A statistical comparison showed that the B-17 had a 30% longer combat life than the B-24.

In spite of the AAF comparison study, the AAF continued to order huge numbers of both planes. They were needed for the war in Europe and the war against Japan. The Second World War was a time of great urgency and the fact that one bomber or fighter was better than another bomber or fighter was not the primary decision-making factor. Quantity won out over quality.

During World War II the Axis powers, the Americans and the Allied Nations produced many different types of airplanes. No one fighter or bomber was adequate to meet the wide range of requirements. In this chapter we will examine, briefly, some of the other bombers that other nations, both Allies and Axis, used during the war.

America produced and used several medium bombers that were widely used. Generally speaking, the medium bombers could take off from shorter runways. They required less space and smaller hangars and facilities. The medium bombers had their own niche. They were assigned missions that did not have long range requirements. They were assigned missions that did not require the big loads that the B-24s and the B-17s carried.

The table following shows the characteristics of two widely used American medium bombers.

Two Widely Used Two Engine American Bombers

Plane	Empty Weight	Max/Cruise Speed	Range	Bomb Load	Armament
B-25	19,480 lbs	272/230 mph	1350 mi.	3000 lbs.	12 50 cal. MGs
B-26	24,000 lbs	282/214 mph	1150 mi.	3000 lbs.	12 50 cal. MGs

The British had a number of bombers. One of their most important bombers was the long range Lancaster bomber. This bomber was similar to the American heavy bombers in its capabilities. It could carry 12,000 lbs. of bombs and on occasion it carried a huge 20,000 lb. "dam buster bomb." The range of the Lancaster, which flew from RAF bases in England was sufficient to cover every target in Germany, but not sufficient to cover targets in Rumania such as the Ploesti oil fields and refineries. The British lost half of their entire force of Lancasters during the course of the war. They lost 21,000 airmen in those Lancasters.

The British had another, much different, bomber called the mosquito. This bomber was very fast and had less armament than American bombers. It relied on its speed and ability to maneuver as defensive mechanisms. It had an excellent record for precision bombing. Its loss rate was one of the lowest among all Allied bombers. The mosquito bombers were often used in support roles for other heavy British bombers.

The German air force, The Luftwaffe, had no bombers comparable to the American and British heavy bombers. Since Germany was located in central Europe, it was in fairly close proximity to any possible opponent in a future war. During the inter-war period it developed good fighter planes, some of which were for use in close support of ground forces. It developed bombers with sufficient range to bomb potential foes: Britain, France and the Soviet Union.

Perhaps the most significant of the German bombers was the Junkers Ju 88 bomber. It was a two engine bomber with a range of 1450 miles – sufficient range for most potential targets. It could fly 286 miles per hour and carry a bomb load of 4000 lbs. Later models had eight 7.9mm machine guns for defensive purposes. This was one of the most important bombers that the Germans used in their air war against Britain.

The Japanese had a variety of bombers most of which were single or two engine bombers. Many of their bombers were designed to take off from aircraft carriers.

The Mitsubishi "Betty" was one of the most produced planes. It was a long range two engine bomber that could carry a bomb load of 2000 lbs. It had defensive armament of four 20 mm cannons and two 7.7mm machine guns. Its range was 2700 miles. The "Betty" had some notable deficiencies. It had very little protective armor. It had extra fuel tanks on its wings that were not self-sealing. When one of these tanks were punctured by a bullet, the entire plane was likely to explode in flames. Needless to say this plane was not popular among aircraft crews.

The nature of a possible future war in the Pacific region caused the Japanese to concentrate their aviation development in a much different manner from its Axis partners Germany and Italy. Its aviation development was likewise much different from Allied aviation development. The Japanese developed a number of carrier based planes. The Japanese had a good navy and a number of aircraft carriers. Hence, many of the Japanese planes were developed as part of their plan to build a strong navy that would dominate the entire Pacific region. They did not develop or plan to build big four engine bombers designed to heavy bomb loads to bomb large industrial targets.

A comprehensive review of all the bombers used in World War II is far beyond the scope needed for this document. During the period before the War some of the models developed for use in a possible future war did not perform well in actual combat. The answer to that problem was to define the problem and then apply a fix to the plane. Sometimes that solution worked and the revisions kept coming all through the war. For example: there were B-17Bs, up through B-17Gs during the war. Nearly every plane used in the War appeared in revised versions based on combat experience.

<u>Chapter 6 - The B-17 Crew</u>

There were ten men in the crew of a B-17. From a review of the available information, it appears that crews rarely flew short-handed. It probably happened on some occasions, but a B-17 required a crew of ten and every one of those men had an important job to do. Without a crew of ten, it could not perform to its maximum capability.

All of the crew members of the B-17 had specific skills needed to crew a bomber. Among the crew members, there were four officers and six enlisted men. The officers were usually better educated than enlisted men. They had received more training and had higher levels of skills than the enlisted men. The pilot, co-pilot, navigator and bombardier were officers.

From the standpoint of physical location and starting from the front of the plane and proceeding to the tail of the plane, the location of crew members were as follows. In the far front of the plane sat the bombardier. Part of the nose of the B-17 was clear plastic so he could look ahead and down to properly do his work. In addition to his duties as a bombardier, he operated the machine guns in the chin.

Also in the nose of the plane and located just behind the bombardier was the navigator. He too, had an additional duty of operating the chin guns when not doing his work as a navigator.

The cabin of the plane was immediately to the rear and slightly above the nose. In the cabin were the pilot, co-pilot and engineer. The pilot sat in the seat on the left side of the plane and the co-pilot sat in the right hand side. From their cabin they had the broad field of vision necessary to pilot, take-off and land the B-17.

Immediately behind the pilots was the engineer. He also operated the top turret machine guns.

About half was back to the rear was the radio operator. He also operated a single rear-facing machine gun located on the top of the B-17.

In a half or three quarter sphere on the bottom of the plane was the ball turret gunner.

Above and slightly to the rear of the ball turret were the two waist gunners - one on each side of the plane. One of the waist gunners may have had the job of armorer. The armorer did gun maintenance and activated the bombs.

Finally, at the far rear of the plane was tail gunner. He sometimes assisted the armorer. Data from (6-1)

The pilot was either a first or second lieutenant, but some were captains. Actually, all ranks up to general flew on bombing missions. For example there were squadron leaders who were higher ranking officers. Bomb group and wing commanders flew on occasion. So in addition to the lieutenants and captains who were normally the pilots, there were also majors, lieutenant-colonels and colonels that flew planes.

The co-pilot was often a second lieutenant, co-pilots who were first lieutenants were not unusual. After a co-pilot had served enough time and had enough experience he was then rated as a pilot.

Both bombardiers and navigators were officers. They were more likely to be lieutenants and slightly lower in rank than the pilot.

The crew members were, for the most part, sergeants. The men in the Army Air Force probably achieved rank more quickly than any of other services. This was especially true of those men who flew the planes. Achieving rank among those in ground crews was more difficult and about the same as the other armed services. However, rank was given to those soldiers with the most responsibility and with the highest level of skills. Flying a B-17 required a high level of responsibility and a high level of skills.

Each member of the ten man crew had a specific set of duties. Crew members had received training for these duties both in classroom and in practice settings.

The most important member of the crew was the pilot. He was responsible for piloting the plane, but he was also the commander of the plane. He had to know each member of the crew and the duties and responsibilities of each crew member. He had to be skilled pilot and as part of his duties he had to be able to fly in formation and hold his assigned spot in the formation. He had to be able to land the plane even in unfavorable weather conditions. He had to be able to land the plane if it was damaged and not operating correctly. Although the navigator was responsible for navigation, the pilot had to have a knowledge of navigation. The pilot had been through a long and demanding training program. Many of the pilots had never flown before entering the service. They had to take pre-flight training, and later flew in a small, single engine plane at first with an instructor and later, at the discretion of the instructor, he flew in solo flights. After qualifying on a small plane he learned to fly larger planes with two or four engines. It took a long time to train a pilot.

The personal qualities and characteristics of a bomber pilot were different from those required of a fighter pilot. It should be noted that pilots of heavy bombers carried a crew of ten men; they had the responsibility of bringing the crew safely home. Being a bomber pilot was not a job for risk taker. A fighter pilot might do and might be required to do very dangerous things. A fighter pilot did not have the responsibility of a ten man crew. The pilots of bombers were more conservative and less reckless than their brother fighter pilots.

The co-pilot had the same training program as the bomber pilot. Most of the co-pilots qualified as pilots after they had received some seasoning by flying some actual missions.

The navigator was a highly trained professional. Along with the pilot they made a flight plan that took into consideration factors such as cloud cover, directional headings, proposed air speed, fuel and bomb load, altitude, and alternate air fields that might be used in case of emergency. After the mission began, he constantly monitored the position of the plane. He used several navigational systems. One common system and the oldest system was called,"dead reckoning." This means that he knew where the plane started from and the direction and speed that the plane was going. By this method, he could tell where the plane was at any given time. However things like wind speed and direction made it impossible to use dead reckoning as an exact measure of position. The navigator used other methods such as celestial navigation which involved the use of sextant and a very accurate timepiece, and/or other instruments to determine position more exactly than could be achieved by "dead reckoning." During missions the navigator constantly monitored the position of the aircraft and other navigators checked their data with each other to assure correct position calculations. The ship leading the mission had a navigator on board that had overall responsibility for the navigation. A navigator needed a high aptitude for mathematical calculations. The training program for navigators was comprehensive but not as long as that required of pilots.

It was not a requirement for navigators or bombardiers to receive pilot training. However when pilots were in training, some of them "washed out," which means that they were not able to successfully complete pilot training. Some of those men who had "washed out" were sent to school to become navigators and bombardiers. Thus the pilot training program was a good source for identifying potential navigators and bombardiers.

The bombardier was in charge of dropping the bombs. It was his responsibility to release the bombs in the right place at the right time to insure maximum effectiveness. He was in charge of the essential mission: dropping bombs on the enemy. He had a top secret device to help him achieve his mission: the Norden bombsight. It was a mechanical computer with such accuracy that it could place a bomb within a radius of 100 feet from four miles high. . It was a critically important secret device and the USAAF made the utmost efforts to ensure its security. Crew members had to take an oath to protect it with their lives. The Norden bombsight had been developed by a naval engineer named Carl Norden. The bombsight combined a number of factors to achieve bombing accuracy. Here are some of the factors which the Norden bombsight used in calculating time for pressing the button that released the bombs: air speed, wind speed and direction, altitude, and angle of drift. The bombsight was also an automatic pilot. During the time that the bombs were dropped, the plane was in the hands of the bombardier and the Norden bombsight. Data on Norden bombsight is from the Air Power Museum. (6-2)

There were four officers on a crew: pilot, co-pilot, navigator and bombardier. The regular duties of the bombardier and navigator required them to man machine guns when not actively performing their principal duties. There seems to have been no fixed AAF policy in regard to gunnery training for bombardiers, navigators, pilots, and co-pilots. Sometimes they got the full training, but apparently more often they did not receive it. There were some very short orientation courses less than a week in length that some officers attended. Mainly, the officers learned gunnery skills on the job even if they had little or no training.

Although a full crew was the norm, Fourtner (6-2) tells of a bombing mission on which they had no bombardier. A sergeant was assigned as a "toggler" which meant that when the lead plane dropped their bombs, the sergeant hit the toggle switch to drop the bomb load. On subsequent missions they had a bombardier on board.

There were two other crew positions whose duties were often performed by an enlisted men. These positions were armorer and flight engineer. A gunner would do double duty as a gunner and a flight engineer, or as a gunner and an armorer.

The flight engineer monitored the engine and navigation instruments. He also kept a log of the engine functioning. The flight engineer was usually assigned to the gun position of the upper turret. Data source: (6-3)

The armorer had the duty of keeping the machine guns in working order and making necessary repairs. Gunners were responsible for ordinary cleaning and maintenance. The armorer also had some expertise about the different kinds of ammunition such as tracers, high explosive, and incendiary ammunition. The armorer helped to load the bombs in place and shackle them into position. Data from (6-3)

The radio operator was another key position on the B-17 crew. He had to be able to operate the radio equipment on the B-17. On a mission he made position reports every 30 minutes. He helped the navigator take position fixes. He maintained a position log. In some instances he acted as the photographer taking pictures to assess bomb damage. The radio man was also a gunner. Data from (6-4)

The remainder of the crew members were gunners. Those gunners who operated a turret had to have some skill in operating the turret; the guns in a turret were pointed by pointing the turret in the desired firing direction. A smaller man was often selected to be the ball turret gunner because of the restricted space in a ball turret. Data source: (6-5)

Crews had to know other members of the crew and be able to work together as a team. The USAAF knew the importance of cooperation, unity and interaction. To achieve a feeling of unity and cooperation, crews were trained together in the United States and sent overseas as a crew. When a B-17 crew flew their first mission, they were not flying with a group of strangers.

Even though crews usually flew together as a crew, they did not always fly in the same plane. Brother Bob's account of his mission usually mentions the name or number of the plane in which he flew the mission. Sometimes a crew member would be assigned to fly a mission with another crew. On other occasions a crew member might volunteer to fly with another crew. If a crew member was in a hurry to finish all of his 50 missions then he might be motivated to volunteer. On the other hand crew members might avoid, if possible, being assigned to missions hoping that the war would end before they completed their 50 missions. Following are some examples from Brother Bob but without information on whether he volunteered or assigned.

On August 10, 1944 Brother Bob says, *"I flew with Baran's crew in 286."*

On August 20, 1944 Brother Bob says, *"Flew with Blackman's crew in 570, Achtung."*

On August ?,   1944 Brother Bob says, *"Flew with Lt. Burke's crew in 064*

On August ?, 1944 Brother Bob says, *"Flew with Delp and Sibley, a mixed crew in 182."*

Brother Bob also flew with Lt. Worthington's crew several times. When Brother Bob said that he flew with Worthington's crew or Blackman's crew, he referred to the pilot. Bob referred to the plane in which he flew the mission. Some planes he identified by name and others by number.

Every crew member of a B-17 had a specific job to do that was essential to the completion of the mission. Crew members developed close relationships and some continued for many years after the war.

Chapter 7 - Early Missions

Preparing to go into combat is a profound emotional experience. The soldier had to face up to the fact that there is an enemy out there that would try to kill him. Combat was a dangerous business as Brother Bob and many, many other soldiers discovered. There is no prescribed method to prepare for that experience. Brother Bob does not tell us how he prepared for the experience. While he was in Ardmore, Oklahoma he had trained with his assigned crew and all knew one another and had learned to know and depend on each other. They had solved that part of the equation.

In one way or another Brother Bob and the crew prepared for their first mission. They must have been tense, nervous, fearful and hiding a secret panic. They probably wondered if other crew members were as concerned as they were. Bob does not share his feelings. We can only imagine what they were.

The date was 25 June 1944 and the target was Sete, France. If they flew in a straight line, they would cross over Italy and proceed over the Mediterranean Sea. Their planned route might take them over the island of Corsica. Here is Brother Bob's narrative.

"Started for southern France - turned back about 80 miles from the target. The No. 1 engines was feathered. The pilot didn't want to take a chance of getting pounced by enemy fighters. 'Stragglers die in combat.' Sure seemed like a long ride for the first time."

So it was all for nothing. Bob did not get credit for a mission. It was entered in the record books as an ERT, or early return. Bob does not say what happened to the no.1 engine. It must have been a mechanical problem because he does not mention enemy flak or damage caused by enemy fighters. He says the engine was feathered. That meant that the engine was locked in a still position. A pilot could sometimes do something about a failed engine. The best thing to do, if feasible, was to feather the engine: lock it in place. That was not always possible. Sometimes the engine was not running and the propeller would keep turning because of the wind, This condition was called "wind milling." It created a tremendous drag on the plane and caused the other engines to use more fuel.

Maybe the aborted mission was a good practice mission. The crew members did all the things that they later did on real missions. However, they probably would have liked to have had credit for the mission.

On the very next day, the 26th of June, they went on a very real and dangerous mission. Here is what Brother Bob had to say about that mission.

"We hit Vienna; the flak was heavy, intense and accurate. After the run I looked back and boy! Boo-coo flak - a regular cloud of black puffs. Got four or five holes in the ship - one in the nose Plexiglas and several in the wing and tail. None bigger than a silver dollar. I shot about 20 rounds or so at enemy fighters. I saw quite a few but out range. The Krauts shot down a B-24. The tail gunner said he saw 7 or 8 chutes; the 9th got his chute caught in the stabilizer and there was no successful landing for him.
A single bomber is no match for a German fighter - a straggler will probably die in combat."

This was Bob's first combat experience. German fighter planes attacked the B-17s as they closed on the target. Coming in to the target they were saw black puffs of smoke all around them. Those black puffs were flak. Flak was a type of German anti-aircraft defense. A German flak gun fired a fuzed shell or projectile. Inside the shell was an explosive charge and a timing device or fuze. The fuze was pre-set to explode at a certain altitude such as 25,000 feet. When the shell exploded it sent portions of the shell out in all directions and thus increased the effectiveness of the weapon. It was common practice for the crew to gather around the plane after a mission and look to see how many holes the flak had made and to see how big the holes were. Bob says they got four or five holes in the ship. In later missions there were more than that.

Bob shot about 20 rounds at enemy fighters one his first mission. Individual gunners often did not shoot a single round and might go for several missions without firing their guns. Through most of the war German fighter planes flew up to challenge the bombers. In the last few months of the war, American bomber were unchallenged by enemy fighter planes, but until nearly the last bombing raid the American bombers encountered deadly flak.

Here is what the official Air Force history has to say about the mission that Bob had just completed. The raid that he had been on was a very large raid from the criterion of number of bombers employed. This report is a 15th Air Force report.

"677 B-17s and B-24s attacked targets in Vienna, Austria area hitting an aircraft factory at Schwechat, a marshalling yard at Vienna/Floridsdorf; oil refineries at Korneuberg, Vienna/Floridsdorf, Moosebierbaum,Winterhofen and Laban. Fighters fly 260 sorties in support; an estimated 150 to 175 enemy fighters attack the formations. Nearly 30 aircraft, mostly bombers, were lost. US claims a total of 60+ enemy fighters."

Claims of enemy planes shot down are generally unreliable, but counting the number of our bombers lost was a count that the 15th AF could do with accuracy. Note that 30 planes, mostly bombers, were shot down. This was a very high loss rate for this time of the war; the rate was 4.4%. Overall, during this period of the war, the loss rate was about 2%.

Brother Bob says the flak was heavy. The Germans fiercely defended critical targets such as aircraft factories and oil refineries, and this accounted for the higher loss rates. Raids to Vienna and Ploesti were sites of aircraft factories and oil refineries. Missions to Ploesti and Vienna were dangerous and counted for double missions.

The account uses the term, sorties. A sortie is a single trip out do a mission and return. For Bob the mission to Vienna was a sortie. Bombers rarely made more than one sortie a day. A fighter plane might make several sorties in one day. They would return to base and refuel and go again on a second or third sortie.

Brother Bob mentions that one of the targets was a marshalling yard. A marshalling yard is a train yard where the Germans put trains together. In Austria they may have assembled trainloads of equipment for German soldiers fighting in the Russian front, or the trains may have carried food, fuel, ammunition, vehicles, clothing and other equipment needed by frontline soldiers. If the Allied bombers could destroy the trains and tracks, it would hurt the German war effort. Marshalling yards were common targets.

Another American, a fighter pilot named John Voll, had an interesting day on that same day - 26 June 1944. John Voll was the second highest ranked fighter pilot in the 15th AAF. The following data was used as a basis of the account of what happened to him on that day. (7-1) (7-2)

John Voll had finished his pilot training in January of 1944 and arrived in Italy in the spring of 1944 and received an assignment to the 31st Fighter Group. This group was an element of the 15th AAF and as such one of their missions was to escort 15th AAF bombers, B-17s and B-24s on raids over enemy territory.

On the mission on the 26th of June where Brother Bob was a gunner on a B-17 that bombed Vienna, John Voll was doing escort duty by flying escort in a P-51 Mustang. The record shows that 30 Me210s and 30 Bf109s attacked the formation. John Voll shot down one Me210 and one Bf109 - an extraordinary accomplishment. A good days work

Brother Bob's initiation into the world of combat was an immediate and complete immersion. On three consecutive days in June the schedule assigned him for missions. On 27 June, 1944 he went on a mission to Brod,

Yugoslavia. Here is his account of that mission.

"Flak not as heavy of the date, 6/27/44 as yesterday. Some enemy fighters were present. I took a potshot at a 109 - never got him but a P-38 was sure on his tail. He   (The German pilot) was a brave guy - he attacked middle ship in element back and below us. So far, as ball gunner, I'm the only one who has fired their guns.
Boy, I got airsick, or sick anyway. Today it was pretty bad - had orange juice and coffee running up over my Plexiglas window, but I stuck it out.

Here is what the Air Force history has to say about the raids that day. *"Around 300 bombers attacked targets in Hungary, Poland and Yugoslavia. Some B-17s bomb marshalling yards at Budapest, Hungary; B-24s hit marshalling yards in Yugoslavia and oil industry targets in Poland; 75 to 90 enemy fighters attack the formations: 3 bombers are lost; the bombers and escorting fighters claim 30+ enemy planes shot down; 90 P-51s sweep Budapest area claiming 7 fighters destroyed."*

Once again it was heavy combat for Brother Bob. Certainly there was flak and the official report says that at least 75 to 90 enemy fighters attacked the formation. It was not a good day for Brother Bob. He was airsick and vomit pervaded the small space inside the ball turret. Yet, Brother Bob kept at his assigned task. Flying in combat was a dangerous task and full of hazards.

Brother Bob tended to be thrifty with words. He stuck to factual material. He does not tell us much about how he felt about flying these missions. It would be nice to have his account of how he felt about the war and his perceptions of how the other crew members felt about the war.

How did air crew members like Brother Bob feel when mission assignments required them to go to Ploesti - probably the best defended and dreaded target. Did they get a sick feeling in the pit of their stomachs? After only a few missions, they knew the dangers of flying over Nazi Europe. They knew the hazards of enemy flak; they knew the hazards of enemy fighters; they knew the hazards of accidents, mishaps and the many things that could and often did go wrong. How did they feel about their chances of getting all the way through the rest of their missions. It must have been a discouraging prospect. The 50th mission must have seemed a nearly impossible attainment. Did they hope that the war would end before they had to complete all their missions. Did they hope for a partially disabling wound that would keep him from flying, and send him back to the states. It would indeed be nice to know these things, but we can only imagine their feelings.

On 30 June 1944 Brother Bob went on his next mission. He, says,

"Started for Blechhammer, Germany - high clouds persisted to 23,000-24,000 feet so changed target and thus went to Budapest (500 lb bombs) The flak was light, but rather accurate. We got only a couple of holes, one in flap that was pretty good size. I got airsick first part of this trip. Like to died for an hour or so. Tail gunner Williams got sick too - he took over radio gun of Pietrolungo; Hawksly then took tail and Piet the waist. Saw a few fighters. They stayed out of our range. We saw P-38 giving them rather rough time.

We learn a few things about this mission and other missions by reading between the lines and making some inferences and guesses. The original target was Blechhammer, Germany, but the overcast caused a change in mission. This particular change in mission was drastic. Blechhammer is mostly north but slightly west of Foggia. Blechhammer was a deadly dangerous place and the crew probably was glad for the target change. Their secondary target was Budapest, Hungary. They must have turned and gone in a southeasterly direction to get to Budapest. It was a long mission because of the target change.

Brother Bob had trouble with airsickness again, but this is the last time that he mentions the problem. Apparently it was like seasickness - one gets used to the unusual motion after a time. Note that Brother Bob is already becoming an expert on flak. He notes that is was light, but accurate. Again he notes what the inspection of the plane showed after the raid. There were only a few holes in the plane.

It appears that the enemy fighters held off from attacking the bombers - perhaps because of the escorting P-38 fighters. It is quite possible that the German fighter planes were looking for stragglers that they could attack, but got chased off by escorting P-38s.

Here is what the AAF history says about the raid. *Bad weather causes 450+ bombers and fighters to abort missions; 188 B-17s and B-24s escorted by 138 fighters hit an airfield at Zagreb, Yugoslavia and targets of opportunity in Hungary and Yugoslavia including marshalling yards at Kaposar Osztopan and Split, a highway bridge at Brac Island, airfield at Banjaluka and the City of Budapest, Hungary.*

Brother Bob had an interesting, but perhaps not so enjoyable July 4th. Here is his account of his mission on the 4th of July.

"Quite a 4th, yes we dropped some 500lb firecrackers today - good job - smoke 12,000-15,000 feet in the air. We lost a ship from our squadron, 851 called Thunderbird. Missions of 6/27 and 6/30 were made in that baby - saw at least 9 bail out. Yes, one crew is erased from operations board and there are ten empty bunks tonight. Today we flew in 068 called

"Heaven Can Wait." It lived up to its name guess you would say. Flak was moderate, heavy and tracking."

Brother Bob must have found it dispiriting to watch a plane go down that he had flown two missions in. He would certainly have known the men in the plane. This was a raid on an oil refinery. Here is the official AAF account of the mission. *"250+ bombers attack targets in Rumania; B-24s bomb a bridge and a railroad repair works at Pitesti and B-17s bomb an oil refinery at Brasov; 350+ fighters escort the bombers and carry out sweeps over the target area;*
claims of enemy fighters destroyed total 17; one fighter group strafes 2 landing grounds and a troop train in Yugoslavia on the return trip to base."

Oil refineries were always heavily defended. Note that there were more than 350 fighters escorting the bombers. On the return trip some of the fighters strafed a troop train.

On the very next day Brother Bob is sent on another mission. The targets were in the vicinity of Montpelier, France. A good guess is that these missions had some connection to the upcoming invasion of southern France. They flew this mission about one month after the invasion of France on the Normandy beach. The northern invasion was making progress with much difficulty and the plan for the invasion of southern France was all set and ready to go. Here is Bob's account of the mission on 7 July, 1944.

Really and long one - 9 hours and 35 minutes. My butt got plenty tired riding that Ball Turret. (We) crossed the Anzio Beachhead. you could see three or four ships that looked like Liberty ships that had been scuttled. That probably happened during the landing at Anzio.

Brother Bob flew over the Anzio Beachhead. After the Allies had invaded southern Italy and secured the area around Foggia, they found it difficult to advance farther north because of the intense German resistance. The front line between German held Italy and Allied held Italy was not too far north of Foggia, the headquarters of the 15th AAF. The Allies were not comfortable with situation. The Allied plan was to land a sizeable force at Anzio and get in behind the German front line. The Anzio landing strategy did not work as well as the Allies hoped and the Allies suffered heavy losses. Brother Bob saw some of the Allied Liberty ships that had been sunk in the shallow harbor.

Here is the account of the mission according to AAF historical sources. *"Almost 500 bombers attacked targets in France; B-17s bomb the Montpelier Marshalling Yards; B-24s bombed the Beziers Marshalling Yard. and Toulon submarine pens and harbor installations; close to 200 fighter sorties are flown in support of operations. "*

On the 7th of July, 1944 brother bob flew on another very dangerous mission. Dangerous missions were becoming commonplace. Here is Brother Bob's account.

(We) carried 500 lb bombs and flew in ship 201, Patches. The flak was heavy and accurate. We only got 3or 4 holes in old Patches. We saw a straggler B-17 get shot down. It salvoed its bombs - it couldn't keep up with the formation and was attacked by 4 or 5 Me110s. After the attack they came in under and behind our ship. I took a potshot at them of 30 or 40 rounds but they were a 1000 or so yards out so I couldn't hit them. This is the second time I've had it put across to me "Stragglers die in combat."We had a little close call after coming off target. The bomb bay doors wouldn't close. Pilot called for reserve rpm 2400. This kept us in formation. Waist gunner, Hawksley cranked up the doors; at the same time engineer bones had turret stuck - either fuse blown or clutch came out.

This was quite a hair-raising mission. Brother Bob dismisses the damage with his statement, " We only got 3 or 4 holes in old Patches." He has a good view of a straggling B-17 that falls behind and is attacked by enemy fighters. He must have watched as it went down and watched to see if there were parachutes and how many there were. Brother Bob tells about still another problem. The bomb bay doors did not close after they had dropped their bombs. This sort of thing was a common failure. Continuing on home with the bomb bay doors open was not an attractive option. The open bomb bay doors created a tremendous drag on the plane and made if difficult or impossible for the plane to keep up with the formation. Brother Bob had just seen what happened to a straggler in their formation. In this case the pilot increase the engine rpm to 2400 and that extra rpm enabled the bomber to stay in formation. The waist gunner, Hawksley cranked up the doors manually. The problem may have been caused by a blown fuse. In this case everything turned out right and they got home safely. The literature on the B-17 bombers is filled with incidents of bomb bays not closing and the usual solution is to crank the bomb bay doors closed by hand.

Reprinted elsewhere is an actual picture of the plane that Brother Bob flew that day, "Patches." The plane is shown in flight. The number on the tail and other markings show it is the identical plane. It is possible that Brother Bob was in the ball turret at the time the photo was taken.

Here is what the official AAF report said about Brother Bob's mission. *560+ bombers attacked Germany and Yugoslavia; B-17s bomb 2 synthetic oil plants at Blechhammer, Germany; B-24s also hit Blechhammer and a synthetic oil and coking plant at Odertal, Germany and Zagreb, Yugoslavia*

Airfield and marshalling yard; the bombers and fighter escorts claim 50+ aircraft shot down during fierce battle with 275-300 fighters mainly in the Vienna-Budapest area; 18 US aircraft are listed as destroyed and larger number missing.

Chapter 8a - Strategy -Part 1: Introduction - Thinkers and Theorists

We have seen in previous chapters that Brother Bob flew on his missions in a B-17. He went on dangerous bombing raids to targets in Germany, Hungary, Italy, Rumania, France and other Nazi occupied countries. They bombed tank repair and ball bearing factories at Turin, Italy. They bombed oil refineries at Ploesti, Rumania; they bombed marshalling yards at Mantua, Italy, they bombed aircraft assembly plants at Gyor, Hungary, at Budapest, Hungary, and at Weiner-Neustadt in the Vienna area.

He often mentions the fighter planes that escorted the B-17s on their way to and from their targets and notes the type of fighter and praises their presence and their courage.

Bob flew from a base in Italy: the Tortorella field of the Foggia complex. We know that flew as a member of the 15th AAF. We know that, in the European Theater, there were two other strategic air forces of great importance: the RAF and the US 8th. They were stationed in England.

This is an appropriate time to ask and provide some answers to questions. Who figured out how airplanes were to be used in war? Did these thinkers realize that the advent of the airplane would change the manner in which nations fought wars? Did these early thinkers and theorists envisage the problems that fighter planes and bombers would encounter? Did they foresee weapons such a flak guns? Searchlights? Supplemental fuel tanks? Range problems? The use of Radar? Rapid increases in aviation capability? Armor for airplanes? The answer is almost certainly no. They were thinkers and theorists and they never thought their theories through to the extent that they could envision all of the consequences of the further development of aerial warfare.

In this chapter we will first look at the very general strategies developed by thinkers and theorists from several different countries. Those strategies, for the most part, were general in nature and not specific to their own country. Then we will look at the strategies developed by each country in the period between wars. For the most part each country developed a strategy that reflected its own experience in the first World War. In the next section, we will see that as the war went on the strategic concepts began to change. As the war continued, each nation had to allow their own strategy to evolve as a result of their experience. As an example, they saw the importance of the range of bombers. They found it was necessary to get the home base of the bombers close enough to the enemy targets so that they bombers could carry an effective bomb load. Another example: they learned that bombing raids were too costly if the bombers were unescorted.

And last, a jump ahead to the end of the war to assess the effectiveness of the aerial strategies developed and used by those who won the war: the Allies.

This chapter will supply some information or answers to specific questions about why those particular targets were selected by the G3 operations planners. Why an aircraft factory rather than an electrical plant. Why bomb marshalling yards? Why did the Axis powers defend the targets at Vienna, Blechhammer and Ploesti so resolutely? Here we will find out why it was so important for the Allies to have a strategic bombing base in Foggia, Italy. We will learn how the Allies learned a very bloody lesson regarding the criticality of having fighter planes as escorts.

Strategy, as used in this document, refers to large scale, long time plans for military related actions. Strategy does not deal with finite details; it is conceptual. The terms strategy and tactics need further explanation. As regards the Army Air Force in World War II, one of the overall strategic concepts was to deprive the Axis powers of their ability to produce petroleum. To implement this strategy, they send heavy bombers to destroy those petroleum refining plants. Other Army Air Forces, such as the 12th Army Air Force had a tactical mission. That tactical mission was to support Army land forces and they tried to drive the Germans out of Italy. It difficult to draw a specific line between strategy and tactics. Strategy is a goal. It is big and overall in concept. Tactics are the actions that a nation takes to achieve that goal; they are lesser in scope.

From time to time we will consider how these national strategies affected individual soldiers and especially one single airman, Brother Bob. We will see how he fit into the overall picture. Most individual airmen had little concept of complex national strategies. They knew that bombs killed people; they knew that bombs that landed on factories caused problems for the enemy. They knew that victory was one step closer when they shot down an enemy fighter. Brother Bob may not have had any idea of the specifics of Allied strategy. He obeyed orders and went on dangerous missions and hoped to live through the missions and return home safely. The Secretary of State, the President and the general officers did not consult Brother Bob. But without Brother Bob and millions more like him, achievement of their strategic goals would have been impossible.

The period between World War I and World War II was relatively brief. World War I ended in November of 1918. The starting date for World War II is often given as September 1, 1939. Hitler invaded Poland on the 1st of September in 1939 to begin World War II. A period of 21 years elapsed between the two wars.

Important political changes took place in Europe between the wars. These changes created a whole new set of political realities. The balance of power changed and new alliances were created. Relationships between nations changed. Traditional relationships changed or eroded. New alliances emerged from the chaos left by World War I.

The nations that had fought in World War I had learned some painful and hard-earned lessons about warfare. Some nations drew differing conclusions and developed different strategies for the next war even though they had been fighting each other in the same war.

Two new weapons developed during the first war assumed much importance and were given considerable attention in the period after the first Great War. One was the tank and the other was airplane. In the interwar period the major powers gave more attention to the airplane than to the tank. There was one notable exception: German planners gave armor a great deal of attention and developed that aspect of their armed forces to a greater degree than other nations.

Probably the most influential thinker and air strategist was an Italian, Giulio Douhet. Douhet had some early experiences in the use of airplanes in warfare. In a 1911 war between Italy and Turkey, both sides used airplanes for reconnaissance, transport and in artillery spotting. After that war, Douhet commanded an aviation battalion in Italy. He served in the Italian air service during World War I and criticized the army for incompetence and its unprepared status. The Italian Army court-martialed Douhet and sentenced him to a year in prison. On his release he went back to active duty and had an important command in the aviation service. After the war was over, he got his court-martial overturned and received a promotion to general. He later left the Army and in 1921 and wrote and published his ideas in a book, <u>The Command of the Air.</u>

In his book Douhet pointed out the fact that combatants fight air wars in three dimensions. Early wars had all been fought on the surface of the earth or the sea. (Submarines may have been an exception to Douhet's generalization.) Both land and sea were essentially two dimensional. Perhaps his most critical concept was this: **if one combatant can control the airspace over the enemy's home country, then that nation is condemned to perpetual bombardment and would therefore lose the war.**

Douhet listed the most important targets as follows: industry, transport, infrastructure, communications, government and "the will of the people." Douhet believed the entire population of nation involved in an air war would participate in combat. Douhet believed that an air war would be so terrible that it would not last long. Douhet did not see a tactical use of air for direct support of troops.

As modern experts consider the strategic concepts of Douhet, they credit him with the development of the concept of air superiority as a basic requirement for success in warfare. However, he seemed to believe that air power alone could win wars. World War II proved the importance of air support and control of the air, but it also showed that wars are finally won by land and sea warfare and forcibly taking and controlling the enemy's territory.

Douhet was important because he was the first strategist who concentrated on the aerial aspect of war. He was important because all of the other strategists from other nations read m and developed their own strategies, in full or in part, based on Douhet concepts. Material on Douhet from (8-1)

An important British strategist was General Sir Hugh Trenchard. He must have been familiar with the concepts propounded by Douhet. He said that strategic bombing should have two effects on the enemy. First, it should disrupt the supply chain that kept front line troops supplied. Secondly bombing should destroy the morale of the enemy population. Later we shall see some direct application of Trenchard's strategic concepts.

In Germany there were no dominant strategists, but a number of good military minds that had read Douhet and the other primary thinkers and were ready to apply the strategic concepts. Wever, Hans von Seeckt and later Albert Kesselring were the foremost military men who acted put some of the strategic concepts to use in the real world of the German armed forces. These men were aware of the importance of strategic bombing but did not consider its role to be paramount. Other nations had designers who concentrated on developing bombers for strategic bombing; the Germans successfully developed the concept of tactical support for ground forces. They developed a dive bomber, the Stuka, a most successful adjunct to ground forces. It is not clear who developed this potent concept. The Germans also developed some fighter/bombers that could perform as either a fighter or a bomber. Data on Britain and Germany from (8-2)

America had two influential thinkers and strategists, one was General Billy Mitchell. He said that airpower would change the way that nations fight wars and it would also change they way they conducted international relations. A summary of his ideas was exemplified by this quote, " In the future, no nation can call itself great unless its airpower is properly organized and provided for, because air power, both from a military and

economic standpoint, will not only dominate the but the sea as well."
Mitchell said that no longer would wars be fought only by naval and ground
forces. Air power could operate over both land and sea forces. Nations
would no longer conduct long wars that exhausted one nation to the point of
surrender. He believed that air power could conduct a siege to isolate and
prevent egress of ingress of supplies. He said that a ground force could
hold ground but not conquer it unless it had the ground force and the
supporting air power to hold and control the land and the air above it.
Mitchell's ideas had considerable validity, but he was in error by stating
that nations would no longer fight long wars. Mitchell data from (8-3)

Russian born American Alexander de Seversky was another influential
strategist. He thought and wrote about the importance of air power. In the
early stages of World War II he wrote a very famous book, Victory
Through Air Power. Seversky tried to educate the American public about
the value of airpower. Writing after the war had begun in Europe, he said
that airpower had helped Germany to win campaigns against Poland and
France. Seversky asserted that the traditional forms of warfare had been
diminished by the new weapon, the airplane. He considered airpower to be
a revolutionary factor of warfare; he wanted America to recognize the
revolutionary importance of air warfare. He considered American fighter
planes deficient and said that America needed more and better fighter
planes. He wanted America to build better planes that would enable
America to compete with Axis powers. According to Seversky, America
needed a bigger and better air force since air superiority was now an
imperative for winning a war.

Seversky did not say that airpower alone would win the war, but he
thought that airpower was a critical element. He did not believe that
airpower alone could destroy civilian or military will to fight or survive.

Seversky was a profoundly important thinker and strategist because he
was successful in communicating the concept of air power to the general
public. Hollywood made a movie that increased public awareness of the
importance of air power. Not only did awareness grow, but support from the
general public increased greatly. Seversky material from (8-4)

In the first Great War France had an excellent air force. After the first
Great War, France adopted a strictly defensive strategy. That strategy was
built around land fortifications, the Maginot Line. The French saw the air
arm as an adjunct to the Maginot Line. In the interwar period, French
strategists and thinkers concentrated on French defensive strategy and
therefore their strategists had little international influence.

Chapter 8- Strategy - Part 2 National Strategies

The next section describes the strategic decisions that each country made in the period between the two great wars. These decisions were made, at least in part, as a reaction to each nation's experience in the first Great War and in response to specific conditions that existed in each individual nation. It had been a long and costly war for every participant. There had been no real winners even thought the Allies claimed victory.

Some nations, such as Germany, had lost territory; some nations, such as Serbia disappeared from the map of Europe; some nations such as Poland were re-constituted; some nations such as Austria-Hungary were dismembered into separate nations; some nations such as Russia had entirely new economic systems. It was a profoundly different Europe. The Treaty of Versailles had ended the first Great War, but had created a whole new set of problems.

Each European nation struggled to deal with the reality of the post-World War I world. They developed different strategies to deal with the new conditions.

France, though a nominal winner in World War I, had come out of the first Great War nearly bled dry. They wanted to concentrate on living in peace. When the French considered the lessons learned in World War I, they were fearful of another long and costly war like the first Great War. France, thinking they had learned how to fight a war, developed a defensive strategy bases on the construction of the Maginot Line, an expensive, elaborate and very strong system of fortifications on the border between Germany and France. The French got ready to fight their last war and the Germans got ready fight the next war.

France concentrated it resources on defense. They built an adequate air force that had some good planes and well-trained pilots, but the overall emphasis of French air strategy was that the airplane was a defensive adjunct to a permanent defensive Maginot Line. They did not see air power as the critical answer to their strategic problems.

The **British** too suffered greatly in the First World War. The British had the advantage of being an island nation and that advantage combined with their powerful navy made their island kingdom a hard place to invade. This affected their strategic thinking.

They felt some comfort in being an island nation, but only a narrow English Channel separated them from quarrelsome nations on the European mainland, and they could not be comfortable. They had managed to hang onto their overseas possessions and wanted the keep the mighty British

Empire intact. They saw an alliance with France as a good strategy to prevent any future German aggression.

The British strategic concepts centered on keeping their empire and defending their island. They were aware of the importance of modernizing their armed forces. They developed some good war equipment between the wars. They build some aircraft that turned out to be very effective. Their Spitfire and Hurricane fighters were excellent examples. The British had always depended on the having a large and powerful navy for defense of their island nation.

Russia had become the **Soviet Union** with a communist system of government. During the period between wars, under the leadership of Joseph Stalin, the Soviet Union had changed their entire economic system from a capitalistic system to a communist system. They saw the whole future of the world as belonging to Communism. A central strategic concept for the Soviet Union was to install a communist system in every country in the world. To implement this concept they made every effort to support Communist parties in every country in the world. There were strong, important Communist parties in most of the major countries of the world. Communism was more than just the economic system in the Soviet Union; it was a world-wide force.

When Russia became the Soviet Union, it changed some of their relationships with European powers. The communist philosophy was a threat to capitalist, democratic nations. The Soviet Union was no longer an ally of the British and other European countries who were democratic and capitalistic. The Soviet Union would, if the occasion demanded, tolerate interaction with democratic and capitalistic nations. The Soviets had few strong allies during this period. However, in 1935 the soviets made an alliance with France. The practical results of this treaty were of little importance.

The Soviet Union had a strategy of modernization but the program lagged far behind that of other European nations. However, they did develop some new fighter planes, tanks and other war-making equipment. In one area they excelled. They developed some excellent rockets that proved to be effective weapons. The Soviets, possessing a large population, were in the position of having the potential for creating a very large army, but not necessarily a good army. The Soviet Union was, territorially, the largest country in the world. In a war, it could afford to lose some of its territory. Since it was so large, a conqueror would find it hard to police and control.

In **Italy** Benito Mussolini came to power not long after the firs World

War ended. He became the dictator of Italy. He called his system of government Fascism. This was a form of government without individual freedoms and no democratic institutions. Nationalism, a kind of super-patriotism was an important element in the system. It was tightly structured and highly centralized and allowed no disagreement. It aggressively opposed Communism. Since anti-communism was a basic tenet of Fascism, both Hitler and Mussolini strongly disliked the Soviet Union and all other Communist countries. Italy had a strategy of expansionism. In the period between wars, the Italians acquired some new territory. They conquered the African nation of Ethiopia. The Ethiopians were poorly equipped to resist the Italian takeover.

Between the wars the **Americans** had only limited participation in world affairs. They sat between two oceans and tried to follow a policy of isolationism. Their strategy was to avoid entanglement in European affairs. Since the Pacific Ocean separated America from Japan and the Atlantic Ocean separated America from the Axis powers in Europe, the Americans felt a certain degree of safety.

Their strategic thinking was mostly in terms of hemispheric defense. They did little to increase the size of their Army. However, they did begin the development of important war-making equipment capability between the wars.

Perhaps because of the influence of General Billy Mitchell and other proponents of air power, the Americans did some very useful developmental work in aircraft development. The Army Air force developed and tested a new bomber, later called the B-17, which would turn out to be a formidable weapon. The Army Air force made considerable progress in the development of fighter planes. These fighter planes were much better than the biplanes of World War I, but the British and German fighter planes may have been superior in the inter-war period.

On the other side of the world **Japan** followed an expansionist strategy. Japan needed raw materials, especially iron and petroleum for the expansion of its economy. It had few natural resources and saw Southeast Asia as a prime source of needed raw materials. Many of these areas in southwest Asia were controlled by the colonial nations: Britain, Holland, France and America. The Japanese coveted these areas with their extensive resources and raw materials, but knew that they could only gain control of these areas by going to war against the colonial nations.

As part of their expansionist strategy, Japan had occupied Korea earlier in the 20th Century. They continued that strategy in the 1930s by making war on China. Japan had built up a formidable navy and an excellent air force. Japan emerged as a powerful international force.

In the inter-war period there were three nations who followed aggressive expansionist strategies: Japan, Germany and Italy. The three nations were bound together in an alliance called the Axis powers. The agreement, or alliance, bound each nation to go to war against any nation that was at war with any one of the Axis powers. This was extremely significant in regard to later events.

Germany had been on the losing side in the first Great War. Adolf Hitler came to power in Germany by means of a legal election and some dubious maneuvering. Hitler permitted no more elections during his tenure in office. He immediately set up a Fascist system in Germany influenced by the model provided by Benito Mussolini in Italy. Hitler initiated a series of strategic policies that limited and vitiated the hated Treaty of Versailles; he modernized and increased the size of German armed forces and laid the groundwork for building a "Greater Germany."

The Germans improved and expanded their air force, the *Luftwaffe*. They developed some excellent fighter planes. They also developed bombers but their bombers were not as good as their fighter planes. The Germans developed tactics that entailed close air support for ground troops. The Germans developed the Stuka dive bomber, a tactical weapon for close air support of ground forces. The Stuka had a frightening siren that sounded as it dived. This sound had an important psychological effect. The Stuka and the *Luftwaffe* became part of the *Blitzkrieg* concept. Blitzkrieg combined elements of psychology to intimidate enemies Man for man, at that time, the German Army was arguably the best in the world.

A brief examination of Hitler's emotional prejudices provides some insight into the motivation of Hitler and the influence of these prejudices on German strategy. At least three guided his strategic planning. Hitler had an abhorrence of communism. As soon as he came to power in Germany he took steps to limit and control the strong Communist party in Germany. He wanted to destroy the entire German Communist party. At a later time this emotional prejudice was an element in his decision to make war on the Soviet Union. Later events showed that, for some short period of time, he was able to put aside his abhorrence for a short period of time in order to deal with some other problems. A second was his anger at the terms of the Versailles Treaty that ended World War I and exacted severe penalties on the German government. This strong feeling was, without doubt, a reason for his territorial aggressions. A third motivating factor was his hatred of the Jews. All of these three factors influenced German planning and strategy. The first two, the Versailles Treaty and his hatred of communism were paramount in his strategic thinking. His hatred of Jews had only limited influence on his international policies, but came into play on the international arena when Germany invaded and occupied nations with large Jewish populations.

Hitler knew the value of psychology and psychology played an important part in Hitler's expansionist strategy. Hitler made his first territorial grab in 1938 when he bullied the Austrians to agree to a union with Germany. None of the major powers made any strong objections and Hitler learned that he could get much of what he wanted by bluffing and bullying. Thus, bullying and bluffing became part of Hitler's strategy to build a greater Germany. Hitler's next territorial grab concerned Czechoslovakia. Many of the people in the Sudetenland region of Czechoslovakia were Germans or of German descent. Hitler made a demand that Czechoslovakia cede the Sudetenland to Germany. This time there were objections to Hitler's demands. Some of the major powers of Europe met to iron out the problem. The major players: Hitler for Germany; Daladier for France; and Chamberlain for Great Britain. By the power of his personality and by bullying the fearful Chamberlain and Daladier, Hitler forced them to agree to the annexation of part of Czechoslovakia. Chanberlain and Daladier believed that by giving in to Hitler's demands, they could prevent another world war; instead, they set the stage for another war.

In the next year Hitler's armies invaded Poland and the second Great War began.

Chapter 8 - Strategy - Part 3-Changes in Strategy

The next section is an examination of the way in which unfolding events of the second Great War caused Allied and Axis strategies to change. Hitler's invasion of Poland is generally regarded as the starting point of World War II. Before invading Poland, Hitler had done some strategic planning. He had to be sure that if he went to war with France and Britain, he would not be fighting them in the west and the Soviet Union in the east. Hitler took steps to avoid that problem. Hitler made a treaty with the Soviet Union. The treaty included elements that both countries needed. The agreement arranged for the exchange of goods between the two nations that was mutually advantageous. A secret protocol on the agreement stated that if Hitler invaded Poland, the Russians could occupy the eastern half of Poland.

This strategy allowed Hitler to invade Poland and once Poland was defeated and occupied, he could prepare to fight against his enemies in the west, Britain and France, without worrying about fighting a two front war. Initially, this strategic concept worked very well. Hitler defeated and occupied Poland before the end of the month of September,1939. He waited until spring before he moved against the French and British. Rather than make a direct attack on the Maginot Line, Hitler drove his forces drove into Belgium and easily penetrated the Belgian defenses. Thus he avoided the Maginot Line which ran from Switzerland to the border of Belgium. Once the Germans had defeated the Belgians and occupied Belgium, it was easy for the German armies to wheel and attack the French without having to go through the Maginot Line. The Germans successfully used their *Blitzkrieg* tactics combined with close air support to defeat the Belgian, British and French armies. The British forces retreated to Britain and fought in a in a defensive mode.

When World War II broke out, the whole world watched in wonder and fear as the Axis war machine went from victory to victory. In less than a year they had defeated the Belgians, Dutch and the French. They had driven the British from the mainland of Europe. The Germans had occupied Holland, Belgium, Norway, Denmark, Greece and part of France. Those nations who chose to be Hitler's allies retained a degree of independence. Rumania and Bulgaria belonged in that category. Italy was Germany's major ally, but Italian armed forces never matched the achievements of Hitler's Wehrmacht.

After the British had withdrawn their forces from the continent in June of 1940, the land battles between the British and Germans were, for the time being, at an end. Germany had defeated and occupied France. America was still a sympathetic neutral on the other side of the Atlantic Ocean. The Soviet Union, at that time, had a treaty with Hitler that guaranteed no Soviet interference. Britain stood alone with no major allies.

Hitler's generals developed a plan to invade the British island kingdom. Their invasion strategy required Germany to assemble a tremendous force of men, material, equipment and war machines. The invasion, to be successful required the assembly a very large force. The Germans would have to make an enormous effort to successfully invade England. With the force and equipment assembled, they would have to transport it across the English Channel. The force had to include a large number of transport ships to carry men and equipment across the English Channel. These transport ships had to be defended by German naval ships and German airpower. The Germans knew that the British Navy was a formidable force. Therefore, German airpower superiority was an absolute requirement for the success of their planned invasion of Great Britain. The Germans knew the British would attack them with their maximum effort as they crossed the English Channel.

Hitler knew that he had to control the air over the English Channel and over Great Britain before he could risk an invasion. To achieve his strategic goal, Hitler had to first destroy the British fighter force. Hitler had set the date for the German invasion of Britain for August of 1940. The leader of the German air force, the *Luftwaffe,* was Hermann Goering. Goering boasted to Hitler that he could destroy the British air force in three weeks. But Goering's boast did not work out. After three weeks the British fought as formidably as ever. Goering sent fighters and bombers to attack British targets on the coastal region and other targets further inland. When the Germans attacked, the British sent pilots up to attack the German planes.

The German and British planes fought the " *The Battle of Britain*." It was the only battle ever fought exclusively in the air. The battle was continuous; with no pause for rest. Both sides had brave pilots and good fighter planes but the British may have had a slight edge. The Germans had the Messerschmidt 109 and the British had the Hurricane and Spitfire fighters. Casualties mounted on both sides. It was common for pilots on both sides to fly three, four or even five sorties in a day. Brave men fought on both sides. Pilots flew until they were exhausted. Even when they were able to go to bed, they could not sleep because of the intense strain of a whole day spent fighting. Combat fatigue was more common than the common cold. Injured pilots flew and fought if their injuries did not keep them from flying. Every possible pilot was in the air fighting to the maximum of his endurance. The British may have gained an edge, but they began to run low on pilots. Casualties had been so high that a pilot shortage faced the British commanders. First they assigned some navy pilots to take the place of killed or wounded pilots. When the Germans had occupied Czechoslovakia, Poland and France, some of their pilots had escaped to Britain. Now Britain filled their pilot ranks with pilots from other nations and continued the "Battle of Britain."

The British found an advantage. A Scot, James Watt, developed one of the first useable radar systems. It enabled the British fighter pilots to learn of the approach of German planes. It gave the British an edge. The radar alerted the British of the approach of the Germans. The radar provided directional information and data on the size of approaching formations. The British were no longer taken by surprise. When they knew when the Germans were coming and where they would be, they could effectively plan to intercept the invaders. They could alert the anti-aircraft batteries. It helped to turn the tide.

Prior to this time the Germans had attacked British shipping, port facilities and factories. Then, apparently not by intention, a German plane dropped some bombs on London. It is possible that the German plane did not intend to attack London. Maybe it was a crippled bomber that had to get rid of a load of bombs and salvoed them over London. In reprisal Churchill ordered an attack on Berlin and in a counter-reprisal Hitler ordered more attacks on London. The German bomber campaign against London became the principal thrust of the Luftwaffe effort. The German fighter and fighter bomber attacks ebbed as the main Luftwaffe effort switched to bombing London and other major cities. Oddly enough, the German attacks on London enabled the British to regroup and refresh their fighter command. Hitler had not gained control of the skies. The Battle of Britain" was over. Some sources give German losses as 1733 planes and the British losses at 915 planes. Another favorable factor for the British was that when a German plane shot down a British plane, the pilot often was able to bail out and land safely. That pilot would live to fight another day. A German pilot who was shot down would be POW until the end of the war (8-2)

A stalwart band of very brave British pilots, with some assistance from pilots of allied nations, and a new radar system had stymied Hitler's invasion plans. The "Battle of Britain" illustrates the concept that the individual soldier, or airman, is ultimately responsible for the implementation of strategy. The general, admirals, leaders, analysts, thinkers and strategists may conceive and develop great strategic ideas, but even though the strategic concepts may be excellent, thorough and memorable, the great thinkers do not implement those strategies. In the case of the "Battle of Britain" the pilots had much assistance. Many servicemen and civilian workers kept the pilots flying. The aircraft mechanics serviced, repaired and kept the planes flying. The cooks, bakers, bartenders, girl friends and a whole host of supporting personnel helped to keep the pilots in the air. Mainly, it was the pilots who foiled Hitler's strategic plans and made the British defensive strategy work. The great British leader, Winston Churchill, said of those brave pilots who fought the battle of Britain, "Never in the course of human history have so many owed so much to so few."

Without air superiority Hitler decided that he could not risk an invasion of Great Britain. With air superiority, he could invade Britain; without that superiority he knew an invasion would fail. Faced with his inability to invade England, Hitler turned his attention elsewhere. Hitler hated Communism and the Soviet Union was the exemplification of Communism. The Soviet Union was next door to Germany and in Hitler's mind, uncomfortably close. This hatred predisposed his strategic thinking and moved him to action.

On Hitler's orders, the German General Staff began their planning for an attack on the Soviet Union. Hitler's strategic concept of not fighting a two front war was partially successful. He had not succeeded in destroying the British Air Force but, to a large degree, he had succeeded in his strategic plan not fight a two front war. Great Britain, reeling from the "Battle of Britain," was not likely to invade the continent and Hitler was free to plan an attack on the Soviet Union.

Hitler invaded the Soviet Union in June of 1941. This created a new strategic situation. Prior to the invasion, the Soviet Union and Germany had been allies, but the relationship had been perfunctory and temporary. When this important development occurred, it made the British position more tenable. They then had the Soviet Union as an ally. Before the German invasion, they had stood alone. The Americans had been sympathetic and helpful, but not willing to declare war on Germany or to commit forces to combat. They could, and did, send supplies and equipment to the British. The Americans did not actively participate. The British knew that the German invasion of the Soviet Union would require a substantial part of the German ground and air forces. It offered the British some breathing space and an opportunity to rebuild and strengthen their air and ground forces.

In December of 1941 a second major event changed the world situation profoundly. The Japanese attacked Pearl Harbor in the American owned Hawaiian Islands. Following the attack the Japanese and the Americans declared war on each other. Japan, Italy and Germany had been partners in a three-nation Axis alliance. The agreement among the three Axis nations was that if one of the nations declared war against some nation, then all of the Axis powers would declare war. Following their commitment, Germany and Italy went to war against America and America declared war on Germany and Italy.

Again this favored the British. Now they had a very powerful ally, the United States of America. It required several years of build-up before the United States played an important part in the European war. The Americans had to fight two wars: one in the Pacific against the Japanese and another in Europe against the Axis powers.

Before the advent of war, the American aid to Britain was a trickle. After the declaration of war, American aid increased greatly in volume.

In the middle of 1942 the first B-17s arrived in Britain. These American planes became the nucleus of the American 8th Air Force. Over a period of several years, 1942-1944, the British and Americans built two great strategic bomber forces in Britain The British built the RAF and the Americans built the 8th Air Force. Both had a series of bases in the southeast of Britain. Eventually they were of about equal size, but the British had the larger force in the early years. Later the 8th Air Force grew to approximately the same size.

The commander of the RAF was Air Marshall Arthur Harris, nicknamed "Bomber Harris." In the early part of the war 1940-1942, the RAF conducted raids on Germany and German occupied territory. The early raids on Germany were not very successful. The RAF conducted many of their early raids during both day and night-time hours. As a result of their experience they decided to concentrate on night bombing. In the early raids the British uncovered a serious problem: the limitation of range of British fighter planes. Raids on areas close to Britain were more successful because fighter planes escorted and protected the bombers all of the way through the mission. The British had no long range fighter planes that could escort bombers to targets deep in Germany.

The British began to understand that they could not win the war through air power. They realized that it was to be an adjunct means of winning the war.

But the British were learning the art of air warfare. The size of the British raids got larger. They were able to mount larger raids and they increased the size of attacking forces to as much as 1000 planes. They developed a better long-range navigation system, GEE. They developed new, improved tactics to improve bombing results. Under the leadership of Air Marshall Arthur Harris, they began a psychological warfare against

Germany. "Bomber Harris" cared little if bombs missed intended targets and hit civilian areas. Sometimes the RAF bombed areas with no targets except the civilian population. Members of the British Parliament and other prominent figures criticized Bomber Harris for his attacks on the civilian population of Germany. This is a good time to recall the air strategy propounded by General Sir Arthur Trenchard who emphasized the psychological, or terror effect, of bombing. In general the Americans opposed targeting civilian populations and concentrated on daylight precision bombing.

In order to develop a bombing strategy that was maximally effective, Allied Strategic planners met and developed a great strategic plan that set up priorities for bombing targets. They wanted every bomb to be effective and part of an overall bombing strategy. This priority system insured that the bombing campaign would concentrate its efforts on the most critical targets and not "waste" time, money, bombs and material on lesser targets.
Priority 1: electric power, transportation, and petroleum
Priority 2; air bases, aircraft factories, aluminum factories and magnesium factories
Priority 3: submarine bases, surface sea craft, invasion ports

Implementation of this strategy meant that there were often primary targets and secondary targets. For example, if it was not possible to bomb a priority one target like the synthetic oil refinery at Blechhammer because of overcast conditions, then a priority two or three target could be substituted and bombed so as to not "waste" a bomb raid.

In January of 1943, Roosevelt, the President of the United States, and Winston Churchill, the Prime Minister of Great Britain met for a strategic planning conference in Casablanca in Morocco. Joseph Stalin, the dictator of the Soviet Union was not able to attend. They formulated strategic plans to conduct war against the Axis powers. A major decision was a declaration that the Allied powers would accept only an unconditional surrender of the Axis powers. The Allies did want to fight another war against a resurgent Germany in another 20 years. They intended to arrange Europe and the world in such as way as to avoid another painful war.

They made important strategic decisions. They decided to make the main effort an invasion of the European mainland at Normandy. In southern Europe they would invade in a somewhat lesser effort. They would first invade Italy and at a later date invade southern France. When the southern part of Italy was in Allied hands, then Allied forces could move their air bases to Italy and be nearer targets that were out of range for the 8th Air Force and the RAF. Therefore, the Allies could reach more Axis targets because more Axis targets would be reachable and vulnerable. The Allied powers saw the oil fields at Ploesti in Rumania as a major target.

There was much discussion about day and night bombing. The British already followed a plan of night bombing. Churchill wanted the Americans, the 8th Air Force, to do night bombing. General Ira Eaker, speaking for the Americans opposed it. He said that daylight bombing was more accurate and therefore more effective. He said that Americans had designed and constructed planes for daylight bombing; America had trained their crews for daylight bombing. His arguments won the day. The final decisions called for a new strategic concept, " around the clock bombing," with the British doing the night bombing and the Americans doing the daylight bombing. This new concept also had the name of Combined Bomber Offensive or CBO.

One of the great early efforts of the CBO strategists were the raids on Schweinfurt. Allied strategic planners knew that the Germans produced approximately half of their output of all ball-bearings in Schweinfurt and in Regensburg. The planners thought that if they could destroy the majority of ball-bearing production, it would cripple the many other segments of German industry that relied on ball-bearings. Ball bearings were used in every tank, armored vehicle and every plane manufactured in Germany.

The American 8th Air Force made two raids on the ball-bearing targets. They made their first raid on 17 August of 1943. The American 8th Air Force sent 200 bombers to attack Schweinfurt. They lost 36 bombers of a force of 200. The loss rate was 18%. The 8th AAF mounted a second raid on the 14th of October on the same targets. On the second raid the Americans lost 82 of 291 bombers a loss rate of 28%.These were painfully high loss ratios and not sustainable over a long period of time. .

Although the strategic concept of the raid on the ball-bearing factories was a good idea, the planners and strategists had not solved a critical problem. Schweinfurt and Regensburg were beyond the range of Allied fighter escorts. The bombers would have to approach the well-defended targets without fighter escort. The missions were extremely dangerous and extremely costly. The Allied forces paid a heavy price in human lives for a strategic concept that did not work out very well. At this point the Allied planners began to acknowledge the fact that unescorted bomber raids were too costly to continue. They had to revise their strategic thinking to include the concept of fighter escorts for most bombing raids.

After war was over, the Allies were able to assess the value of the Schweinfurt raids. They had cut ball-bearing production, but the Germans took countermeasures to decentralize the production of ball-bearings. They had some stocks of ball-bearings on hand and they quickly moved to restore production capability. This aspect of the CBO was only marginally effective.

.   Take a moment to empathize with the feelings of the airmen on their way to Schweinfurt. Imagine how they felt when their escorting fighter planes veered off and started for home. The bombers were left to their own defense. Bombers had limited repertoire of defensive techniques. The pilot had to stay in formation; the bomber was big and loaded with fuel and bombs and could not take evasive maneuvers. Even if the pilot revved the engines to maximum speed, it could not speed away from the attacking German fighter planes. The fighters were fast and the bomber was slow. The armament differed. The bombers had 50 caliber machine guns and the German fighters had with 20mm or 30mm cannons that were much more potent and had a greater range than the 50 caliber machine guns on American bombers. Air crews watched in dismay as bombers straggled - soon to be target of enemy fighters. On those raids on Schweinfurt, the German pilots had great success in shooting down allied bombers.

If the bomber was hit, the pilot might try for a crash landing. Or, the crew might bail out. However, if the did bail out, that would be the first parachute jump for most of them. . If they got down safely, they might face extreme hostility from the German civilian population. A hard life in a German POW camp was the best they could hope for.

An airman who went on a dangerous raid such as Schweinfurt had only a 45% chance of surviving three such raids. The obverse statistic is that he had a 55% chance of getting shot down if he went on three such raids.

Those strategists, generals, and analysts who sat in offices in London or at Air Force headquarters knew of the high loss ratios and understood that the Allies could not sustain loss ratios of 20% to 35% over a period of time. They could not tolerate the loss of life nor could they tolerate the loss of so many planes. They had to plan corrective strategic actions.

A critical element was the fact that bombers had a much greater range than the range of fighter planes. When 8th AAF bombers and RAF bombers raided places within the escort range of fighters the loss ratio was quite low. As an example, some of the German ports and submarine facilities were close enough to British airfields so that fighter planes could escort bombers all the way to the target and all the way home. Such targets could be raided successfully without great loss of planes and airmen

In the latter part of 1943 the 8th USAAF Operations Research section made a study of losses incurred in fighter escorted missions compared with losses incurred in unescorted missions. They found strikingly significant results. They found that unescorted bomber missions had <u>seven</u> times greater losses than escorted missions. They also found that unescorted missions incurred 2.5 times greater damage to bombers on such missions. The results were so impressive that decisive action was imperative. Research data from (8-2)

The strategists overcame the problem of high loss ratios by a combination of three different solutions. They needed more range for escorting fighters. At that time the British had two important fighters, or escort planes, The Spitfire and the Hurricane. In the earlier part of the war, the Americans used the P-47. All were good fighters but handicapped by limited range. Aircraft designers and engineers came up with a very simple and moderately effective solution. They developed a disposable gas tank. They called this tank a "Tokyo Tank." When the fighter took off on an escort mission, the fighter plane used the gas in the disposable tank first and then dropped the tank and finished the mission on fuel in the regular tank. When the fighter returned to base, mechanics equipped it with new disposable tanks.

A second solution was to develop newer, better, and longer range fighters. The Americans developed two such fighters. Both of these fighter/escorts were very successful. The planes were the single engine P-51 and the twin engine, twin tailed P-38. Both had ranges sufficient to complete escort missions all the way to the target and all the way home. There is some information that the P-38 had some mechanical problems in its early stages. The Americans rushed both plane into production and by 1944 they were the primary escort fighters for American bombers

Strategists developed another new tactic to cut the loss ratio. The original tactic for escorting bombers required fighters to stick close to the bombers and to fight off German fighter attacks on the bombers. The new tactic called for escorting fighters to attack German planes whenever and wherever they could. This tactic was an offensive method rather than a defensive method of defending the bombers. Using this tactic, Allied fighter planes challenged the German fighter planes to come out and engage in combat. They attacked airfields and other facilities used to shelter and service the fighter planes. This change in tactics increased the number of battles between Allied and Axis fighters and increased Axis losses. By the latter part of the war, the Axis were less able to stand high losses. Here is an example of the change in tactics. Early in the war American fighter planes stayed close to the bombers and protected the bombers. They did not go after fighters in the vicinity. A German tactic was to follow a formation of bombers at a distance and wait for one or more of the bombers to straggle.

Then they attacked the straggler. With the new tactics, all German fighters in the area were attacked. They could not wait for stragglers.
Data from (8-3)

The Allies developed another very effective strategy to allow bombers to be escorted all the way to the target and all the way home. They obtained air fields closer to their targets.

The African based strategic Air Force was the 12th Air Force. The Allies used the bases in North Africa in two ways. Sometimes the 8th Air Force or the RAF would go on a long range raid deep into Axis territory. If they went as far as Ploesti in Rumania they did not have enough fuel to get back to bases in England. They sometimes used the one way trip. They left bases in Britain and went to Ploesti and dropped their bombs. Then they continued on to bases in North Africa: a one way trip. See map in appendix. It was also possible to launch raids on Ploesti and other European targets from bases in North Africa. The Allies used both of these strategies, but the magnitude of the effort was not great.

As the Allies reclaimed territory and drove the Axis forces back , the Allied strategy changed as Allied forces captured bases nearer to targets. In 1943 the Allies had driven the Axis forces out of Africa. Therefore it was possible for the Allies to set up bases for use in bombing Europe.

When the Allied Forces invaded Sicily and Italy in 1943, Italy surrendered and was no longer a factor in the war. However, the German troops in Italy opposed the Allied landings in Italy. The Allies landed on the far south of Italy and began a long and difficult movement northward upward along the Italian boot. The Allies made the German airbase facility in and around Foggia, Italy a prime objective. Its location was about halfway between Rome and the bottom of the heel of the Italian boot. After its capture the Allies quickly converted the airfields and other facilities into a major Allied air base.

By the time that the Allies began to use bases in Italy, they had organized a new Air Force, the 15th AAF. It combined the old 12th Air Force, RAF elements, and other elements into the new 15th Air Force. This Air Force was never as large as the RAF or the 8th Air Force, but it was a major force.

One of the targets the Allies wanted most to destroy was the oil fields in Ploesti. These oil production facilities were primary providers of petroleum for the Axis armies. Look at the map in the Appendix and the comparison chart. . It shows that the distance from Foggia to Ploesti is much closer than the distance from southeast England to Ploesti. A trip from Foggia to Ploesti and back was shorter than a raid that started in England and ended in Africa.

The bombers went a shorter distance and carried more bombs and less fuel.

The creation of the 15th Air Force gave the Allies a great strategic advantage in bombing the Third Reich, but it had other advantages. The allies planned two invasions of France- a major cross channel invasion of northern France from Britain to occur in June of 1944 and the second invasion of southern France. The RAF and the 8th Air Force were in position to provided tactical support for the cross channel invasion to land on the Normandy beaches of France. The 15th Air Force would be in a very good strategic position to provide tactical support to troops landing in south France. This invasion of southern France occurred in August of 1944.

By the time of the Allied invasion of northern France on June 6, 1944 the Allies had complete control of the air. The German air opposition was present but it was inconsequential. The Normandy invasion was a success. It probably would not have been possible unless the Allies had control of the air over the invasion site. The invasion of Normandy was difficult. The Germans had built numerous defensive positions on the coast of Normandy in anticipation of the invasion. The invasion was difficult and costly but achievable. It may not have been successful without the Allied control of the air.

On August 15 the Allies invaded the southern part of France. Here again control of the air was a critical factor. Brother Bob's account of the day says,

" It was the earliest H-hour ever for me - 2400 midnight. The most planes I ever saw were in the sky that morning. It was sure hard to see at night especially in the ball turret because the superchargers (contrails?) gave off so much light. I saw large groups of B-24s and B-25s and also saw B-26s, P-38s and P-51s, and various Navy planes and Spits (Spitfires) and Hurricanes. We saw the ships and barges of the invasion. It was the darndest bunch of ships I ever saw. There was a partial overcast, but we saw a lot of the ships. Saw the guns shelling the coast. ... Col. Seeman told us the briefing that this invasion 50% greater than the Normandy invasion and I could 0easily believe that. If something happened that we didn't make it to the target at 7:30 AM we were not to drop bombs. We reached target at 7:10 and - bombs away. The H-hour was 7:30 when the troops hit the land. I saw several planes blow up that collided. It really lit up the sky with the flames from the collision. The Barges and boats were only a short distance from the shore. They were heading for shore as we left the coast. The reports were that they were exactly on time. We also heard that there were the most airman in the air in at the same time in all of history. The report said 14,000 airmen in the air at the same time."

This was a much easier invasion and the Allies took fewer casualties and met less resistance than at Normandy. From Brother Bob's account it appears that the Axis air force was not present on that day. Considering the number of Allied aircraft in the air, it would have been most unhealthy for an Axis plane to venture into the area.

There was another instance of the Allies obtaining bases closer to targets in Germany. As the Soviets drove the Germans back toward Germany, the front line in the Soviet-German conflict moved westward and closer to Germany. The Soviets began to launch raids against targets in Germany. They were able to bomb Berlin and other targets in eastern Germany within the range of Soviet bombers.

By mid 1944 at the time of the two invasions of Europe the strategic situation in Europe had changed greatly and all of the changes favored the Allied Powers. On the eastern front by August of 1944 the Soviets had regained control of nearly all of the Soviet territory that Germany had taken in the early part of the war. The Soviets had advanced into Rumania and before the month was over, the Soviets had taken the oil fields of Ploesti. This was a deadly blow to the Germans; it worsened an already critical shortage of petroleum. After that the Germans had to rely almost entirely on synthetic fuel and Allied bombers constantly bombed the German synthetic plants.

The two invasions of France made important progress. Allied planes bombed the enemy more frequently than ever with ever larger and more deadly forces of bombers. Allied bombers encountered enemy fighters less frequently on missions, but the *Luftwaffe* was still a factor, but a factor of lesser importance. Sometimes bomber formations came home without ever seeing a single enemy fighter. The flak gunners were as active and deadly as ever. The mission of bombing was still a deadly dangerous assignment, but the probability of getting shot down decreased to an average 2.05% rate per mission- still a great hazard, but a world better than the 20-30% rate of some of the early missions.

As the war began to wind down in 1945, the Allied air raids continued and the Allied forces continued their march into Germany. For all of the war up until the final months the war had been fought in Poland, in France, in the Soviet Union, in Italy and other places, but it had not been fought in Germany. The German population had much experience with being the recipients of bombs, but now the land war came to Germany.

Chapter 8 - Strategy-Part 4 - Assessment of Strategy

The second Great War ended in May of 1945. Much of Germany lay in ruins. Allied forces occupied the western part of Germany and the Soviet forces occupied the eastern part of Germany. A hard earned, costly peace returned to Europe.

At the war approached its end the Allies began to consider an assessment of their strategies for winning the war.

Brother Bob did not write about his assessment of the success of the bombing war. He certainly did see the results of each bombing raid, providing there was no overcast, but he was not in a position to make an overall assessment of his contribution to the defeat of the Axis powers. He could not know, with any degree of exactitude, the effectiveness of the raids he made on Ploesti, Blechhammer, Vienna and other raids. He noticed sometimes that there were great towers of smoke; he noted that that they did a good job on some particular day, but he could not evaluate the overall effect of the raids he went on. He could observe, at the invasion of southern France, that Allied air power was a dominant factor, but he did not know the reasons for the great success of that invasion except in very broad, general way.

It is reasonable to ask the question: what effect did individual soldiers like Brother Bob have on the outcome of the war? What was nature and importance of their contribution? It is now time to do what Brother Bob did not do and could not do - assess the value of his contribution to the Allied air war and in turn the effect of air power on winning the war. Following data from (8-4)

Near the end of the second World War the Secretary of War appointed a group of experts to do a survey of the effectiveness of Allied Bombing. This project and the resulting document was the United States Strategic Bombing Survey (USSBS) or Summary Report. (USSBSSR)Of the 12 names, several may be familiar to readers: John K. Galbraith, George W. Ball and Paul H. Nitze. The survey included a great many additional staff people both civilians and military. They did on the spot inspections, reviewed photographs, evaluated Bombing Damage Assessment (BDA) documents, and interviewed Allied and Axis participants in the war.

They developed some amazing statistics concerning the volume of the bombs dropped during the war. During the war, the Allies dropped 2,700,000 **tons** of bombs on the Axis countries. More than 1,440,000 bomber sorties were flown. More than 2,680,000 fighter sorties were flown There were a total of 28,000 combat aircraft and 1,300,000 men in the combat commands.

They determined that, in Germany, Allied bombs damaged or destroyed 20% percent of dwelling units. They estimated that strategic bombing killed 300,000 civilians and injured another 780,000 people. Some cities in Germany were reduced to piles of rubble.

In the early part of the war 1940 -1943 the Allies were not able to mount large raids against the German heartland. Some of the early raids were not very successful. The most outstanding example was the raids on the ball-bearing factories in Schweinfurt and Regensburg. They did have some effect but the long term effects were overcome by German dispersal of manufacturing facilities and by a rapid program of repair of damaged factories. These were very costly to the Allies and did no long term significant damage to German war production. The Allies did not repeat such costly raids because of the tremendous cost in planes and trained personnel.

Another priority target was the German aircraft industry. Both sides knew that control of the air was a critical factor. Hence they placed a high priority on destroying the enemy's capacity to build planes. The Allied attacks on German aircraft factories began in 1943. The German aircraft production had been distributed widely over Germany. Therefore it was a difficult targeting situation because Allied planners had to plan raids on a large number of aircraft factories widely distributed over Germany. Germany had some excess, unused capacity that made the problem more difficult.

In 1943 the Allies made a special effort to bomb aircraft production facilities. The USSBSSR report shows that aircraft production of the fighter plane, the ME109, decreased from 725 in July of 1943 to 357 in December. However this was only a short-term affect and the Germans were able to take actions to restore aircraft production. Because of the success of attacks in 1943, the Germans vigorously subdivided and dispersed their production facilities. The German program of subdivision and dispersal of facilities must have been successful. When the USSBSSR looked at overall aircraft production they found that during the whole year of 1944 the German military received 39,807 aircraft of all types. In 1942 the German military had received 15,596 aircraft of all types. One can only conclude that the Allied attacks on German aircraft factories contributed only slightly to winning the war.

The Allies bombed steel production facilities, but it appears that the Allies never made the German steel industry a high priority target. Some Allied planners thought that Steel production was not an effective use of airpower. After-the-war interviews and evaluations show that Allied raids had no critical effect on German steel production. Allied damage to German steel production was not a crucial factor in the defeat of Germany.

Attacks on German tank and armored vehicle production were not a high priority. The early Allied attacks on these facilities in 1942 and 1943 caused the Germans to disperse their production facilities and near the end of the war the Germans still were producing a large number of tanks and armored vehicles.

The Allies targeted the German transportation system and gave it a high priority. The Allies bombed road and railroad bridges, especially those over rivers where alternate routes were not easily available. The Allies bombed marshalling yards where trains were assembled for transporting supplies to factories and to supply front line soldiers on both fronts. Ships and port facilities were also targets. On a tactical level, fighter planes sometimes attacked trains and military convoys. Although big bridges could not be rebuilt quickly many of the other targets could be repaired in a relatively short time. Hence it was necessary to repeat bombing of targets in order to be effective. The USSBSSR concludes that Allied attacks on transportation system disorganized the German economy. The Allied attacks substantially reduced German factory output. The Allied attacks on canals and waterways were most successful. In some cases canals and waterways were completely closed due to the effects of Allied bombing. The Allies gave special attention to supply lines that supported front line troops and the after war survey showed these attacks were effective in interdicting materiel to front line forces.

In summary, the Allied bombing of the German transportation facilities was quite successful. However, it did not win the war. It had the effect of creating a shortage of critical materials. The critical materials such as food, ammunition, raw materials, and finished goods were delayed. Spare parts did not arrive on time because a bridge had been bombed and the convoy was delayed. Ammunition was in short supply because the convoy delivering the ammunition had been strafed by Allied fighter planes. Multiply these examples over and over and the German situation comes into better focus. The German war machine was slowed, crippled, damaged, but not destroyed by Allied bombing.

The Allies could have targeted the German electrical system, but the system was the target of a limited number of raids. Allied planners thought that the German electrical grid had a very high capacity for re-routing electricity. They concluded that if one electric plant was put out of commission, then the Germans would just switch the transmission to other lines and there would be no net negative effect. Hence the Allies did not bomb the electric plants very much. Post war analysis showed that Allied attacks might have created great problems in the German economy.

The Allied attack on German oil production and oil refining facilities was a major factor in defeating Germany. It was the Achilles heel of the German war machine. The main sources of natural petroleum for the German war machine were the oil fields in Ploesti, Rumania. Some oil was also produced in Hungary and in Austria, but Ploesti was the main source of natural petroleum. In addition to the natural petroleum production, The Germans had a number of plants that used coal as the basis for producing synthetic petroleum.

The Allies made the first important attack on German oil in 1943. This low-level attack was extremely costly for the Allies. It had little long term effect on German petroleum production. In April of 1944 The Allies resumed attacks on Ploesti. By that time the 15th AAF had been activated and was capable of making raids on Ploesti. A look at the map shows that Ploesti was easily accessible from the main base of the 15th AAF, Foggia, Italy. By that time P-51 fighters and P-38 fighters were available to escort bombers all the way to and from Ploesti and this factor made Allied raids from Foggia much more feasible. The 8th AAF and the RAF bombed German synthetic plants in Germany that were in easy range. Beginning in the spring of 1944 the Allies were able to bomb all German production and refining facilities of both synthetic and natural petroleum. Allied raids had negative effects on the German fighting capacity. Speer, Hitler's industrial production expert, is quoted in the USSBSSR as saying, "The enemy has succeeded in increasing our losses of aviation gasoline up to 90% by June 1944. Only through speedy recovery of damaged plants had it been possible to regain partly some of the terrible losses."

Remember that petroleum production facilities were a number one priority for Allied strategic planners.

Hitler was so concerned that he appointed an expert, Edmund Geilenberg to repair and reconstruct the oil plants. Geilenberg had first priority on his requirements for the repair and reconstruction of German oil facilities. He had as many as 350,000 men available to disperse, rebuild and strengthen production facilities. Geilenburg dispersed the reconstruction of plants and began some new underground construction. Geilenberg's project was a long term solution and he did not complete all of his planned constructions before the war ended.

Even in the early part of the war petroleum had been in short supply and had been a controlling factor in planning military operations. This problem was especially difficult for a war machine that relied on sudden, powerful and rapid attacks. Such tactical moves called for enough petroleum to fuel the attacks.

John Ellis in his book, Brute Force (8-5) presents the thesis that brute force, the great power exerted by Soviet, American and British forces decided the war. He presents, in graphic form, some relevant data on the effects of Allied bombing on the synthetic fuel production in Germany. In January through May of 1944 German synthetic fuel production was approximately 300,000 metric tons per month. Until May the Allies did not drop large quantities of bombs on oil targets. In May and June the Allies dropped about 200,000 tons on bombs on oil targets. By June German oil production dropped to 150,000 tons per month. Allied raids had halved German petroleum production. In June, July and August the Allies dropped an average of about 200,000 tons of bombs per month. By August German synthetic oil production had dropped to 47,000 tons per month. By the following March German synthetic oil production was down to 12,000 tons per month. This created a critical oil shortage.

On page 205, in Brute Force Ellis illustrates in tabular form the effects of the fuel shortage on the training of German pilots. In the period of 1942 to 1943 the Germans allocated 220 flying hours to the training of pilots. In that same period the British allocated 360 hours and the USAAF allocated 300 hours. By late 1944 the Germans allocated only 125 flying hours for pilot training and the British allocated 360, the same as earlier in the war, and the Americans increased the time allocated to 400 hours. British and American pilots were much better trained than their German counterparts.

Theo Boiten and Martin Bowman are the authors of Jane's Battles With the Luftwaffe. (8-6) This is a first person narrative by a young German combat pilot, Uffz Fritz Wiener, who tells about some of the deficiencies of his training.

"When I joined JG11 in the beginning of October, 1944, I had never flown the Me 109 with the additional 300 litre belly tank. I had never practiced take offs and landings in formation; and I had never fired the Mk108cannon and MG151 machine guns with which my Me109G-14 was equipped. Combat tactics, combat formation flying and combat maneuvering in formation were entirely new tasks to be learned. All of this occurred during a period of about two months with severe restrictions on flying time, because the gasoline supply was already very limited even in combat units."

On page 200 a German officer, Lt. Karl-Heinz Jeismann explains that extreme efforts were made to conserve fuel. He says that as a safety measure, fighter planes were kept in an area with berms of earth piled around them. He says, "Due to the shortage of fuel the aircraft were not to be moved under their own power, but were dragged by teams of oxen. We had some 20 to 25 (oxen) which the local farmer had been required to supply."

The two citations given previously provide dramatic examples of the effects of Allied bombing on the German air force. As the war period lengthened for the Germans they lost more and more of their experienced pilots. They could not replace the lost pilots with pilots of the same quality. The petroleum shortage created new group of German pilots who were inexperienced and poorly trained. All the while American pilots received more flight training before going into combat. This gave Allied pilots an important edge.

In summary of the USSBSSR, it is safe to say that air power helped the Allies to win the war. It is not accurate to say that Allied air power won the war. It seems that the early theorists of the interwar period, Douhet, Trenchard, Mitchell and others were only partially correct. Those who said that air power could be the weapon that could win a war were not correct. However, most of the theorists saw air power as a critical adjunct to winning the war.

One of the members of the USSBSSR was a very well known economist, John K. Galbraith. He had a different opinion on the value of airpower. He stated that land forces were the principal factor in winning the war. He differed from the other members of the panel in regard to the value of air power. Galbraith noted that most German industries continued to operate at some level and he noted that Germans kept fighting up until there was no more land to retreat to.

The USSBSSR reached these conclusions. Even a first class military power like Germany cannot function capably if subjected to a powerful continuing air attack. Control of the air over any territory is a most decisive factor in the outcome of a war. If a nation is well organized and forceful, it can disperse and reorganize in an effective manner so as to limit catastrophe. Careful selection of targets is a critical element of air warfare. A single large attack on some target cannot put a single industry out of commission. Repeated attacks on critical targets are necessary for success. The development and use of new technology was a critical element of success in air warfare.

Brother Bob did not have access to the conclusions of the USSBSSR. If he had, perhaps he would have understood the critical importance of the American attacks on Ploesti, Vienna, and other oil related targets. It might have helped to explain to him why the Germans defended those oil targets so ferociously. Perhaps he would have had an extra feeling of accomplishment as his B-17 limped home after a raid on Ploesti. Had Brother Bob known that knocking out bridges and marshalling yards would greatly damage the German war effort, it might have motivated and energized Brother Bob.

The great gods of strategy plan; the lowly airmen perform,

Chapter 9 - A History of the Fifteenth Air Force

When Bob arrived in Italy, the Army Air Force assigned him to the 346th Squadron which was a part of the 99th Bomb Group and which in turn was a part of the 15th Army Air Force. As Army Air Forces go, it was a relatively new Army Air Force.

A little review of history will make the mission of the 15th AAF more clear. Some of this information is based on a History of the Fifteenth Air Force prepared by Gary Leiser. Some information is from the 376th Heavy Bomb Group Association. (9-1)

Before World War II, the British had a continuing presence in Egypt and that part of the world. They, along with the French, owned the company that operated the Suez Canal which was a critical world waterway. In 1941 German forces invaded and occupied most of North Africa except for the substantial British presence in Egypt. .

In November of 1942 British and American forces invaded north Africa. This invasion was called Operation TORCH. One of the units of this force was the American 12th AAF. It operated as a support unit for American and British armored and infantry units. On the 13th of May in 1943 the last of the Axis forces had either surrendered or had been driven out of Africa.

Following the retreat of the Axis forces, the Allied forces next attacked Sicily and later attacked the mainland of Italy. During these operations the 12th AAF continued as a tactical support unit supporting these operations first in Sicily and later on the Italian mainland.

In October of 1943 the 15th AAF came into existence as a strategic air force. The 12th AAF continued its support of Allied land operations as a tactical arm of the invading American and British forces. From that time onward its mission was tactical. It did not do long range bombing raids. The components that were merged into the 15th AAF came partly from the 12th AAF, partly from British RAF units in the theater, partly from the US 8th AAF based in Britain and also a collection of other units. Some of the units were fighter units - both British and American. Also added were support units such as reconnaissance and photography units. Shortly after its formation, Major General Nathan Twining was appointed as its commander.

The main function of this new air force was to serve as a strategic arm. In other words its mission was to bomb Axis infrastructures such as oil fields, aircraft factories, tank factories, ball-bearing manufacturing sites and any other Axis structures that would cripple the economy of the Axis nations and help the Allies to win the war. When the 15th AAF moved onto the Italian mainland to bases such as Foggia, they were in an excellent geographical position to conduct bombing raids on parts of the Axis empire that the RAF and the American 8th AAF in England could not get to. As a specific example, it was not feasible, or barely feasible, for the RAF and the American 8th AAF to bomb a target such as Ploesti because it was at the limit of their range. (See Comparison chart in Appendix.) The curse of the balance between bomb load and fuel made productive raids barely possible but not feasible. Moving the 15th to the Italian mainland changed all that.

The new 15th AAF had other functions as well. One was to destroy the German Air Force. Another was to support the continuing Allied attack in Italy. Still another was to weaken the Axis position in the Balkans.

By the spring of 1944 the 15th AAF had begun full scale bombing raids on a wide range of targets. A study of the map in the appendix shows that certain targets were better situated for one AAF than another. For example, Berlin was within the range of the 8th AAF and the RAF in England. All the targets in north and central Germany were within their range. On the other hand the 15th AAF was well situated for raids on the Balkans countries and such important targets as Budapest, Vienna and Ploesti. Part of Germany was within the range of all three of the major strategic AAFs. The Fifteenth Air Force began its raids on prime Axis targets such as Ploesti, Blechhammer, and Vienna as soon as April of 1944. As previously stated the 15th AF bombed targets easily within its range, but on at least one occasion, on 24 March 1945, it bombed the Daimler/Benz tank works in Berlin. On that day some of the new German jet fighters shot down two B-17s. Those two bombers were the last aircraft lost by the 15th AF until the end of the war.

The 15th AF flew its last strategic mission on 25 March 1945 when it bombed targets in the vicinity of Prague, Czechoslovakia. From that time until the end of the war, the 15th flew tactical missions in support of ground actions. The last of these missions ceased after 1 May. The Germans surrendered on 8 May, 1945.

After the surrender of Germany, the planes and equipment of the 15th AF were deployed to either to the US or to the far east for use in the war against Japan. Later, after the surrender of Japan the 15th was deactivated. At a still later date it was reactivated.

During its short existence, the men and planes of the 15th AF made a great contribution towards winning the war. According to Leiser's History of the 15th AF, it dropped more than 303,000 tons of bombs on Axis targets in 13 different countries. It flew more than 148,000 sorties; it destroyed 1946 enemy aircraft; it destroyed 1600 enemy locomotives and 1400 rail cars. During the same time it lost 3400 of its own planes. Its own casualties were17,615 men killed, wounded, or missing in action. A statistic nearly unique to the 15th AAF is the number of men missing men returned to duty. These were airmen who bailed out or crashed landed, mostly in Yugoslavia, and made their way back to their home base. In many instances they were helped by partisans. The number of returned airmen was 5650 men.

One way to summarize the strategic function of the 15th AAF is to note that prior to its inception, some parts of the Axis empire were nearly immune to attacks by Allied strategic bombers. After the formation of the 15th AAF and its move to the Italian mainland, there were no safe havens for Axis oil production, aircraft production or any other type of industrial activity. After the advent of the 15th AAF, those areas were no longer exempt from aerial surveillance. Hence the 15th AAF made a critical contribution to winning the war.

Chapter 10 - Counting Parachutes - Prisoners of War.

When combat veterans of the United States Army Air Force prepared their memoirs, it was common to see a recurring statement about an ordinary, but tragic event. They counted the parachutes coming out of a falling, damaged plane.

When bombers were hit or crippled, the pilot might decide to try for a crash landing and ask crew members if they wanted to bail out or stick with the plane for a crash landing. If there was still a good measure of control and if crew members had a great deal of trust in their pilot, then crew members were likely to stick with the plane rather than bail out. Crew members had received some training on the use of a parachute, but practice jumps were not part of the training. In many circumstances, there was little hope of a successful crash landing and the surviving crew members would bail out.. When we read accounts of such events the authors will say that they saw four parachutes or six parachutes and in some instances no parachutes and if luck was with the crew - ten parachutes.

Bailing out did not guarantee a safe landing. There were many hazards for those airmen who had to bail out. First of all they had never actually bailed out of a plane and they knew little about how to bail out. They had hardly any control of where they landed. They might land in the Adriatic Sea or the Mediterranean Sea. They were equipped with a flotation jacket that kept them afloat for some time. They might come down in a mountain region that was not inhabited and they might get their chute caught in a tree on landing. If they came down while flying over Yugoslavia, there was a good chance that partisans such of those of Tito, would find them and care for them and return them to the Allies. Officially the Germans occupied Yugoslavia and the Germans captured some airmen who landed in Yugoslavia. Those who flew out of Britain with the 8th Air Force might crash land or bail out over Netherlands, Belgium or France. All of those three countries were occupied by the Germans. However, many of the people of these countries were sympathetic to the Allies and often hid or helped downed flyers to escape back to Britain.

Many of the airmen who went down over Germany or German occupied territory became prisoners of war. It is probably safe to say that the Germans captured a majority of those who went down over Germany or German occupied territory. Nearly all of those who landed in Germany spent the rest of the war in a German POW camp. They stayed alive as German prisoners of war. It was a difficult life, but most survived the ordeal and got safely home.

Brother Bob, like other crew members, carefully watched for flak, enemy fighters and carefully gauged the distance from their plane to other nearby planes. As a group they were extraordinarily alert. Damaged bombers were one of the things that they watched and reported on. Bob, in his narrative of his experiences, counted parachutes a number of times.

On a mission on 26 June, 1944, his first mission, he says, *"Krauts shot down a B-24. The tail gunner said he saw 7 or 8 chutes and the 9th got caught in the stabilizer so the landing of the 9th man was not successful."*

On 4 July, 1944, Bob says, *"We lost a ship from our squadron- 851 called Thunderbird. My missions of 6/27 and 6/30 were made in that baby - saw at least nine bail out. Yes, one crew is erased the operations board and there are ten empty bunks tonight."*

About 28 August, 1944, Bob says, *"Ship 570 went down - quite a few old gunners on it - none were intimate acquaintances, but I knew some of them. Reports seem to indicate that ten of them got out.*

Stephen Ambrose in his book, <u>Wild Blue</u>, (10-1) has this to say, " When a B-24 got shot and started to tumble or crash…the men are looking out and they're counting the parachutes, one, two, three - sometimes it got up as high as five. Sometimes there no parachutes at all."

Roy F. Statton tells of an experience that happened on a raid on Germany. "After our bomb run, we had two engines shot out and we fell behind the formation. We were attacked by German fighters. The pilot ordered the crew to bail out which I and the enlisted crew did. But as I heard later, the pilot and co-pilot remained in the plane for awhile and eventually bailed out in Free France. The rest of us were captured and became POWs. (10-2))

Robert Billings had this to say about bailing out or staying with the plane. " But what happened if both pilot and co-pilot were disabled? The first choice was to bail out and hope all the parachutes opened (and this was no hundred-percent certainty). But on many occasions one or more of the wounded could not jump and their comrades would not want to leave them to be killed in the inevitable crash. Then there was only one hope."(10-3)

Leslie VanderMeulen has prepared a narrative concerning her grandfather's experience as a tail gunner for the 15th AAF. His name was Charles Waldo Anderson and he flew out of Foggia Italy, With her permission, here is a long excerpt from her work. In a few instances the narrative has been paraphrased.

"Though the crews tried to make the best out of life in the camp, wartime certainly did not consist of fun and games. My grandfather's flight crew performed many missions during their time in Foggia. The crew was part of the 15th Army Air Corps, specifically in the 364th Bomb Group, 772nd bomb Squadron, where my grandfather did his job as a tail gunner on their B-17. A tail gunner's job is to shoot from the rear of the plane. Their final mission took place on February 13, 1945. This mission included bombing Vienna, Austria and proved to be quite successful. The plane received a shot in the fourth engine, causing the third engine to catch on fire. This sent the plane crashing down in flames, and the entire crew bailed out over the city of Vienna at 15,000 feet. The report sent to my grandmother regarding the crash stated "plane sighted going down in flames- no parachutes sighted.'

My grandfather experienced a stroke of luck that day which saved his life. After he bailed out of the plane he landed in a tree, while the other crew members landed on the ground. When Viennese civilians found those six crew members, my grandfather watched as they lynched his friends right there.

The civilians took this action because German soldiers had convinced them that the Air Corps planned to bomb their villages and homes, thus they were very angry at these soldiers. Germans soldiers did find my grandfather's extra pair of shoes that had fallen off his belt when they went to look for survivors. However, seeing no footprints in the snow, they concluded that this man must be dead. Luck for my grandfather, they did not look up to see him sitting there in a bare tree.

In a report taken after the war, my grandfather stated that he evaded capture for three days, but a farmer turned him in and he was then taken to Weiner Neustadt Airfield, Austria. He was held there from February 16 to March 5, where he was interrogated for two days (March 8-10). After the interrogation, he was transported to three more camps. From March 12 through March 16 he stayed at Dalagluft, March 18 through April 4 held at Nuremberg, and from April 4 to April 219 at Moosburg.

My grandfather never spoke to his children about the treatment at the camps. He did say they were given very little to eat, so that they would be too weak to fight back. Most imprisoned soldiers involuntarily participated in prison detail, which consisted of any hard labor that could be found to keep the prisoners occupied. Most of this work (was) done outside of the camps, thus the Army Air Corps could not participate. The reason was that angry civilians would throw stones at or otherwise harass USAAF personnel.

In some of the marches between camps Air Force personnel were stoned or otherwise harassed. They encountered other unexpected dangers. Once on a 100 mile march to Munich, they feared for their lived when Allied planes dropped bombs on them. They were also the targets of Allied planes when they were being transferred in boxcars in the Nuremberg rail yards. Travel between camps was more dangerous than being held in enemy camps.

Charles Anderson was captured near the end of the war. He felt that the German guards knew that the war was soon to end and the guards were fearful about mistreating prisoners. Therefore treatment was more humane as the end of the war got closer. Anderson says that when the war ended and American troops freed the prisoners, some of guards who had mistreated prisoners were shot.

There were many American soldiers taken prisoner and their accounts of their treatment vary. Carol Hipperson author of the book, Belly Gunner, (10-4) was a prisoner and indicates that his treatment was better than that received by Charles Anderson. Hipperson flew with the 8th Air Force out of England. His ship was hit and several crew members were killed. He bailed out and pulled his ripcord and started floating down. He saw water below and thought he was coming down in the English Channel. However the water was a canal in Holland. He saw people below waving at him and cheering as he came down. He floated on past the people and landed in a meadow with two of his crew mates. While they were considering what to do next, a uniformed man appeared. He was a Dutch policeman. He asked them if they wanted to get in contact with the underground. They said yes! The Dutch policeman told them to go and hide in the woods and he would contact an underground member. They went into the nearby woods and considered their good stroke of luck of meeting a policeman who knew about the underground. They hid and waited for some of the underground people to appear. Then, they heard the Dutch policeman shouting for them to come out. They came out and found that the Dutch policeman had brought a dozen armed German soldiers with him. They were prisoners of war.

The Germans set in motion the process of getting the prisoners to a prisoner of war camp. They transported the prisoners first by truck and then by train to a prisoner of war camp. While they were traveling on the train, the German guards came along and pulled down the window shades so the civilians could not see who was in the railroad coaches. They told the prisoners that inhabitants of the cities were so incensed against Allied prisoners that they might not be safe if city residents knew the train carried Allied prisoners of war. When they disembarked at Frankfurt a group of civilians gathered around the prisoners and called the Allied prisoners "Schweinhunds" and spit on them. The German guards hurried the prisoners out of harms way and on their way to a prisoner of war camp.

The Germans took the prisoners to another camp and interrogated them. Then the Germans shipped them to Stalag 17 where they remained until the end of the war. There were about 4000 American prisoners of war there. There were also British, French, Italian and Russian prisoners of war. Each national group was kept separate from the others.

Prisoners settled into a routine. The day began with a roll call the purpose of which was to be sure that all the prisoners were there. Sometimes this took a long time. The diet in the camp was sparse, bland and tasteless. One of the main items on the menu was rutabaga soup. This was the morning and noon meal. Occasionally there would be some sort of bread or potatoes. The highlight of their diet was the once a week Red Cross parcel. It was the most important event of the week. The individual parcel contained a can of instant coffee, some powdered milk, a six ounce package of sugar, a half pound of cheddar cheese, a can of salmon, a semi-sweet chocolate bar and some crackers. Initially, each prisoner got a parcel, but later in the war, each parcel had to be shared with five prisoners. The POWs thought that the Germans kept some of the parcels for themselves. Hipperson said that Red Cross parcels were the difference between surviving and starvation. He noted that the Russians did not get any Red Cross parcels and they were in bad physical condition and their mortality rate was much higher than the American rate. The Red Cross also sent some clothes to help the prisoners stay warm.

They had a guard named Corporal Schultz. He had been born in America and spoke perfect English. He had gone to high school in Chicago. He had gone home to Germany to visit his parents and had been drafted into the German Army.

Hipperson really did have a guard named Corporal Schultz and he really was in Stalag 17. He just recorded the facts.

Boredom, bad food and a shortage of food were the main complaints of the American prisoners. Hipperson's experience was probably fairly typical. The Germans had little food to spare. This author's research covered numerous instances of Allied airmen being captured by the Germans. In those situations, concerning American airmen, the Germans did not systematically mistreat American airmen who became prisoners of war.

Chapter 11 - The Prototypical Mission

Every mission was different from every other mission. Some were much longer than others. Some were different because of weather conditions. But the factor that differentiated among missions and made some especially memorable was the danger factor. The mission with the highest count of flak holes at the end of a mission might be the most memorable. If an individual gunner had shot down an enemy plane, or helped to shoot down an enemy plane then that mission was memorable.

It was reasonable to classify missions as to danger. In the 15th AAF at that time there were two kinds of missions. When strategic requirements made it necessary to assign missions to Ploesti or Vienna, then crew members were worried and fearful. American airmen dreaded such assignments. However, such missions counted as double missions and helped the airman build his count of missions and made his day of departure for home that much closer. Other missions, less hazardous were often called "milk runs." They were missions where the bombers encountered no enemy fighters and little or no enemy flak. Even the "milk runs" sometimes turned out badly.

Information resources for a prototypical mission: (11-1) (11-2) (11-3) (11-4)

Crewmen scheduled to go on a mission were awakened early. An awakening time of 0200 was not uncommon.. Crew members lived in tents. Their tents were primitive and only lit by a candle or a kerosene lamp. By the light of the kerosene lamp they put on their clothes - it was not a simple task. They started with woolen underwear and put on two pairs of trousers and two of shirts. They put on two pairs of woolen socks, fur-lined boots and a warm cap and heavy coat. It would be cold where they were going.

They went to the mess hall for breakfast. If their barracks were a long way from the mess hall, a truck carried the men to the mess hall. Crew members going on a mission might get a special treat - real fried eggs. Other airmen got powdered eggs.

While the crew members slept, mechanics had repaired, and refueled their airplanes. They had loaded the plane with bombs. The number and type of bombs depended on the distance they had to fly and whether they wanted to start fires, blow things up, or kill enemies.

After breakfast all crew members assembled for the general briefing. Up until this time the crew members did not know where they were going. They were anxious to find out. If it was a "milk run," there would be a huge collective sigh of relief. If it were a fiercely defended target such as Ploesti, orVienna, then there were no cheers, and many of those present had a tight feeling in the pit of their bellies. The officer who gave the briefing, usually an operations officer(G3 or S3) would uncover a map showing the target. He presented information about the target location, the IP, initial point and the RP, rally point. The IP was the place where the planes began their bombing run. It was just a few miles from the actual target. The RP was the place where the planes would rally, reassemble, for their trip home. The briefing officer provided information about cloud conditions and weather. He might add some motivational material on the importance of the target. Following are some briefing notes regarding a mission to Novi Sad. *"Our target today is the bridge at Novi Sad. It is the main route by which German Armies in Rumania are supplied. If we succeed in knocking it out, this route will be impassible for at least a week and perhaps as much as a month. It is a large six span steel bridge and knocking out any span will present a difficult repair problem for our Axis enemies."* The last item on the agenda was the synchronization of watches. Actions had to be done at specific times and all watches had to have the same time. (This was a long time before accurate quartz watches.) This was the general briefing for all crew members, officers and enlisted men.

When the general briefing was over, There would be a series of special briefings. For example all the bombardiers would assemble and receive additional and more detailed specific information that they needed to know - information about cloud conditions, wind speed and direction, time of expected arrival over the target and other data necessary for a bombardier to do his job.

The same would happen for the navigators. They would get much of the same information as the bombardiers. They would get exact geographic coordinates of their targets. In every formation, there was always a lead pilot, a lead bombardier, and a lead navigator. The lead pilot led the formation and the rest followed. The lead navigator set the precise course necessary to arrive at the target. It was his duty to make sure that the pilot had the right information to get the formation over the target at the right time The lead bombardier located the target; when he released his load of bombs then that was the signal for the rest of the formation planes to release their bombs.

Pilots and co-pilots had their own briefing. They would get much of the same information about weather, coordinates of the target and information that navigators and bombardiers received. They received information about the defense capabilities of the enemy. The briefers supplied information on the expected kind of anti-aircraft batteries and the amount of flak expected.

The briefer supplied information about the expected fighter strength, or the possibility of not encountering fighters. The briefers had access to intelligence gathered from higher command levels and data collected from debriefings of other crews who had made the same bomb run. Photo and weather reconnaissance units had collected weather information and photos for presentation at the briefing. The briefing data was a best estimate; certainty was not part of the package.

While the officers attended their special briefings, the enlisted men checked out their needed special gear - things such as electrically heated suits and footgear, parachutes, and life jacket that every soldier called a Mae West. Some of the men elected not to use the heated suits and instead doubled up on conventional warm clothing. Some feared failure of the electrical system and being left in a cold suit. Others are wary of electrical shocks resulting from electrical shorting Every airman had his own oxygen mask and a .45 caliber pistol with holster. The .45 caliber pistol presented a problem. If a crew member bailed out and landed in enemy territory, he might be considered an armed invader. As an armed invader, he would be shot. Should he take it or not? – It was not an easy decision. They also checked out a flak jacket which was an armored vest. At this same time all the gunners checked out the 50 caliber machine guns and installed them on mounts on the plane.

The crew assembled for the mission. The pilot reminded crew members not to carry wallets or other material not relevant for the mission. An Air Force chaplain was present to offer comfort and offered prayers for those who felt the need for divine assistance. The crew waited nervously; some hope for a last minute decision to "scrub" the mission. It seldom happened.

At a specified time engines were started. Taking off for the mission was not a simple process. Planes were positioned to taxi onto the runway in a specified sequence and to take off with very little time between planes. Take-offs had to be done exactly right so as to avoid accidents. The bombers did not leap into the air. They carried very heavy loads of fuel and bombs. Often they carried nearly the maximum permissible load. On return would have neither the bombs nor the fuel.

When a bomber left on a mission it did not fly directly to the assigned target. After take-off, the bombers had first to assemble into a group and get into the planned formation. On many of the missions planes from several bases would come together for the assembly of a great 200 plane, 300 plane or larger formation. Planes flew to a high altitude and circled and waited for all planes to get airborne and then the assembly process began. A basic building block of formations was a three plane V shaped unit with a lead plane and two following planes behind and on either side of the lead plane. Behind the leading group of three would be two more pairs of three planes. The pattern repeated over and over. All the planes did not all fly at the same level: their exact elevation differed. Some crew members looked up and saw the bottom sides of the planes above them and some crew members looked down and saw the top sides of planes below. The design of the formation is such that planes were not directly above or directly below other planes. The formation design was such that dropped bombs should not fall on a plane below, although there are records of such accidents. At the far rear of the formation there was one last plane. That last plane was called, "Tail End Charlie," and it was not a prized position. German fighters approaching a formation of B-17s often attacked the last plane in the formation.

Once the entire formation had assembled, they were probably flying at about 25,000 ft as they made their way to the target. Sometime early in the mission, the gunners received an order to test fire their guns - a final check to make sure they were ready for enemy fighters.

If their targets were the Ploesti oil fields, they began to cross the Adriatic Sea soon after they reached altitude and completed the assembly process. Crew members did not like to fly over water because they thought their chances of survival were not very good if they had to ditch over the ocean. If the target was in Germany, then they flew across much of northern Italy and over the Alps. They may have enjoyed looking at the snow capped Alps.

As they flew they looked at whatever scenery they could see. The crew members looked to see if their escorts are present. Escorts were either P-51s or P-38s. By this time of the war escort planes accompanied bombers all to the target and stayed with them all the way home. Escorts tended to keep their distance from formations of B-17s.

The navigator was busy with his work. One very common method of finding the way was called, "pilotage." This is a very simple system of navigation similar to what a driver uses with a road map. The navigator looked for prominent landmarks such as the junction of two rivers, or he looked for the town at the junction of the rivers. He looked for roads, and prominent landmarks and checked that visual sighting against his map. He also used dead reckoning. The main responsibility rested with the lead navigator who led the whole formation. He in turn checked with navigators in individual planes and with so many navigators they seldom got lost. If they flew inside clouds, that was a different story. If there were clouds below them then the pilotage system did not work. Then other skills had to be used: dead reckoning or celestial navigation.

It was very cold at the high elevations. As the planes got to elevations of 25,000 feet, crew member might don additional clothing or put on their heated suits. There was not much for the gunners to do. The engineer kept close track of the performance of all four engines and checked fuel levels and fuel consumption. The pilot and co-pilot were busy. The pilot would turn the flying duties over to the co-pilot from time to time. It was a time of apprehension and fear. Not the actual fear present in actual flak and fighter attacks, but the anticipation of flak and fighter attacks.

Sometimes formations made directional changes as feints to deceive the Germans. They might head for Brasov in Rumania and the defenders in Brasov would be alert and waiting for the attack. As they got close enough to expect to get some flak, the formation would make a turn and go toward the oil refinery at Ploesti hoping to catch the Ploesti defenders unaware. A last minute change like this might help to keep enemy fighters away.

The fighters scrambled for the defense of Brasov when the bombers actually were on their way to Ploesti. Such feints had some value, but probably were most successful only the first few times.

There was apprehension as the bomber approached the IP where the actual bomb run began. The lead plane fired off a flare. This was the signal for crew members to remove the bomb pins that ensured that the bomb could not explode unexpectedly. The flare also was the signal for enlisted men to open the bomb bay doors. Open bomb bay doors created considerable drag which increased fuel consumption. The bomb bay doors were open only during the actual bomb run.

As the formation approached the target, the enemy flak gunners began firing at the bombers. German flak gunners fired in a box or area just above the target. When American bombers got to the IP, they were ready to begin the bomb run. German flak gunners did not know where the IP point was, but they began their fire as the bombers approached the target.   To the crew members the visual signal was the appearance of spherical black puffs of smoke as the flak shells exploded and sent pieces of metal in all directions. The experience of flak was first an experience of seeing rather than hearing. When they could hear the flak explode and see the red flash that marked the initial explosion, they knew they were in an intense danger zone. Crew members had terms for flak. One was whether it was heavy, medium, light or no flak. Heavy flak meant that there was flak everywhere the crew member looked. Not only that, there was a great magnitude of flak. The density was great. Everywhere a crew member looked there were black puffs of flak. Accuracy was another element. If the flak was close to the planes, then it was accurate. If there were puffs of flak inside the formation, then the flak was accurate. If planes were being hit by flak, then the flak was accurate. If crew members could hear the flak explosions then the flak was close and accurate. A third quality of flak was tracking. Tracking flak followed a plane and sometimes caught up with the bomber. Tracking flak meant that the flak gunner had a specific plane in his sights and adjusted his aim to get more of a lead, or adjusting it in some other way to score a hit. If all three flak qualities were present, then there would be human casualties and airplane losses.

As the bombers approached the target, the job of the bombardier became critical. He had entered all relevant data into the Norden bomb sight. Relevant data was plane speed, wind speed, wind direction, altitude, and other factors. The Norden bomb sight took all these factors into consideration as the bombardier peered into the bomb sight. The bombardier was in control of the bomber as they approached the target. It must have been a nerve-wracking experience. The bombardier had to concentrate on entering data into the Norden bombsight and give his full attention to preparation for dropping the bomb load. He had to work while planes in his formation were being hit by flak and other planes in his formation were damaged and were going down or dropping back because the could no longer keep up. He worked while flak was exploding all around the plane. The entire success of the mission rested on the shoulders of the bombardier.

Generally speaking, German fighters did not attack bombers during the time they were over the target. This was not always true, but the air over the target was an extremely dangerous place to be. German flak gunners were filling the air space above target with flak and if a German fighter attacked a bomber in the formation, the fighter ran a high risk of being hit by flak.

The lead bombardier determined the exact moment to release the bombs. "Bombs away!" As the bombs were released, the crew members felt the plane appear to jump up because suddenly it weight has been greatly reduced. As soon as he released the bombs out of the lead plane, the remainder of the bombers in the formation released their bombs.

Sometimes there was an undercast of clouds as the bombers flew over their target. The Allies had a radar system called "Mickey Radar" that they used to determine the exact time to release bombs over the target. Apparently this device was not in use until later in the war.

The Germans were clever and used many stratagems to maximize their chances of shooting down allied bombers. They had one trick that they used on at least some occasions If a B-17 bomber crash landed in Germany, it came into the possession of the Germans. The Germans sometimes repaired the B-17 and made it flyable. They then tried to sneak the B-17 into an approaching or attacking allied formation. The German B-17 sent information about air speed location ahead to the defenders so that flak batteries and fighter planes were alerted. It was a nasty tactic, but not a war winning tactic

When all bombers had released their bombs, the formations took evasive actions. They could take little evasive action when they approached the target as it was necessary to keep organized and go in together for maximum effectiveness. Evasive actions were a rapid turn in one direction or another, or dropping in altitude to get below the level at which the German flak gunners had set the flak shells to explode. They might fly on through the target area to get out of the area of flak coverage. In some instances if the approach to the target had not taken the formation over the target, and no bombs dropped, then the whole formation might circle around for a second run. This doubled the danger of a mission.

After the bombers completed their bomb run they would reassemble at the RP, rally point to begin their trip home.

.   All of this time enemy fighter planes had been active. They may have attacked the formation on the way to the target. They usually did not attack the formation over the target. . German fighters liked to attack the lowest planes in the formations and the last plane or planes in a formation. Sometimes they waited until the bombers had completed their bomb runs and they could see which of the bombers were crippled. A crippled bomber lagging behind the formation was an easy target for a German fighter. On an incoming formation of bombers, there were no stragglers, but after going through the flak above the target, many bombers were hit and not able to fly fast enough to keep up. They may have lost an engine or received enough flak damage so that they could not function well enough to keep up with the formation. German pilots looked for such opportunities.

However, allied pilots in escort planes knew that some of the bombers would straggle after the raid. The leader of the formation might help the stragglers by slowing the formation so that damaged bombers could catch up with their formations. The allied pilots of fighter planes, as well as the German pilots usually stayed out of the flak zone above the target. It was too dangerous for American fighters and too dangerous for German fighters. Allied pilots had learned to respect the courage and skill of German pilots. Some of the German pilots were very skillful and very brave.

After the raid was over, the bombers reassembled and started for home.

Each plane checked for damage. If the only damage is a few flak holes, then the bomber stayed in formation and with the escort fighters protecting them, they stood a good chance of making it home safely. But many planes had substantial damage. Flak may have caused damage to an oil line, a fuel line, or an electrical system. Often the damage affected only one engine. If so, the engine could be feathered and the bomber could stay in formation and limp home safely. For the bomber so badly damaged that it could not keep up with the formation, the situation was more critical. Possibly, it might ask for and get fighter escorts to guard it safely home. If it straggled by itself, its chances of getting home safely were very poor. "Stragglers die in combat."

The time after the raid was over was the time when there might be air-to-air combat between Allied and German fighter planes. The job of the American fighters was to protect the straggling, wounded bombers. The Germans wanted to pick off the stragglers. There would be aerial combat. Such combat between fighters was called a "dogfight." There were many on the way home.

The pilot did checks on each individual crew member to see if they were alive and active. The pilot would check for major and minor damage to the plane. The pilot and bombardier wanted to know if all the bombs had been dropped. If some had "hung up" it would be necessary to salvo the bombs. For those returning home over the Adriatic Sea, the decision was easy. Otherwise it was a serious problem. If a crew member had been injured, then crew members administered first aid. They first tried to stop the bleeding and applied sulfa powder. Then they bound up the wounds. If the problem is very serious, they gave the wounded man a shot of morphine. They applied first aid; kept the crew member alive until they got home where the crew member could get first-class treatment.

Starting for home was a time of intense perception. They were on guard for enemy fighter planes The gunners had their fingers on the triggers of their 50 caliber machine guns and fired at enemy fighters that came within range. They watched the dogfights between Allied and German fighter planes; watched the actions of wounded bombers; watched for men bailing out of planes and counted parachutes; they checked to see if their plane was keeping up with the formation; they looked back to see what is happening to stragglers; looked back at the results of the raid; checked their own equipment to see if electrical flight suit and other gear were working; they began looking for landmarks that marked progress on the way home. The pilot and navigator paid attention to and stayed away from enemy flak centers on the way home.

As the formations got well away from the mission site and got away from the enemy fighters, an attitude of relaxation began to prevail. The pilot came down to a lower altitude where oxygen masks were no longer needed. It was possible to smoke a cigarette and talk to other crew members.

Crew members rejoiced as they approached their home base. As they neared the base, those planes carrying injured airmen fired off a flare to alert waiting medical personnel. Planes carrying wounded men received a priority for first landing. Planes that might not be able to land safely were sometimes delayed until later so that a unmanageable plane did not crash land and block a runway.

After landing safely, crew members dismounted their guns. Trucks picked up crew members to attend a post briefing session called the debriefing. In the debriefing area there would be a series of tables. Each crew gathered around the table for the debriefing. Each crew was debriefed as a group. The Intelligence officer, S-2 or G-2, asked questions about the apparent success of the bombing mission, the numbers and types of fighter planes encountered, the type, amount and accuracy of flak. They asked about B-17s that had gone down and tried to determine where they had gone down. They asked questions about the identity of B-17s that had gone down.(Bombers carried tail markings that helped to identify planes.) They asked if parachutes had been seen and how many were seen coming out of damaged planes. Intelligence officers used this information to alert partisans to the presence of allied airmen. In some instances it was feasible to send in rescue teams. In a rather strange but humane action, they sometimes alerted Germans to the presence of allied airmen. This would occur if planes went down in mountain regions where they could survive only for a very short time. It was better to have the crewmen be POWs rather than frozen corpses.

After the debriefing, the air crew turned their equipment in. Some of the materials used in the mission were classified materials and had to be turned in for safekeeping.

When all material had been returned, the mission was over and it was time to relax, discuss the mission on an informal basis with other crew members and with other crews. Their relief at finishing the mission may have been tempered by the fact that some planes had not returned safely.

Sometimes those crew members who had got home safely waited and watched by the runways to see if any stragglers had returned. They searched the sky and listened for the sounds of a wounded B-17. Rarely, the waiting men were rewarded with a returning straggler, and there would be great joy for the returning stragglers, like the joy on the return of prodigal son. Too often they waited in vain.

Trucks returned the crews to the mess hall. It usually had been a long time since they had a last real meal and they were hungry. Returning crew members were sometimes rewarded with one or more shots of whiskey or some other alcoholic beverage. It was a reward much appreciated by thirsty, weary, nervous airmen.

Each returning airman kept his own mission count and had his own personal musings, prayers and coping mechanisms. We can guess that Brother Bob may have had some of the following thoughts: *"Thank God I got through that mission. That was a really tough mission. That makes 24 trips and 32 missions for me. I wonder what my chances are of getting through to 50. My old buddy, Kelly Rasmussen, who flew with the 463rd squadron got shot down on his 45th mission. We have had one crew member suffering from combat fatigue and he has not been able to fly for the last five or six missions. I notice that I am getting a little testy and short-tempered. I never seem to be able to get enough sleep. It is hard to know how to cope with the system. Should I volunteer for additional missions. If I do, I mighty be able to make it home for Christmas this year. But, if do all that volunteering for extra missions, it may shoot my nerves which are already bad. Maybe it would be better for me it I just take missions as they are assigned to me and hope for a whole batch of milk runs. That way I may not get home in time for Christmas, but my mental health will probably be better. The war seems to be going quite well and I am quite sure we are going to win the war and I would like to be around to enjoy the peace. Once the war is over, there will be no more missions to fly. Maybe I should try to convince the docs that I am suffering from combat fatigue. If I could get a couple of months off to recover from combat fatigue, then maybe the war would be over by that time. Yet, I know I would not feel right about faking combat fatigue. Lots of other guys are nervous and scared, but they keep on flying."*

Each man had his own individual coping mechanism. Some worked better than others. Alcohol was an important element that helped many to get through a tremendously difficult time. Human companionship was a critical element for many. It may have taken the form of a game of pinochle, or poker or some other game. It may have been ordinary conversation. Some found solace in religion. Some who found solace in religion had never been religiously inclined before their experience in war. Some who had been religious leaned on existing religious beliefs to sustain them through their tour of duty.

Chapter 12 - More Missions

On the 13th of July in 1944 not everyone in the world was worrying about the next bombing mission. There were other things going on in other parts of the world. Back at Brother Bob's farm home in Nebraska, his father was just beginning the wheat harvest and it was a better year than most. Harvests and prices were good during wartime. For Bob's father the war period and the years immediately afterward were times of relative prosperity. In Budapest, Hungary the inventor of Rubik's Cube was born on this day. At Yankee stadium on that day two major league teams comprised of older men, pre-draft age men, and men classified as 4F played baseball. The Boston Red Sox beat the New York Yankees 8 to 4. Over in the Pacific theater US Marines were beginning an operation to take back the island of Guam which the Japanese had taken during the early part of the war. On this day the famous author and aviator, Antoine de Saint-Exupery, who wrote the children's book, The Little Prince and adult books about aviation, was killed when he was shot down by German fighter planes while he was on a reconnaissance mission in the Mediterranean area. In Europe the Allies had invaded the European mainland, but were still bottled up in a relatively small area in France. The Allies were, however, building up forces for later drives into Europe.

On the 13th of July 1944, Brother Bob took off for the 8th time and the target was Pinzano in northern Italy. It was an easy target. They called such easy targets "milk runs." A milk run was an easy mission that counted as a mission but involved little danger.

Bob's account says, " *Flew 068, "Heaven Can Wait." We carried 500 pounders and bombed a railroad bridge. It was an easy mission - no flak, no fighters.*

The official diary of the Fifteenth Air Force says this of the mission. *591 bombers attack targets in NE Italy; B-17s hit marshalling yards at Maestro and railroad yards at Latisana, Pinzano, al Parliament and Venzone; B-24s bomb marshalling yards at Brescia, Mantova and Verona; and oil storage at Parto Marghesa and Trieste; P-38s and P-51 fly escort; other P-51 carry out a sweep over the Po River valley.*

So it was an easy day and the mission counted toward the magic number of 50 missions. . On this day the crew had encountered no flak and so they did not walk around the plane and count the flak holes nor were there any holes to measure. It was a welcome respite from the dangerous missions completed and dangerous missions yet to come.

Missions to destroy railroad yards or marshalling yards were of considerable value but, from a strategic point of view, not of lasting value. Rail yards could be repaired in a relatively short time and be functioning in a matter of a few days. Even so rolling stock and freight were often destroyed and denied to the enemy.

On the very next day, the 14th of July, Bob was on the operations schedule. This mission was no milk run. The 15th AAF hit oil refineries at Budapest and the Axis defenders were ferocious in their defense. Bob has this to say concerning the mission to Budapest.

We flew in the "436" (Vicious Vixen) The flak was heavy, intense, accurate and tracking. We got 15 or 20 holes in our ship the size of a quarter.

Had it a little rough - if any of our crew could be blamed - guess it was me. ___?___ hose (probably oxygen hose?) twisted around support column of ball turret and all oxygen leaked out of right waist. Waist gunner Hill passed out from lack of oxygen. Radioman Pietrolungo and waist gunner Bones gave him emergency treatment in the radio room and brought him back to consciousness. . My turret ran out of oxygen and I had to go up in the nose right after the target run. We hit an oil refinery - looked like we did a good job.

No Fighters were encountered. The P-38s flew with us going off the target - sure did look good to me. When I was afraid we would be attacked with only two gun positions working - I indeed can say as another gunner of 50 missions said, "God Bless American and the P-38s."

The official 15th AAF report was less dramatic. 430 B-17s (sic) and B-24s attack oil refineries at Budapest and Petfurdo, Hungary and Marshalling yards at Mantua, Italy; P-51s and P-38s provide escort; P-38s fly an uneventful sweep of the Budapest area; and P-38s strafe trains north of LaSpezia and dive-bomb Ghedi Airfield in Italy.

On a personal basis the 14 July mission illustrates one of the many types of problems that can cause casualties or cause a mission to fail. In this case the twisted oxygen hose did not cause any severe problems, but if they had been subjected to a powerful attack on the right side, they would have been nearly defenseless with possible dire consequences.

In the big picture, this raid shows the possible scope of a single mission. The main targets were the oil refineries, but the mission also hit the marshalling yards at another site, and the fighter planes made a strafing attack on some trains. The last probably was a target of opportunity.

Brother Bob got not one day of rest before his next assigned mission. He was, by this time, a seasoned veteran. He had been on some "milk runs' and he had bombed oil refineries which were the most dangerous of all targets.

By this time Bob had gotten over his airsickness and he did not have further problems with this malady.

His mission assignment on 15 July was the oil refineries at Ploesti, Rumania. This was perhaps the most dangerous target of all the dangerous Axis targets. It was vitally important to the Axis Powers. It was their main source of petroleum products and it was critically important for them to hold on to this system of refineries in and around Ploesti. Consequently they defended it to the utmost.

The Allies had long known of the importance of Ploesti and knew that it was a target that must be destroyed. Allied planners as early as 1942 wanted to bomb the oil refineries at Ploesti. It was not feasible to bomb Ploesti from bases in England as it was beyond the range and capability of bombers and bases.

However, there was at least one Ploesti raid in 1942. It came about through a set of complex circumstances. (Data from(12-1)In May of 1942 a Colonel Halvorson left Florida with 23 new B-24s bound for China as part of a plan to bomb Tokyo. He took off from Florida and headed east. When he got to Egypt, which was then held by the British, he received orders to use the planes to bomb Ploesti. Late on June 11th of 1942 the planes took off to bomb Ploesti. They arrived near the target early on the 12th. They actually dropped some bombs in the Ploesti area but did little important damage. Some of the B-24s got back but others ended up interned in Turkey. The first Ploesti raid was not a success.

By summer of 1943 the Germans had been driven out of much of North Africa and the Allies had some air bases closer enough to targets such as Ploesti, but the bomber bases were still in North Africa. In 1943 the situation was more promising and bombing raids to Ploesti began to both possible and at least partially feasible.

In 1943 another group of 154, or perhaps 177, bombers made a raid on Ploesti. That raid is described in the chapter on Hazards.

Brother Bob had been on a very intense and trying schedule. On the 15th of July, he was assigned to fly on that most dreaded of all targets: Ploesti. It was his third day in row to fly a combat mission. Such schedules quickly added to the individual mission total, but were hard on nerves of those who flew such difficult schedules.

Here is what Bob said of that mission on 15 July. *Went to Ploesti - 500 pounders I believe it was - hit oil tanks and depot. It looked like a good job; smoke must have been 15,000 to 18,000 feet high - highest I've ever seen smoke. Flak was heavy, accurate and tracking. When off the target a trail of flak puffs were following us about 100 yards below and behind us.*

When we turned the flak turned also. We saw on plane go down just after passing over the target - couldn't tell what kind but looked like a straggler B-17 who made bomb run by himself. A flak burst in a vital spot - could see big flames after falling about 1000 feet. No enemy fighters seen.

The official AAF report on the raid had this to say. *In Rumania 600+ B-17s and B-24s bomb 4 oil refineries in the Ploesti area and the Teliajenul pumping station; P-51s and P-38s fly 300+ escort missions.*

It was a difficult mission but perhaps not as bad as it might have been. The flak was very heavy and the flak gunners were doing a good job of tracking the bombers - but not quite good enough. There was one bomber that came in late - straggling but able to make a bomb run by itself. This gave the flak gunners a single target to shoot as instead of a whole flight. They hit their target. The gunners were rewarded by bringing down an enemy bomber. Later. in America, ten families would receive the dreaded letters telling families that their sons or husbands had been lost.

Bob's schedule did not get any easier, on the next day the 16th of July there was another mission. This was his 4th day in a row. The mission on the 16th was another very dangerous mission. Vienna was the target: oil refineries and aircraft factories. This mission was probably more hair-raising than his mission to Ploesti on the previous day.

We carried 400 lb. Frags in 570 ship called, "Achtung." We had plenty of escort and we saw no enemy fighters. Tailgunner Williams said he saw four 109s. We saw two B-17s of the 301st collide over the target. They went down in flames. Another went down on the edge of the target; we only saw two chutes - pity those poor boys because they must have landed right in the city of Vienna.
Flak was intense, tracking and accurate - worst flak I've encountered in my 14 missions.

Our ship got hit in left wing with other scattered holes. The left wing had to be removed and replaced as well as Tokyo tanks.
(name undecipherable) flew in a another plane and I'd say he was lucky to get back. He came home from target on 3 engines. The no. 4 engine had a big hole in it. When he landed, they found a big hole in the rudder; rudder wouldn't work on landing but the brake worked. They had to leave the plane setting on the edge of the runway. The brace that supported the no.1 engine was hit pretty bad.

That fourth mission in four consecutive days ended the intensive string of Bob's missions. Here are his comments on the following day. He also tells about a visit from an old friend named McGee.

... (on) the day after this last raid it was non-operational. I heard that

only 5 planes in our squadron were in a condition to fly. Yeah, I'm thinking stronger now, "combat is rough."

*My old friend McGee was here today. He had quite an experience. Their plane came from the target with only two engines working because their oil systems were shot out. One of the propellers was wind milling. They hardly got over the mountains on their way home and they were about to ditch into the Adriatic Sea. In a final effort to keep from ditching, they threw guns, ammo, radio equipment overboard; they salvoed the ball turret into the Adriatic Sea. (*It was possible to detach the ball turret and drop it. It required special tools that not all B-17s carried. It took 15-30 minutes work to detach the ball turret.) *They managed to lighten the plane enough to enable them to make it home. Mc Gee said when they got back the S2 interviewed them to get the full story of their adventure. He said the crew might get to go back to the United States.*

Brother Bob had a four day respite for crew to rest and rejuvenate to whatever extent rejuvenation was possible. Mechanics, armorers and maintenance men repaired planes, replaced parts and got the planes into flying condition again.

On the 20th of July, the planes of the 346th Squadron and Brother Bob were again scheduled to fly. This time their target was Memmingen, Germany.

We carried 500 lb. Bombs to Germany today - flew in ship 055 called, "Dynamite."(also identified as Dinah Might) Yes, old "Dynamite" let go of some firecrackers. We dropped them on an airdrome and repair depot. It looked like a pretty good job. We saw quite a few planes on the ground. We encountered no fighters, but we did see a few dogfights. No flak today. We flew over the Alps today - just about 50 miles from Switzerland. They are high and snowcapped. We heard a reliable report that four men from 851 have returned. I guess they met partisans in Budapest who gave them help to get out.

Brother Bob's first trip out was an Early Return and did not count toward his mission total. His first mission that counted was a mission to Vienna and Bob had flown in plane 851. Bob had noted on the mission that "851" had been shot down and he had concluded that all the men were probably dead. Not so! At least four of them had survived.

Bob got another four day respite before his next mission: Northern Italy. Bob says of this mission:

Carried 1000 lb. Bombs and flew in "286." It was a new ship that had only flown on 5 missions. No fighters sighted; flak was moderate but accurate. In fact a piece of flak came through the nose section and went through the floor and table and hit Lt. White's computer breaking it into a 100 pieces. We hit a tank repair depot. (At Turin, Italy)

Here is the official report from the 15th AAF. *200 (sic) bombers attack targets in France and Italy; B-17s attack tank repair and ball bearing works in Turin, Italy; B-24s attack the harbor at Genoa, Italy and airfields at Valence/LaTresorerie and Les Changoines, France; fighters hit troop concentrations at Sjenica, Prijepalje, Pljeulja and Andrijevica; fighters provide escort and strafe the Prizren, Yugoslavia area.*

The mission to Turin, Italy should have been an easy mission, but as long as there were flak gunners there were no easy missions. It took only one lucky or very accurate hit to make the difference between life and death. Lt. White or another crew member could easily have been killed in this mission.

With one day's rest Bob was sent to Wiener Neustadt on another hair-raising mission. Here is his report of the 26 July mission.

Went to Vienna (listed in official records as Wiener-Neustadt near the city of Vienna) *We hit a plane factory at the edge of the city. Flak was about like my second trip there. There was Boo-Coo flak - heavy intense and accurate.*

*We had numerous holes in our ship; one was about the size of a fist. (The flak) went right through the side of the ship hit our good old armor plate. We had another go through the right tail hitting and breaking deicer line for the right elevator surface. (*Deicer not used in combat*) Another ship from our squadron, "182" came from target on two engines; they salvoed all armor plates and flak suits. Boy those flak gunners are plenty good at Vienna. They say that they graduate from schools there. One bombardier got wounded and one engineer was wounded bad enough so that he had to go to the hospital. Another man got a piece of flak in his butt. I also heard that a tail gunner and a radio operator had been killed by flak.*

The official 15th AAF report: Fighters on the second shuttle mission leave USSR operations FRANTIC bases; strafe enemy aircraft in the Bucharest, Ploesti, Rumania area and return to bases in Italy. In Austria 330+ B-17s and B-24s attack the Wiener-Neustadt aircraft factory, the airfield at Markersdorf, Thalerkof, Zwolfazing, and Bad Voslan, and targets of opportunity in the Vienna area. Also hit are Szbathelp Airfield, Hungary and oil storage at Berat, Albania. Fighters fly escort and carry out patrols and sweeps in Brod, Zagreb, Yugoslavia and Ploesti - Bucharest, Rumania area; bombers and fighters claim 70+ enemy aircraft shot down. (operation FRANTIC was a special operation to set up a system so that American planes could land in Soviet territory and refuel and return home.)

After this Bob got a four day rest and when assigned to another mission it was relatively easy.

Flew in "570" and we started for Budapest but overcast caused us to hit Brod marshalling yards. Flak was light to moderate. No enemy fighters seen.

The 15th AAF report had this data on the Brod mission. *300 bombers attack targets in Hungary and Yugoslavia; B-24s bomb Duna Airfield; B-17s bomb the aircraft factory at Budapest and marshalling yards at Brod, Yugoslavia. P-38s and P-51s escort the missions.*

Sometimes a mission that seemed to be easy turned into a very dangerous mission and sometimes a mission that really was not overly dangerous could be very hazardous for a single plane that happened to be in the wrong place at the wrong time. After the mission to hit the marshalling yards at Brod, Yugoslavia, Bob got a long respite he did not go out for nine more days. He must have thought that to be the equivalent of a small vacation. However, if he had enjoyed relative safety for those nine days, he encountered a perilous situation in his next mission on the 9th of August.

Flew "182" to a target between Vienna and Budapest. Flak was light - for most men they chalked this mission up as "milk run," but not for me or I should say us. We had a full regular crew except for Bones who has a nervous system on the bum; and is grounded for a few days at least. Anyway, a flak gunner scored a real hit on no.1 engine just after releasing our bombs. Engine caught on fire as oil leaked down onto the supercharger wheel. I was out of my turret in a flash - in fact I had my chute on before the waist gunner of radio man. Guess we lost a whole tank of oil. Fire died down quickly in about a minute after I got out. Engine wind milled all the way home. We were a straggler - no enemy fighters sighted - had quite a few P-38s escorting us on the way home. I was sure glad to see them. When we were on the ground we examined the hole. It went in at the bottom and made about a 5 inch diameter hole. It came out at a 36 inch diameter hole. Major said it was the biggest hole he had ever seen.

The 15th AAF report lacks the drama of Brother Bob's report. *Around 400 bombers with fighter escort, hit targets in Hungary and Yugoslavia; B-17s bomb an aircraft assembly plant and a rolling stock plant at Gyor, Hungary and marshalling yard and oil refinery at Brod, Yugoslavia; B-24s bomb 2 airfields and an oil refinery in Budapest, Hungary.*

Brother Bob had noted previously that "stragglers die in combat." Fortunately, there were no fighter planes in the area to attack them and even though they straggled behind the formation, the P-38s stayed with them and protected them on the way home. On most missions the navigator did not have much to do. The pilot simply stayed in formation following the lead plane or lead formation. But on this mission the navigator earned his pay and used his navigational training. He was responsible for setting the pilot on the correct course to get home. He apparently did an excellent job.

On the next day, the 10th of August Bob made another mission to Ploesti. He flew with another crew. He writes - *I flew with Baran's crew in "286." We saw no fighters and bombed from 28,000 feet and encountered little or no flak. We had five out of our 16 bombs hang up. We carried them over to the Adriatic and dropped them there. It was a pretty good mission. It sure seemed easy after previous missions. I was what you might call a little jittery, nervous, or just plain scared from previous missions.*

The 15th AAF report said, *"B-17s and B-24s with fighter escort hit 6 oil refineries in the Ploesti, Rumania area...*

Next, on the 12th of August, Bob flew an easy mission to Savona in northern Italy. It was as ordinary as far as bombing missions go

On his next mission on the 15th of August, Bob took part in an important historical event. Much space in history books tells of the invasion of France in June of 1944, but a second, and nearly comparable invasion took place when the Allies invaded southern France on August 15th. Here is Bob's account of that mission.

We flew in "570" Achtung and carried 100 lb. Demolition bombs. We had 38 bombs in our plane. It was "D" day. It was the earliest "H" hour ever for me. They roused us up out of bed at 2400, midnight. The most planes I ever saw in the air were assembled together that morning. It was very hard to see from the ball turret that night as we approached the target. We saw large groups of B-24s, and B-25s and also saw B-26s, P-38s and P-51s and many kinds of Navy planes; we also saw lots of Spits and Hurricanes. (British fighter planes). We saw the invasion ships and barges of the invasion fleet; it was the darndest bunch of ships that I have ever seen. We saw the fleet even though the sky was partially overcast. We were able to see the Navy ships shelling the coast. There are huge flashes of flame when the big Navy guns fire. Col. Seeman told us at the early morning briefing that this invasion was 50% greater than the Normandy invasion and I could easily believe that. If something happened that we didn't make it to the target at or before 0700, we were not to drop bombs; we reached the target at 0710 and "bombs away." The H hour for the infantry to hit the beaches was 0730.

We saw several planes collide and blow up and go down in flames; they really lit up the sky.

The invasion barges and ships were only a short distance from the shore. We heard reports that the landing took place exactly on time: 0730. We heard that there were the most airmen in the air together than at any other time in all history. The report said we had 14,000 American airmen in the air that morning. We encountered no flak.

The day after this mission, Williams; Bud and I went to town and saw Marvin Bates, who we had known previously. He flew with a different Squadron, the 463rd, the flew to a target inland about 90 miles. Their target was some bridges and they encountered flak and lost 2 of 7 ships. Bates was really sweating on that mission. That flak is not popcorn.

The Official 15th AAF account says: *In the Fifteenth AFs first mass night raid, 252 B-17s and B-24s took off before dawn and pounded beaches in the Cannes/Toulon area in immediate advance of operation DRAGOON. 28 other fighter escorted B-17s sent against coastal gun positions abort the missions owing to poor visibility; and 166 P-51s escort Mediterranean Tactical Air Force C-47s carrying airborne invasion troops. (*Operation DRAGOON was the code name for the invasion of southern France.)

The mission flown in support of the invasion of southern France was, from a historical point of view, the most important mission the Bob flew in. For him it was not the most dangerous mission, but a most interesting spectacle to see from the air. How many people have the opportunity to get a really good view of important historical events? Unfortunately, many of those who took part in the great battles and events of the Second World War did not live to tell about their experience.

In the great wars of history there have been great actions of important historical significance that have been long remembered because of the heroism, determination and courage of one or both sides. An individual veterans presence, or participation, in these battles marked that veteran as an extraordinary person; a veteran worthy of respect and honor. Here are a few examples.

Agincourt: a famous battle fought in 1415 in which the British prevailed against the French

Waterloo, another battle that decided the fate of Europe, in 1815.

Gettysburg, a battle in the American Civil War in 1863.

San Juan Hill, a battle in the Spanish American War of 1898

Muese-Argonne, a battle in the World War I

The Great Invasion of Europe in 1944

Ploesti, an air battle of World War II

The foregoing list is by no means exhaustive, but rather a representative sample biased in favor of Anglo-American culture and history.

<u>Chapter 13 - A Look at The Enemy Side</u>

When nations fight wars, the conflicts are less personal than conflicts between individuals who know each other. It is somewhat ironic that personal conflicts between individuals seldom result in permanent or fatal injuries to either of the parties. In wartime the individual airman or soldier probably did not personally know any of the individual enemy personnel. In spite of the lack of individual animosity, armed forces personnel undertook, with great zeal, the task of killing the enemy.

American soldiers varied greatly in education and some were very well informed about the aims of the war and others knew very little about our nation's war aims. Every soldier in the United States Armed Forces knew that the Japanese had made a surprise, unprovoked, sneak attack on Pearl Harbor resulting in great loss of life - both civilian and military. They knew that the US Navy had suffered grievous losses in that attack. Suddenly, all over America, a sense of patriotism that had been partly dormant, emerged as a tremendous motivating force. After the attack on Pearl Harbor both young and middle aged men rushed to enlist in the Armed Services. The attack on Pearl Harbor was a prime motivating factor to enlist; to seek vengeance; to even the score.

Additionally, American soldiers were motivated to fight against the Germans. Most knew that the United States had participated in the first World War. They knew that America had been on the side of the British and French in that war. They were, for the most part, informed about Hitler's aggressive actions against Austria, Poland, and Czechoslovakia. Hitler's outright annexations and aggression against these small and nearly defenseless nations created a sense of outrage against Hitler and against Germany. The Germans had violated the American sense of fair play.

The Japanese sneak attack on Pearl Harbor and Hitler's aggressions and annexations created a strong patriotic motivation on the part of American servicemen to put the situation right. Putting the situation right would require battles, attacks, bombings and many other acts of violence. People get killed in wars and American soldiers were prepared to kill the enemy when required to do so.

This created a situation, perhaps common to other wars, that motivation existed for soldiers to kill the enemy, but they felt little or no individual animosity to enemy soldiers.

In Germany the situation was similar in some respects and different in others. The Germans felt that the Treaty of Versailles had been unfair. They hated the provisions of the Treaty. They felt impoverished and humiliated

by the provisions of the treaty. Hitler, with his aggressive policies and
nationalistic actions, offered a possible way for Germany to emerge as a
stronger and more successful nation. Instead of a surprise attack from
another nation, the German territorial recoveries and expansions provided
patriotic motivation for German citizens and soldiers. Although Americans,
then and now, looked on Hitler as an evil aggressor, the typical German
citizen saw Hitler in a much different light. When Hitler's initial
aggressions gained or regained territory for Germany, it created a
tremendous patriotic motivation for the people of Germany.

Hitler and his chief propaganda minister Joseph Goebbels controlled the
amount and kind of information available to the people of Germany. The
German people heard some anti-Jewish propaganda but they knew little or
nothing about relocation, death camps or any of the rest of Hitler's deadly
anti-Jewish policies and programs. They did not know about his harsh
policies of treatment of mentally deficient or physically defective persons.
Information about his outrages was not available to the people of Germany
until after the war was over. In the early part of the war and in the middle
part of the war, Goebbels and Hitler fed only positive propaganda to the
people of Germany.

Looking at the situation in Germany from a 21st Century point of view,
we are convinced that the Allies were on the right side of World War II. We
can site mountains of evidence of the criminality of the Nazi regime. After
the war ended the Allies conducted War Crimes Trials and convicted a
number of prominent surviving Nazis and some were put to death.
However, during the second World War, the Germans, Japanese and Italians
were convinced that they were on the right side. They knew that they were
right and the Allies were wrong.

Now we will take some time to look at what life was like on the German
side. We will give special attention to the German airmen, the counterparts
of Brother Bob, but we will look at other aspects of life in Germany during
World War II.

*On his second mission Brother Bob says, "Flak not as heavy of this
date 6/27/44 as yesterday. Some enemy fighters* (were in the area) - *took a
potshot at a 109 - never got him but a P-38 was sure on his tail - he was a
brave guy - he attacked middle ship in the element back and below us.*

This was a typical contact that Brother Bob had with the enemy. He saw
only the fighter plane. Gunners reported that they sometimes caught an
imperfect glimpse of a pilot in a fighter plane.

Now we switch to the point of view of the German fighter pilot. This is
an account of the actions and feelings of a German fighter pilot. The

following is a narrative tells of his actions and feelings as participated in combat against American bombers raiding Germany. Material from (13-1)

I started behind the Gruppenstab[II.Gruppe] as leader of 9,Staffel JG 54 from the airbase at Oldenburg on April 16th, 1943, 12:29 CET for reported American B-17s. Around 12:40 CET we recognized 120 to 150 four-engine Boeing-type bombers, altitude 7-8000 meters, (about 20-23,000 feet) *to west of Wilhelmshaven. The enemy unit flew course S to SE. We passed the enemy bombers on the left, to attack him frontally. As we had just enough lead to set up an attack, the enemy turned left, so that we now had a right-hand position to the bombers.* (The German formation approached the American bombers from behind and then passed the formation and turned and attacked the formation from the front.) *Now I corrected my direction a bit and set up a frontal attack with the whole Staffel. At the same time the enemy continued turning left, so that I was in a very bad attack position. I did not expect an effective attack. Meanwhile, the B-17s attacked Bremen and turned back South, then turned West. Now I started another attack and flew directly frontal to the leading box. I opened fire on the right B-17 of the leading box from 500 meters up to a ramming-distance; I observed very good hits in the canopy and engines of the Boeing. At the last moment I wanted to push underneath the Boeing, but I failed, ramming the bomber.(* The pilot probably did not intend to ram the B-17.) *My 109 completely lost its tail. The aircraft immediately went into a very fast spin and did not react naturally to any rudder movements. I decide to bail out at once. For that I pushed away the canopy and opened the beltlock. I was immediately catapulted out of the aircraft. I overturned _____(?) and lost altitude from 6000 to 5000 meters, where I could launch my parachute. It took 15 to 20 minutes with strong wind speed, until I reached ground; passing by woods, lakes and electricity wires. In any case, the stormy wind and my wild pendulum swings made the crash so severe that I lost consciousness. I was dragged several hundred meters through a field.*

When I woke up and wanted to disconnect the parachute belt, I could not do it because the rubber dinghy handicapped me. I first stripped off the chute so I could bring the chute down by pulling on the ropes. In the Home Area were stationed home guards, who were former soldiers of WWI. They observed the dogfight and saw the fall of the American bomber from which the crew bailed out. The home guards mission was to catch the Americans. Their mission was successful and they caught me too. German flight-overalls looked like the American ones, although we had strange badges on ours. As a Hauptmann, I had (insignia) to signify my rank. I was still groggy from crashing to the ground, so I didn't resist against being caught.

A little bit later, when my mind cleared up, one of the home guards, said to another, "Look man, there is an Ami, wearing the Knights Cross!!."

So they all turned: they celebrated my victory. In the nearby village of Grosskoren;, the mayor gave a big victory party, where I became honorary citizen of Grosskoren. It was a drunken anticipation of the "Endsieg." (Endsieg means final victory.*) My parachute jump had consequences: My whole body had green and blue fields - IO could not move for the next three days. The victory was proofed and confirmed by the RLM.*

In the foregoing narrative, a German Captain, the leader of a group called a Staffel,(A Staffel is a group of approximately 12 planes) led an attack on a formation of B-17s. They followed the American formation of B-17s and maneuvered so they could make a frontal attack on the B-17s. The German captain intended to attack a B-17 from the front and then fly under the bomber, but he was too close and plane's tail was torn off. He had to bail out and home guards picked him up. Home guards were World War I veterans whose duty it was to pick up Americans who bailed out of B-17s. In this case they, at first, thought the Germans captain was an American before they noticed that he was wearing the Knight's Cross, an important German decoration. The narration indicates that a number of American airmen bailed out of the downed B-17.

The following is another account of a fighter pilot attacking B-17 bombers. In this episode the German fighter pilots, from a German point of view, have a very good day. Here is Hans Iffland's narrative about defending Berlin from 8th AAF bombers in 1943. (Same source as 13-1.)

Normally we got up about 6:00 AM and reported to the operations building a 6:30, where we had our breakfast. Officers and NCOs sat around chatting, some playing cards, other writing letters or reading books.

There were several rooms and offices in the operations building, as well as the main briefing room. There was a large gridded map on one wall of the waiting room, where the position of the bomber stream was marked when it began to come in. Next to the map was a large board with all of the pilots' names, their victory scores, which operations they had flown in, and when pilots had had to break off operations prematurely for any reason. So one could see at a glance which pilots had pressed on with their attacks, and which were liable to break away at the least sign of engine or other trouble. Obviously, if a man had engine trouble had returned early four times in a row, questions would be asked. The board also showed who was sick or wounded, who was on leave, etc. While waiting, I would play cards or ping-pong.

When the bombers were reported coming in we had three states of readiness. First 30 Minute Readiness... This was a loose form of readiness, and meant only that the pilots were not allowed to leave the airfield. Normally martial music was played over the loudspeakers, and the announcements would interrupt this. Next readiness state was 15 Minute Readiness......... Then came more music. On this order pilots walked to the Staffel readiness rooms; next, they went their aircraft dispersed around the airfield. Earlier in the day each aircraft had been run up by the ground crewman, so each was ready for action, fully fueled up and armed. Each aircraft carried a drop tank under its belly. The engine had been warmed up first thing in the morning. At this stage, the pilots put on their life jackets and other flying clothing, although it was often worn throughout the day.

Next stage was Cockpit Readiness:......... The pilots walked over to their aircraft and strapped on their parachutes, did up their seat harnesses, pulled on their helmets, and did up their radio connectors. Each Messerschmitt already had the large crank handle in place, sticking out the starboard side of the engine ready for the engine to be started.

At Cockpit Readiness, the pilots could hear the fighter broadcasts via the telephone line plugged into each aircraft. Cockpit Readiness usually lasted no more than ten to fifteen minutes though it could last for as much as an hour. For me, the minutes before being ordered to Cockpit Readiness and being given the order to take off were the most terrible of all. After the order came to get airborne, one was too busy to think about one's possible fate. But waiting to go with nothing to do but think abut what might happen - that was the most terrible time of all. Would one still be alive that evening, or was this the beginning of one's last day? My own greatest fear was that I might be seriously wounded with permanent injuries. Death was, of course, a fear, but that would have been the end. The thought of being left a cripple for the rest of one's life was, for me, the greatest fear of all.

AT 11:37 came the order to scramble. Single free flare rose up from the operations building. The scramble takeoff was normal for a German fighter unit, with the aircraft of the three Staffeln and the Stab unit dispersed at four points equidistant around the airfield. On the order to scramble, two crewmen hopped onto the wing of the Messerschmitt and began turning the crank handle to get the heavy flywheel of the inertia starter revolving. They would (turn) the crank faster and faster; then the pilot pulled a handle beside his right knee to clutch in the engine, which usually coughed a couple of times before starting with a throaty roar. After engine starting, the Stab took off first, straight out of their dispersal point. As they passed the center of the airfield, the tenth Staffel, situated ninety degrees to the left around the perimeter of the airfield, began his takeoff run Then the eleventh, then the twelfth Staffeln. After takeoff, the Stab turned left, circling the airfield, and climbed away collecting the tenth eleventh, and twelfth Staffeln. Once the Gruppe had assembled, the leader Major Friedrich-Karl Mueller, swung it around to a southeasterly heading for Magdeburg.

When we were within about 800 meters(2300 feet) of the bombers, we felt ourselves safe from the enemy fighters and had only the bombers' return fire to worry about. At such a range it was difficult to tell a Mustang from a Messeerschmitt, and both would be shot at by the bombers' gunners. Our orders were to help the Destroyers punch through the screen of escorts, so that they could engage the bombers. I remember seeing the bomber formation like a swarm of insects in the distance.

It was terrible to have to attack the bombers, which opened fire at very long ranges of about 800 meters, while our Messerschmitts had only limited ammunition - we had to hold fire until about 300 or 400 meters. This interception on 6 March 1944 as one of my first operational head-on attacks against an enemy bomber formation. The head-on attack was adopted because it was a more cost-effective way of engaging the bombers. When we attacked from the rear, there was a long period of overtaking when the enemy gunners were shooting at us, but we were not within range to fire at them. As a result we sometimes lost more fighters than we shot down bombers. When we attacked from head-on, we were able to fire for only about one second, but the bombers were big, and we were relatively small, so that we were far more likely to hit them than they were likely to hit us. Our tactic was to attack by Staffeln in line abreast, so that the enemy bombers could not concentrate their fire against any one of us.

During the firing run, everything happened very quickly. We were flying at abut 450 kilometers per hour,(270 miles per hour) and the bombers were flying about 380 kilometers per hour(240 miles per hour) so closing speed was about 800 to 900 kilometers per hour (around 500 miles per hour) After firing my short burst at one of the B-17s, I pulled up over it. I attacked from slightly above, allowing a slight deflection angle and aiming at the nose. We knew that just a single hit with a 3cm explosive round would have devastating effects anywhere on the nose, but it was hardly possible to aim accurately during the brief firing pass. I aimed at the nose but saw the flashes of the tracer rounds exploding against the Fortress's port wing root. And the whole time we could see the tracer rounds from the bombers flashing past us. I saw four or five rounds exploding around the wing root.

As I pulled up over the bomber, I dropped my left wing to see the result of my attack and to give the enemy gunners the smallest possible target at which to aim. I had also to pull up to get out of the way of the fire from other Staffeln of the Gruppe coming in behind me. Of course I did not want to ram the B-17. I saw the port wing of the B-17 slowly begin to fold up, and the bomber went down. Then I was out in the back of the formation, and my main concern was to join up with other Messerschmitts of the Gruppe for the next attack.

On this day we knocked down thirteen bombers in return for only one of our fighters lost and none of our pilots were killed or wounded. It seemed that we really were able to overcome the massive numerical superiority enjoyed by the enemy. We were astonished by our success, which gave us all new hope. We felt we really had grasped problem of dealing with great formations of bombers.

I tried to join up with machines from my Staffel, which carried white numbers. The eleventh Staffel had yellow numbers. If one was alone, one was highly vulnerable to attack from the Mustangs, and many of our fighters were lost that way. The Gruppe pulled around in a sweeping turn to the left of the formation, and then the fighters sped, flying a course parallel to and slightly above the bomber, overtaking them out of gun range as they moved into position for a second head-on attack. It was very important to deliver the second attack in line abreast with sufficient aircraft. If one or two attacked alone, the bombers could concentrate their fire on these and that was extremely dangerous. Our orders were to continue attacking the bombers so long as we had ammunition and fuel. It was frowned upon if undamaged fighters returned with fuel and ammunition remaining. Even if we had only ten rounds of cannon ammunition left we were expected to deliver another attack against the bombers.

I came in for my second attack, but the target bomber made a slight turn causing rounds to miss. At the time of the first attack, the bombers had been flying in close formation. Now there were gaps in the formation, and the bombers were fling further apart so the pilot would have more room to maneuver. The B-17 snaked from side to side when I opened fire. It was enough to make the rounds miss during the brief firing pass. Then I was out of ammunition.

The most dangerous part of the engagement was getting through the screen of escorts. On this day we had done so without difficulty. Our orders were to engage the enemy fighters only when we had to otherwise we had to concentrate our attack on the bombers which represented the greatest danger to our country. The only exception was when we were escorting the Destroyers.

Once one was out of ammunition, it was important to join up with other German fighters, because it was very dangerous if one was attacked by American escorts, If there four or five of us together, the Americans would be more careful about attacking us. Also, being short of fuel, it was important fix our position and decide where we were going to land.

On breaking away from the bomber, we went down in a rapid descent to about 200 meters to get well clear of the enemy fighters. At that altitude our camouflaged aircraft were very difficult to see from high above, while we could see the enemy machines silhouetted against the sky. A 200 to 300 meter altitude also gave us good R/T range, so we could contact our base. Sometime we flew back even lower than that and climbed only when we wished to call our base to make sure it was safe for us to land there since it might have come und enemy attack. When we arrive back over Salzwedel, we flew low over the airfield, and those pilots who claimed victories waggled their wings. I saw another aircraft in front of me doing it. We knew we had been successful even before we landed. When we were overtaking the bombers for our second attack, we had seen some going down, other streaming fuel or smoke. One went down about 1000 meters (3100 feet) and then exploded. It made a vivid impression.

After landing and taxiing to the Staffel dispersal, the first to meet me was my mechanic. He had seen me rock my wings, and when I had shut down the engine and opened the hood, he stood by the trailing edge of the wing, clapped his hands above his head, shouted, "Herr Leutnant, gratuliere!" and offered me a cigarette. Obviously if a pilot scored a kill, that counted for the mechanic also; it meant he had done a god job of preparing the machine. No shortage of cigarettes for the Luftwaffe; we were looked after very well as regards food and drink. I do not remember any problems when we operated in Germany, though there had been some difficulties in getting supplies through when we were in Italy.

When I reached the Gefechtsstand, our commander, Major Mueller, was already there receiving the report from his pilots. I awaited my turn then marched to the table. I clicked my heels, saluted and proudly said, " Melde Gehorsamst. Vom Einsatz zuruck. Eine Fortress abgeschossen!" Then I explained how I had hit it and seen the wing fold up on port side before it went down. "Ach, das war Ihrer! Hab ich gesehen!" exclaimed one of the other pilots. This was important, for without a witness, it was very difficult to get credit for a victory. Several other pilots said the same thing: The bomber had gone down in a spectacular manner, and several pilots remembered seeing it. "Gratuliere!" smiled Mueller. After me other pilots reported kills. Each one was marked on the board beside the pilot's name, so soon it was clear we had hah a very successful day.

Salzwedel was a permanent Luftwaffe airfield. Mueller announced, when the Gruppe stood down from readiness, "Tonight we celebrate!" After a bath and changing out of my sweaty flying suit, I was at the officers Kasino for dinner at 7:00 PM. Jagdegesechwader 3 had links with the Henkell wine company, which ensured that we never ran short of wine. Whenever a pilot was killed, it was usual for the Kommandeur to deliver a short requiem after dinner; then the pilots drank a toast to his memory before hurling their glasses, which were special cheap ones, into the fireplace. But there had been no losses on this day. The party would have gone on until after midnight, but it came to an end when Mueller said, " Jungs, that's enough. We must be ready again tomorrow." At a Luftwaffe officers' party we did not have violent games. We sang songs, but did not sing Nazi party songs. " Es ist so wunder winder schon, hoch in den blauen Luftigen Hohen." "Oh, du schoner Westerwald" "Auf der Luneburger Heide, in den wunderschonen Land." (The foregoing are names of the songs that the German officers sang.) *One of the officers would accompany the songs on guitar. A pleasant comradely evening, with the other officers steadily getting more and more drunk, then off to bed.*

Another German fighter pilot, Lieutenant Otto Stammburger's story is told in the book, Battles With the Luftwaffe by Theo Boiten and Martin Bowman, page 10. (13-3)

From October to the end of the war I served with Geschwader JG26 'Schlageter' on the western front. In May 1943 I was shot down for the first time by a Spitfire and seriously wounded. In December 1943 I was allowed to fly again. On 31 December I brought down my sixth American viermot(four motor), and was seriously injured again in the process. I was on operations as a fighter pilot from January 1941 to January 1944,with a few breaks in hospitals. In all I was shot down four times twice being seriously wounded with lengthy stays in hospitals. I shot down two Spitfires and six American viermots all in the period from October 1942 to May 1943 after which my flying ended.

These narratives by German pilots demonstrate the fact that German pilots often were very skilled at their craft; they were human beings; they enjoyed having a good time; they liked to celebrate success and they hoped to get through the war and enjoy life in a post-war Germany.

The narratives reveal much about the Luftwaffe, the German air force. The second account notes that the Luftwaffe had good food and other amenities such as wine. The Luftwaffe pilots, were, at least to some extent, the elite of the German armed forces. According to the account, - their food and treatment was probably better than the food other amenities available to the average German soldier.

The Luftwaffe had worked out tactics to deal with American B-17s. They made it a point to get in front of the bomber and attack it head on and then fly under or over the bomber. This required a high level of flying skill and as noted in one account, the pilot did not successfully fly under the B-17 after he had attacked it. However, Lieutenant Stammburger who fought B-17s earlier in war tells elsewhere in the Boiten and Bowman book about attacking B-17s from the rear. Apparently the Germans changed tactics later in the war.

The Luftwaffe had problems with an ammunition shortage. The pilots had been trained not to waste ammunition. They were under orders not to fire until they were close to the target. The American gunners could fire from a long distance and might get lucky and knock down a fighter from a long distance. The American gunners were not restrained by a shortage of ammunition.

German accounts from late in the war show that, in addition to the ammunition shortage, the German pilots were short of fuel; they could not always respond to Allied attacks because there was no fuel to use in a defensive action against Allied bombers.

As previously noted, the two main causes of American casualties were from fighter attacks and flak damage. We have looked at the German side regarding fighter attacks. Now for a look at the German side in regard to the people who manned the flak guns.

In World War II Germany suffered from a shortage of manpower. Every able bodied man had to served in the armed forces. And, almost without exception, every able bodied man was in the armed forces. Even so, Germany did not have enough manpower to fight the war, manufacture war equipment, raise food, and keep schools in operation and all the other things that needed to be done. To get the additional manpower they recruited manpower from groups that were, at least at that time, a little unusual.

Westerman in (13-4) provides a breakdown of the personnel in the 14th Flak Division which had a total of 62,550 people. This division was responsible for the defense of a synthetic oil refinery at Leuna. The breakdown looks like this: Regular Luftwaffe personnel - 44%, Labor Service personnel - 28% Male Luftwaffe auxiliaries - 10%, Female Luftwaffe auxiliaries - 5%, Hungarian and Italian volunteers - 1.5%, Soviet POWs - 6%, and Others - 5%

Manning the flak guns did not necessarily require the cream of German manhood. Hence the flak gunners came from many sources. Some women served as flak gunners. One of the most unusual sources was the use of Soviet prisoners of war as flak gunners. (One wonders if the Soviet flak gunners were conscientious in their aiming.) The Germans sometimes used women as flak gunners. They also used older men and young men under draft age. The following material about one such young German, Gustave H. Roosen, has been extracted from this source: (13-5) In the narrative Roosen explicitly makes a statement that his account of his experiences cannot be construed as an endorsement of Hitler of Hitler's policies.

Gustave was recruited at age 16 and became a flak gunner, or Flakhelfer. He was a former student at Monschau High School. He had been posted as a Flakhelfer at several sites in the east of Germany. His third posting was at an anti-aircraft tower in the area of Hamburg Germany, or Hamburg-Wilhelmsburg. Gustave had grown up in Hamburg and knew his way around the area.

He noted that the city had received considerable damage due to bombing raids earlier in the war. He noticed that camouflage nets had been placed over important targets such as railway stations and bridges.

The authorities assigned Gustave to help man a flak tower in Wilhelmsburg. Wilhelmsburg was some distance from the city of Hamburg and the dock area.

There were two flak towers sited close together. One was the gun tower. It was a square tower about 140 feet long on each side. It was about 125 feet in height or a total of nine stories high. The top floor was the gun platform from which they fired their anti-aircraft guns. They lived on the floor just below the gun platform.

The other tower was slightly smaller and had the function of fire control. It had radar and range finding equipment. The distance between the two towers was about 500 feet.

He says that his duties were not especially difficult. He sat on a metal seat, like a seat on tractor, and operated a hand wheel that had a power assist mechanism so that the power for moving the gun did not come from his muscles. The gun had some sort of aiming device that Gustave does not adequately describe.

Gustave said that they had air raids almost every night at approximately 8:00 PM. Hamburg was a port city and often the target of the raids, but it was also on the route that Allied bombers used to go to bomb Berlin.

Gustave used several different anti-aircraft weapons. On was a 128mm anti-aircraft gun. The 128 was a two barreled weapon and it was usually sited in flak towers such as those described by Gustave. This gun fired about 10 rounds a minute and could reach up to 35,000 feet. Through most of the war the Germans used time fused high-explosive shells; they were not able to develop an effective proximity fused shell before the end of the war He complains about the quality of the ammunition. Prisoners and other "forced laborers" worked in the factory that made the ammunition and they often sabotaged the ammunition in such a way as to cause it to explode prematurely and destroy the barrel of the anti-aircraft gun. He had had such an experience in his earlier posting. Although times were not clear inGustave's narrative, he also used another well-known and effective weapon. The 88mm gun was a very effective anti-aircraft weapon. It was such a good weapon that Army infantry and artillery units needed it for use as an anti-tank weapon. The eastern front were desperately in need of "88" Anti-aircraft units were not always able to get all of the 88mm guns that they wanted. The "88" required a crew of 10 people to operate it. It could fire more than 15 rounds in a minute and was effective in altitudes up to 31,000 feet which was the approximate altitude of the B-17 bombers.

Gustabe was a teen-ager during his service and most of his comrades were teen-agers. He tells of some of the events that happened that might have been typical for any teen-ager. Once a truck delivered 30 crates of wine for storage. The wine was to be used later for a celebration of Luftwaffe personnel. While unloading the wine, the flakhelfers managed to lose one of the crates so they could drink it themselves. In another instance he tells about a "secret door" that went into a room filled with electrical cables and used to service equipment. It was not ordinarily in use. Gustave and his friends used it as a hideout when trying to avoid being found. Later one of the officers found out about the hiding place and sealed it shut with heavy nails. That was the end of their hiding place.

Gustave and his young friends found time to visit with young girls who lived near the towers. They never went far away from the towers so that they could immediately get back to the towers if the air raid warning sounded.

Gustave mentions a very heavy bombing raid in March of 1945. After that time, the military gave him his discharge and he left to area to rejoin his family in a small German town, Detmold. His family had moved to a smaller town to escape the bomb raids that nearly all the major cities suffered. (The following data is from 13-6)

.   The Germans had fragmentary shells that exploded and broke into fragments in all directions. Later they developed an incendiary shell with incendiary pellets inside the shell casing. When it exploded, it might penetrate a flammable spot on a B-17 and set it on fire. It was a very effective weapon.

The Germans had railway mounted flak units that hey could transport from place to place to defend cities likely to be attacked or to defend places where flak units had been disabled or destroyed.

The British did much of their bombing at night and the Germans had searchlight batteries sited next to their flak batteries. The German searchlight batteries would seek out a British bomber and when one searchlight caught the bomber in its beam, then the other searchlights would concentrate on that one bomber. The flak gunners would give their full attention to the bomber in the searchlight. Woe to the bomber caught in caught in an accumulation of searchlights and flak batteries! Searchlights provided an excess of light to pilots and bombardiers who were partially blinded by the brightness and the pilots found flying difficult and the bombardiers found aiming difficult.

Next, we shall consider the German civilian condition during the war. Some of the following material is taken from (13-7)

At the beginning of the War, the German civilian population were in the middle of an economic recovery. Nearly everyone who wanted to work was working. The German standard of living was equal or higher than most other European nations.

As the War went on, things were not so good. However, the diet of the average German was still more than just adequate. In the middle of the war some food items became hard to get, but it was not a serious problem. The same generalization applies to other consumer goods such as clothing. It was not until near the end of the war that food shortages appeared and consumer items were nearly impossible to obtain.

The Germans who lived in rural areas did not get bombed and as a whole they were less affected by the war. Their diet was better than those who lived in cites because the rural people raised much of the food that they consumed. Those who lived in cites suffered the most from food shortages and from Allied bombing raids.

The Germans had given some attention to defense against bombing raids and had made plans and the plans covered things like the methods of controlling fires and providing security during air raids. When the actual war started, the volume and intensity of the attacks was much greater than the Germans had anticipated. Consequently, the Germans had to revise and augment their plans. One problem that the Germans did not adequately anticipate was the extreme effect of Allied incendiary bombs. In some cases almost all of some German cities were consumer in a great firestorm created by Allied bombing.

The Germans, famous for being thorough, built some excellent bomb shelters. Some were enormous in size and constructed of concrete. The shelters were excellent and effective, but the Germans did not build enough of them. Many German civilians had to rely on basement shelters - better than nothing but hardly bombproof. Casualties among those seeking safety in basement shelters were high.

The Allies bombed German cities intensively and consequently German bombing casualties were high. The following figures are for civilians, foreigners, and military personnel who were in the cities at the time of the raids. The figures are for the period from January1, 1943 to January 1, 1945. This is not all inclusive, but this period of time was the period of the most intense bombing of Germany. Official German statistics put the number of killed at 250, 253. This figure was later revised to 305,000. The number of those seriously injured was 305, 455. This figure was later revised to 780,000.

Deaths and injuries were not the only negative consequences suffered by the German nation. Many building were damaged or destroyed. According to one source, 485,000 were totally destroyed and 415,000 seriously damaged. Apparently, according to one source, more than 7 million Germans were rendered homeless.

Still another effect of the bombing raids was the destruction of German hospitals and other medical facilities. When hospitals and other medical facilities were damaged, many of the medical personnel were killed or injured. The effect of this loss was the impairment of the German health system to treat injured patients. This in turn meant that many of those injured could not return to their military or civilian occupation and were thus lost for longer periods of time than necessary.

Some of the following material is taken from (13-8) More recently, a German historian, Jorg Friedrich , had published a book with many pictures showing the consequences of Allied bombings. Friedrich puts the total number of Germans killed in Allied bombings at 600,000. He says that Allied bombings of Germany during the late stages of the war were indefensible.

Many historians, and ordinary citizens have looked at World War II as a war between good and evil. Hitler's mass killing of the Jews and other atrocities certainly qualify as one of the most evil figures in all of world history. Even if Hitler was the personification of evil, one can make an argument that the intensive raids on German cities were overkill. Hitler's Germany had already been defeated and no further raids were necessary. In England, near the end of the war, the civilian memory of the German blitz on London and other English cities was still fresh in their minds, and they could feel no pity for the Germans.

During the war the head of the British strategic bombing program was Air Marshall Arthur Harris, better known as "Bomber Harris." Harris advocated a bombing program of nearly indiscriminate bombing of German cities. Fredrich attacks the policy of Harris and Churchill in no uncertain terms. To say that he roundly condemns their policy is a gross understatement of his condemnation.

Fredrich makes an interesting discussion of the morality of Allied bombing of Germany. He says that after the war many Germans did not complain about the indiscriminate Allied bombing attacks because they saw the attacks as retribution for the atrocities committed by Hitler. Fredrich admits that the Germans started the war and initiated the bombings of major cities in Great Britain. He has written widely about the indiscriminate destruction of German cities. He is especially critical of Air Marshal Bomber Harris who planned and conducted the night bombing raids. These night bombing raids did not try to hit a specific military target; they were aimed at general areas and might be described as indiscriminate. The German casualties from these raids were enormous.

There were many facets of life in wartime Germany. The Allies did not bomb every city in Germany. Life went on but there were many changes. (Some of the following material is from (13-9) Religious life continued, but not exactly in the same way as before the war. For example, the Germans celebrated Christmas, but the official Government position was that Christmas should be celebrated as a non-Christian holiday. There was some problems in regard to the positions of the Catholic Church and the Nazi Government. The same was true for the Lutheran Church. The Nazi government never banned religion but the Nazi faithful were generally not Christians. During the war, church attendance increased and the Nazi Government did not like it ; however, they took no steps to ban worship. The German Army continued to have serving Christian chaplains. However the Government exercised some control over the services. They required the chaplains to include a prayer for Hitler as part of their services.

As the war in Germany continued, the need for military manpower increased and every able bodied man had to serve. The Government changed the draft laws so that men with as many as eight children still had to serve in the Military. The Government took other actions to improve and increase productivity by lengthening the work week to as much as 72 hours.

Some things continued very much as in peacetime. For example, musical concerts were held in spite of shortages, bombings and the shortage of musicians.

As the war went on, conditions got worse and worse. The shortage of food was serious and worsened by a partial failure of the potato crop which was an important part of the German diet. Morale began to suffer as Germans heard of defensive battles being fought in areas close to Germany and later inside of Germany. German soldiers who came home on leave provided the civilian population with information on how the actual war was going. It was not going well.

Conditions in Germany during the war were quite good in the early part of the war. That was still true through most of 1942, but things got worse after that time. By the end of 1944 and the first months of 1945 the situation became very serious.

In Great Britain, the conditions were also arduous. They suffered greatly from the bombing raids during the first part of the war. Their situation in regard to bombing improved as the war went on. While it was getting worse in Germany, it was getting better in Great Britain. Food shortages and other shortages were severe, but manageable. In the United States, conditions were much better than in either Germany or Great Britain. Compared to Britain and Germany, things were merely inconvenient in the United States. In the Soviet Union the situation was much worse than in any of the other participant nations.

Chapter 14 - Hazards

Brother Bob flew his missions with the 15th AAF in the latter part of World War II. He had a dangerous job and was lucky to survive and come home safely. An analysis presented later shows that he had about a 50-50 chance of making it through his 50 missions and coming home safely. The following short narrative shows that other airmen had worse odds.

Crawford J. Ferguson III a veteran of the bombing raids on Germany served in the 8th AAF. (14-1) Ferguson learned the hard way about the hazards of flying as a gunner on bombing raids over Germany. He says that, at the time he reported for duty with the 8th AAF, the average life of a B-17 gunner was 6 missions. He mentions a common saying among the gunners, " you're a gunner today and a goner tomorrow." Ferguson frankly admits to being extremely fearful during his bomb runs. He uses some colorful language to emphasize the quantity and quality of his emotional states. Ferguson makes no pretensions as a hero, but he evidently was a hero regardless of his lack of pretension. He flew numerous hazardous missions, and lived to come home and tell about his experiences. Ferguson said that he yet to meet a B-17 gunner who didn't pray for Divine assistance. Brother Bob has this to say about a raid on Ploesti, *"I'm not afraid to say I did some hard praying this time."*

Ferguson quotes from an official report by a Colonel John Doolittle. "While the Royal Air Force bombed by night, Americans in B-17s and B-24s thundered through frigid daylight skies filled with enemy flak and fighters, grappling with the costly demand of high altitude precision bombing. On the most dangerous missions, more than a quarter of American bombers failed to return. Ten hours on oxygen, intense cold, deafening noise, constant vibration, and a one in three chance of completing their tour, were the average prospects of our bomber crews. Our nation paid a heavy price. Over 30,000 United States airmen were lost in the air campaign against Germany alone. The world had never seen combat like this, and I pray it never will again."

One of the most hazardous missions of the entire war was one of the first raids on the Ploesti oil fields in Rumania. (Data from:14-2)

At the Casablanca Conference in January of 1943 the leaders of the Allied Nations agreed on some priorities for future bombing raids. One of the priorities was the bombing of petroleum facilities. Germany had only a limited amount of petroleum and relied on production from fields in Rumania as a major source of petroleum. It also had some capacity for production of synthetic petroleum.

At that time the 15th Air Force had not been formed. This was before Allied forces had landed in Italy. The only bases available to the Allies were those in Great Britain and in Africa. The bombers based in Britain could not make the round trip to Ploesti and back to Britain because of the range limit of American bombers. However, it was possible to fly from Britain to Ploesti, drop a bomb load, and then continue flying to Allied bases in North Africa, then under Allied control. This was not a very successful arrangement. The Allies thought that an attack on Ploesti from fields in North Africa would be more successful.

The task of planning such a raid was given to a Colonel Jacob Smart, a senior Air Force planner. At that time there were two Air Forces based in North Africa - the 9th AAF and a small part of the 8th AAF which was based in Britain. Smart developed a plan for a low level raid on Ploesti originating from North Africa and returning to North Africa. In preparation for the great raid the crews of the B-24 bombers practiced low level bombing raids in preparation for the great raid on Ploesti. Smart had 177 B-24s available for the raid. He needed more than his available 177 planes for a thoroughgoing attack on Ploesti. Lacking enough planes, he selected seven areas within the Ploesti complex as targets.

Smart called the raid "Operation Tidal Wave." On 1 August 1943 177 B-24s took off for the great raid on Ploesti. They left in two different groups or waves. They took with them 311 tons of bombs to drop on Ploesti. The carried 500 and 1000 pound demolition bombs and 430 incendiary bombs. During the first part of the trip, they lost three planes one of which carried the lead navigator. Somehow, the Germans got word of the impending attack and were fully prepared as the B-24s approached the target. Because of cloud cover just before arriving at the Ploesti target the coordination between the two attacking waves was faulty. Errors compounded and specific plans for the attack had to be abandoned and commanders improvised attacks on whatever target seemed available. Some of the second wave attacks were made on targets that the first wave had already hit.

As the groups reformed for the trip home, many bombers were missing. In one group only 15 of 39 planes formed up for the trip home. As they continued home they were constantly attacked by enemy fighters. Some planes landed at Allied bases in Cyprus or Turkey rather than their own home bases.

Only 92 of the original attacking force of 177 planes made it back to their base in North Africa. Others who had landed in Turkey and Cyprus were recovered later. Of the 92 that landed in North Africa, only 33 were undamaged and fit for duty. On the raid to Ploesti 532 Allied airmen were killed, captured or wounded.

Many awards were given to the survivors of this hazardous mission. Five airmen were awarded the Nation's highest honor, The Congressional Medal of Honor. Other important awards were distributed to other brave survivors.

Allied intelligence sources estimated that oil production at the Ploesti complex was decreased by about 41% because of the Allied raid. It was an effective but extremely costly raid.

This raid on Ploesti was one of the most hazardous raids of the entire war. The larger raids on Schweinfurt and Regensburg were other raids with extremely high casualty rates. Allied planners knew that such costly raids could not be continued. They were too costly to do on a continuing basis. The planes, pilots and crewmen were valuable assets that could not be thoughtlessly squandered on multiple hazardous raids.

Two other hazardous raids were those on Schweinfurt and Regensburg. The loss rate on these raids was in the area of 20% to 30%. Such levels of losses were not sustainable over a long period of time. Later in the war, better fighters and increased fighter range got the loss percentage down to 4% in many cases. In Brother Bob's war which he fought in the 15th Air Force, the loss rate per trip was in the vicinity of 2%. That was distressing, but many airmen, with a little luck, could survive a tour of duty and get in their 50 missions.

Flying missions over enemy territory was a dangerous business. It was dangerous even though the tremendous losses of the Schweinfurt and Regensburg were history by the time Brother Bob fought his war. There were many hazards that crews faced on a daily basis. Enemy flak and enemy fighter planes were without doubt the most dangerous and constituted the greatest danger, but there were other dangers less obvious but still present. Accidents were a major hazard. Although enemy actions caused most of the casualties, accidents were an important source of casualties. (Accident data from 14-3)

Major James Carroll did extensive research on problems encountered by B-17 crews. His data and conclusions are interesting and enlightening. In the preface to his study he says, "High accident rates accompanied the bomber force throughout the war, and evidence strongly suggests that the accidents were perceived as the cost of doing business." Overall the war strategists overlooked the most important and limiting component of the air missions, the human being. Stated another way: developing a bomber to carry bombs to the enemy was the first priority. They assigned little or no priority to the safety and well-being of the crew.

Even in the training program in the United States, there were many fatal accidents. Carroll quotes a statistic that lists 850 fatalities in the year 1943. The B-17 was a great airplane that the builders and designers developed rapidly and gave little attention was given to safety.

The following quotation from Major Carroll exemplifies the dangers and the problems faced by the ball turret gunner. In this quotation you will see that there were problems with the design and function of the ball turret that had not been fixed. Brother Bob was a ball turret gunner and he certainly had some of the same problems. . Carroll tells about a ball turret gunner named Shorty Gordon Two thirds of his turret projects from the bottom of the B-17 to meet attacks from below. In it are two 50 caliber machine guns, several hundred rounds of ammunition, a range mechanism, gun sight, switches, buttons, pedals, and petcocks. The gunner gets what room there is left, squeezing between the guns, legs thrown forward, left foot on the range pedal and right foot on the interphone switch. His knees rest so close to the bolt mechanisms that their action during combat often tears his clothes. Remarkable as this strictly GI invention may be, it was not very popular in a particular Fortress Squadron in England for the twenty-year-old kid, Shorty Gordon, who operates it. Shorty hasn't missed a mission yet .

His feet have been frozen and his electrically heated baby blue jumper has failed him at 45 degrees below zero. He has had to work all night inside the wing of a Fortress and go up to fight the Luftwaffe the following day. He has had to beg, wheedle, or steal his way to a gun position in another ship when his was out of commission. He has worked on frozen guns at 24,000 feet while fighters were boring in and flesh was tearing off his fingers each time he touched his guns to coax them back into action. But he hasn't missed a mission yet. Shorty Gordon eases his nerves after a mission by taking a triple-scotch- "more if I can get it."   Then he might go off on a forty-eight hour pass to see his girl. The one he's going to marry after that twenty-fifth mission."

Reading about the travails of Shorty Gordon gives one a better understanding of the flaws of the B-17 that designers could have rectified if they had more time to develop the bomber. Some improvements they could have made: allow more space for the human being who operated the ball turret; allow for more clearance around the bolt mechanism; and develop a better electrically heated clothing system. If they had more time, designers could have corrected these problems and the ball turret gunner would have been safer, and more effective.

Carroll notes that the design of the B-17 was such that it exceeded the capabilities of the human body. It appears that the designers of the B-17 designed the B-17 to complete long distance, high altitude bombing missions and never gave much thought as to the limitations of the human being. The human body can, barely, function at altitudes of 10,000 feet. The B-17 bomber routinely bombed targets from an altitude of 25,000 feet. Anoxia is the name for the physical condition caused by lack of oxygen. In some cases, anoxia can be fatal. On the B-17 some crew positions were more likely to suffer from anoxia. According to Major Carroll belly gunners had the highest number of reported cases and the highest number of fatalities. Next highest was the waist gunner position. Co-pilots were least likely to suffer from anoxia or die from anoxia.

Human beings did not have the capability to withstand the low temperatures of the high altitudes. Over Europe at altitudes of 25,000 feet the temperatures may be in the range of minus 30 degrees to minus 50 degrees Fahrenheit. One airman says that on a trip over Munich they encountered temperatures of minus 85 degrees Fahrenheit. Designers developed electrically heated flight suits to compensate for the extreme low temperatures, but the flight suits slowed and limited movements. However, the greater problem was that damage to the plane might cut the electricity supply to the flight suits and leave the crew vulnerable to the extreme low temperatures.

Still another hazard faced by B-17 crews was Combat Fatigue also called "operational fatigue." This was a condition that could not be fixed by making adjustments to the machine. It was a human condition and not easy to fix.

There is some relationship between ordinary fatigue and combat fatigue. Accounts by crew members often note the high level of fatigue reported by crew members. Some of the writers say that they spent as much time in bed as possible. They slept extraordinarily long hours - many more than they would ordinarily sleep.

But Combat Fatigue was not ordinary fatigue. Major Carroll uses the term "operational fatigue." He says that it is very much like a nervous breakdown that any overworked person might have. It has physical and mental components which combine to create the illness called Combat Fatigue.

Here is what Major Carroll says about the syndrome. It is an illness composed of emotional and fatigue symptoms, generally manifesting itself in a state of anxiety. The syndrome does not appear suddenly among combat airmen but is usually the result of a chain of distressing, harrowing, fatiguing, conflicting and terrifying events. The bomber crews had a higher rate of operational fatigue because of a fear and inability to vent adequate expression of the fear. Every man had to stay at his post and every bomber had to hold it position in the formation. This allowed little chance to act in response to the flee-or-flight responses every crew member experienced. In comparison, the fighter pilots had a lower rate of operational fatigue because they had more freedom of action and could respond to the flee-or-fight response if overwhelmed.

Brother Bob did not suffer from combat fatigue, but a member of his crew did. Bob notes that this crew member was not able to fly several missions because of combat fatigue. There is no evidence that this crew member suffered any long term effects of combat fatigue.

Operational fatigue and ordinary fatigue caused many of the accidents that Major Carroll studied. It is a rational judgment incorporated into laws and regulations that fatigue causes accidents. Truck drivers, for example, are required by regulations to limit the hours of consecutive hours spent driving.   A regulatory system is in effect for present day airline pilots.

Major Carroll made a study of the kinds of accidents and where and when they occurred. He notes that in the Eighth Air Force in 1944 there 2562 aircraft accidents not related to combat. There were 2835 aircraft involved in these accidents and 1692 persons killed in these accidents. Plenty of danger even for planes and people not in combat!

Major Carroll says that a loaded bomber can easily have an accident. When a B-17 prepared for takeoff on a bombing mission, it had a full load of gasoline and bombs - both of which were very dangerous cargo. It was difficult for a bomber to take off with such a full load. When the bomber returned it often came back with damage and holes in vital places. It sometimes came back on two or three engines or with the hydraulic system inoperable. Landings in such situations were very dangerous. The B-17 was a hazardous environment prone to accidents.

Major Carroll calculated where and when accidents occurred. More than 44% of all accidents occurred during landings. Only about 7% of accidents occurred on takeoff. About 23% of accidents occurred in flight. Remember, these are accidents - not events that happened because of enemy actions.

Major Carroll tried to find the cause of the accidents and concluded that morale was an important factor. If morale was good then there were fewer accidents. If many of the crews were borderline "operational fatigued," then there were more accidents. More specifically, Carroll had pilot error as responsible for 53.6% of all accidents. Material failures accounted for 24.5% of the accidents. Personnel, other than pilots were responsible for 8.3% of all accidents.

In defense of the pilots who were responsible for many of the errors, it is fair to state that many of the pilots were newly-trained and by no means were they seasoned pilots. They were college or high school students who had never flown before. They were given a very rapid training program to a very complex task: flying a B-17 bomber. It is rational to expect that high accident rates would occur.

Mid-air collisions were fairly common and perhaps the most important kind of accident not caused by hostile enemy actions. (Data from:14-4) This source tells about a Captain Merrill Green, a B-17 pilot who flew with the 8th AF in Great Britain. Captain Green told of seeing airplanes explode in formation, catch fire and of being attacked by ME-109s. He recounted sighting ME-262 jets and said on all missions except four, his airplane was hit with enemy fire. He once saw four mid-air collisions in one day, a total of 8 B-17s destroyed. His comment was that " We are our own worst enemy" in many respects.

Brother Bob witnessed some collisions. On a bombing mission to bomb oil refineries in Vienna on 16 July, 1944, Bob writes, "I saw two B-17s from the 301st collide over the target - went down in flames. Another went down on edge of target - saw only two chutes - pity those poor boys who bailed out over the city of Vienna."

Other strange accidents occurred. One account tells of a B-17 having bombs dropped on them from another B-17 flying over them. There are many accounts of bombs that could not be released from the bomber. Brother Bob had this happen on a bombing mission to Ploesti," We bombed from 28,000 feet … Flak was below us. We had five of our 16 bombs (250 lbs each) hang up. Carried them over the Adriatic and dropped them there."

The weather caused some of the mid-air collisions. If a formation of B-17s encountered clouds, then they could not see each other, or could barely see each other and that was the cause of some mid-air collisions.

The data source for Table I and Table II is (14-5). The table presents an analysis of 210 B-17 aircraft losses from the 8th AAF. The 8th AAF flew out of bases in Britain. The chart following includes combat losses.

Losses of B-17s - 8th Air Table I - Analysis of 210 Aircraft Losses

Lost in Enemy Territory	Lost At Sea	Lost in Friendly Territory	Lost in United Kingdom
65 Downed by Enemy Fighters	23 Ditched in Ocean	3 Interned in Switzerland	7 Abandoned - Crew Bailed Out
62 Downed by Enemy Flak	1 Other Cause	1 Flew to Italy Salvaged	13 Crash Landing
13 Unknown Causes		3 Flew to Russia Salvaged	6 Mid-Air Collisions
10 Mid-Air Collisions		6 Crash Landings	4 Crashed on Take-off
Total - 149- 67% of Total	**24 - 11% of Total**	**16 - 8% of Total**	**30 - 14% of Total**

Table II - Analysis of 1764 Personnel Casualties From 210 B-17S

Killed in Action	Other MIA Survivors	Prisoners of War
769 in B-17s	67 Evaded Capture	744 Captured/ POWs
32 on Returned B-17s	64 B-17 Ditched/ Rescued	18 Captured/Murdered
8 in US Training Flights -	29 Swiss Internees	12 Repatriated
12 in US Training Flights -		11 Died of Wounds
		1 Escaped and Killed
841 - 48% of Total Killed	**160 -9% Total Survivors**	**764 - 49% Total Prisoners**

Insofar as causes of aircraft losses, action by enemy fighters was the greatest cause of aircraft losses. Enemy flak was a close second. These two causes account for more than 55% of all plane losses. Note that 841 airmen were listed as killed in action. A total of 764 were captured and held as POWs by the Germans or their allies. One can make a guess that if a B-17 went down then there was more than 50% chance that crew members would not survive. Yet, there was a fairly good chance that they would be taken prisoner and survive the war.

The foregoing information shows that enemy fighters and flak were the greatest hazards that Allied airmen faced. For the two most effective enemy tools to be maximally effective, the Germans needed an early warning system that gave fighter pilots and flak gunners time to prepare for an attack. The Germans had radar systems. They had developed radar systems that were able to detect allied bombers as soon as they entered German airspace. They had a system of radar stations that covered all of Germany. The Germans constructed radar stations so each station was 25 miles to 50 miles from the next station. While the Allies had a better radar system than Axis powers, the Germans had a functional system that gave them warning of the approach of enemy planes. The Germans probably used visual systems to detect incoming allied bombers. The bombers flew at high altitudes and left long, white contrails that were easily visible. The bottom line is that Germans had an effective early warning system. Their fighters and Flak gunners had time to prepare for the Allied bombers.

The Allied airmen dreaded the black, spherical puffs of smoke that identified flak. Crew members grew to be experts on flak. Viewed from a distance, the flak explosions looked harmless. They were black puffs of smoke generally spherical in shape. The crew members could not hear the flak explosions until they got closer. When close to the flak explosions, the crew saw a red flash at the moment of explosion and they heard the explosion. They learned that when they heard the explosion of the flak, they were dangerously close to sudden death.

The German concentrated their flak installations around critical targets. The more critical the target, the more flak installations. Some of the targets apparently had no flak units assigned. Allied bombers might encounter enemy fighters on the way to the target or on the way home from the target, but flak was mostly a hazard limited to the immediate area around the target. Flak data from (14-6) Another source of information was material supplied by Robert D. Ekwall.

The word, flak, is a German acronym for Fliegerabwehrkanonen. The word means anti-aircraft weapon. The Germans and their allies had a wide variety of such weapons. Some of the earlier weapons were developed prior to World War II. They developed 37mm(1.47inch) and 20 mm(.79 inch) anti-aircraft weapons. The 20mm flak could reach up to an altitude of about 7000 feet. The 37mm flak could reach up to an altitude of about 15,000 feet. There were few planes in the interwar period that flew at altitudes higher than 15,000 feet. Allied bombers such as the B-17 were designed to fly at altitudes of about 25,000 feet. Therefore the smaller flak weapons were not a serious threat to B-17 and B-24 bombers. However, the Germans were able to use the 37mm and 20 mm flak guns against Allied fighter planes that fought in direct support of ground actions and therefore flew at lower altitudes.

Before World War II began, the Germans had initiated the development of a new and better anti-aircraft weapon. The result of their research and development was the famous "88" an 88 mm anti-aircraft weapon that was both an excellent anti-aircraft weapon and also very good field artillery and naval weapon. It could fire upward for 30,000 or more feet and no allied bomber could fly above the range of the "88". For its time it was the most famous and most successful artillery piece used by either side in World War II.

The German "88" was a crew served weapon that required 10 men to operate it. Later they reduced the number to eight. German manpower was short during World War II and Hitler's war planners did not want to use able bodied men in any place except in combat units. Therefore the Germans drafted under-age boys and older men as flak gunners. They sometimes used women as flak gunners. It seems strange but the Germans used Soviet prisoners as flak gunners. In the Soviet armed forces many of their flak gunners were women.

Anecdotal evidence seems to suggest that early in the war the flak gunners were not very good, and bombers crews were not especially fearful of flak. As time went by the flak gunners improved their skills and accuracy and allied airmen became more respectful and fearful.

The German flak gunners did not fire randomly at bombers coming over them. They had a specified "flak engagement zone." As soon as the bombers entered that specific zone, the place where the bombers were to drop their bombs, the flak gunners opened up on the bombers. The priority target was the bomber leading the formation. When the bombers got through that zone, the gunners quit firing and prepared for the next group of bombers approaching the target.

The shells used in early models of the "88" were time-fused. That means that the shell were timed to go off after a certain number of seconds. The shell then exploded and left a puff of black smoke. The shell fragments would disperse around in all directions. Woe to the B-17 that was in proximity to an exploding "88" shell. As a rough estimate, the shell would be fused to explode after about 10 seconds. That was the approximate length of time that it took the shell to travel to the altitude where allied bombers dropped their bombs. A better arrangement for exploding the shell would have been proximity fused shell. A proximity fused shell is a shell that explodes when it comes into the proximity of some object - for example: an allied bomber. The Germans experimented with proximity fuses but did not develop a successful proximity fuse. For that B-17 crew members can be thankful.

Late in the war the Germans developed another nasty weapon. Inside the shell, or projectile were a number of spherical pellets. These were incendiary pellets designed to set things on fire. When the shell exploded it propelled these pellets outward and forward when the shell exploded. Some penetrated critical spots in bombers such as fuel tanks and set the plane on fire.

The 15th AAF which flew out of Italy and the 8th AAF which flew out of Great Britain did only daylight bombing and rarely, if ever did any night bombing. The RAF, however, did night bombing almost exclusively. They had to fear German searchlights. The Germans developed excellent searchlights and systems for tracking bombers. Bombers caught in the beam of one or more searchlights were in grave danger. The pilots of those planes took every possible evasive action to get out the light and back into the darkness. Failure often meant death for the unsuccessful pilot.

Enemy fighters were the greatest hazard that Allied airmen faced. In the following paragraphs are descriptions of some of the fighters that the 15th AAF constantly encountered on their raids of Germany and German occupied countries. Following data from (14-7)

The Focke-Wulf Fw 190 was an important German fighter plane. Germany produced more than 20,000 of these planes. Some of the early models were not as fast as allied fighters, but in mid-war the Germans developed a new engine for Fw190 that made it an equal of many allied fighter planes. The first models had four 20mm cannon and two 13mm machine guns.

The Me109 was the best known and perhaps the most successful German fighter plane. Its performance was in many ways equivalent to the British Spitfire. It was equipped with 20mm cannon. The famous German pilots who had the most victories used the Me 109. Some of the Me109 pilots who fought on the eastern front had more than 100 kills.

Brother Bob said that a B-17 is no match for a German fighter plane. Consider the weapons that each had. The B-17 had thirteen 50 caliber machine guns. When a Fw190 attacked a B-17, the B-17 could fire at the fighter with only a few of its machine guns. For example, if a Fw190 attacked the B-17 from below and behind, then the B-17 tail gunner and the belly gunner could aim four 50 caliber machine guns at the attacking fighter. The armament of the Fw190 varied from time to time but a common armament was four 20 mm cannon, with two mounted in each wing. In addition there were two 13mm cannon mounted above the engine. Although there is no hard and fixed rule, if the size of the machine gun or cannon is greater than 12.5mm, then it is designated as a cannon. The B-17 had 50 caliber machine guns. That meant that the diameter of the bullets fired was $50/100^{th}$ of one inch. In terms of millimeters(mm) it was about 12mm. The Fw190 had two13 mm weapons plus four 20 mm cannons that it could fire at the B-17. In caliber terms the 20 mm cannon were the equivalent of 79 caliber. Therefore the Fw190 had an advantage of firepower over the B-17.

In addition to the advantage in firepower, the FW190 along with other German fighter planes, was much more maneuverable than a B-17. The B-17 could not turn quickly or take evasive maneuvers to try to escape from a German fighter plane. The German fighter plane was a highly maneuverable airplane that could take all kinds of evasive actions.

However, there were other factors to consider. The B-17s almost always flew in formations. Air Force tacticians designed the formations so the total firepower of a formation of B-17s was greater than the sum of all their weapons. A fighter attacking a formation of B-17s would meet fire from many planes. While the superior armament of a German fighter would probably prevail in a one-on-one encounter, the fighter was probably at a disadvantage when he attacked a formation.

Some German fighter pilots said that they like to hang around formations of B-17s that had completed their bombing raids and look for straggling B-17s who may have been hit by flak and lost an engine and so could not keep up. These were desirable targets. Brother Bob had this to say about stragglers, " stragglers die in combat."

Late in the war the Germans developed the Messerschmidt Me- 262. This was the first German jet plane. It was much faster than any other German fighter plane and in almost every way a superior plane. The Germans did not develop this plane until near the end of the war. By that time fuel supplies and experienced fighter pilots were in short supply. When the first Me-262s came out, the Germans assigned only the most skillful German pilots to fly the new jet planes. Later the Germans were not able to be so selective. The Me-262 was much faster than any American fighter plane. It could quickly and easily overtake an American fighter plane such as the P-51 which was one of America's best fighters. There was one drawback to the Me-262. It flew fast, but if it turned too sharply, it slowed down. German pilots learned to take long easy turns to take advantage of its speed. It was a superior plane and if the Germans had developed the plane earlier in the war, it would have made winning the war much more difficult.

There were many hazards for the crew member assigned to fly B-17s over Germany. The following material is an attempt to calculate exactly how hazardous it was for a single crew member such as Brother Bob, to get through the war without being killed or shot down over enemy territory. Brother Bob flew with the 346th squadron of the 99th Bombardment Group of the 15th Army Air Force stationed in the vicinity of Foggia, Italy. No records are available of how many planes were lost on each mission.

However, the 463rd Bombardment Group was another bombardment group stationed at Foggia. An examination of its records shows that Brother Bob was on many of the same missions that the 463rd Bombardment Group completed. The records of losses of the 463rd Bombardment are available. The available records of the 463rd Bombardment Group begin in March of 1944 two or three months before Brother Bob got to Italy. They records continue until September of 1944 which is about the time that Brother Bob completed his 50 missions.

Overall, the average loss of planes on 96 missions of the 463rd Bombardment Group was 2.05% per mission. That sounds like a man's chances for survival were quite good. However as the following chart will show, if you keep going out on missions the odds are you will get shot down or killed. Brother Bob went out 33 times on his way to 50 missions. Some of his missions counted as double missions and that is why he only went on 33 trips or sorties.

In the following table the first column represents the numbered sortie or trip. The second column represents the average chance of **not** getting home safely. This is the same for every entry. The third column is the cumulative danger; the cumulative chance that a crew member, such as Brother Bob, will make it home safely. The last column is the cumulative chance of **not** making it home safely. It is coincidental that, in the particular case of Brother Bob, at the end of the 33 sorties or 50 missions his chances of making it home safely or not making it home safely are almost exactly the same. If Bob's tour of duty had required 80 missions then the chance of his getting home safely would be perhaps 20-30% as a guess. If an airman went on enough missions, the laws of probability would catch up with him.

Chances of Making it Home Safely
After a Cumulative Number of Missions.

Number Of Mission (Or Trip)	Chance of Not of Not Making It Home Safely Each Time	Cumulative Chance of Making it Home Safely	Cumulative Chance of **Not** Making it Home Safely
1.	2.05%	97.95%	2.05%
2.	2.05%	95.94%	4.06%
.3	2.05%	93.97%	6.03%
4.	2.05%	92.00%	8.00%
5.	2.05%	90.15%	9.85%
6.	2.05%	88.30%	11.7%
7.	2.05%	86.48%	13.52%
8.	2.05%	84.72%	15.28%
9.	2.05%	82.98%	17.02%
10.	2.05%	81.28%	18.72%
11.	2.05%	79.62%	20.38%
12.	2.05%	77.98%	22.02%
13.	2.05%	76.38%	23.62%
14.	2.05%	74.82%	25.18%
15.	2.05%	73.28%	26.68%
16.	2.05%	71.78%	28.12%
17.	2.05%	70.31%	29.69%
18.	2.05%	68.87%	31.13%
19.	2.05%	67.46%	32.545
20.	2.05%	66.07%	33.93%
21.	2.05%	64.72%	35.28%
22.	2.05%	63.39%	36.61%
23.	2.05%	62.09%	37.91%
24.	2.05%	60.82%	39.18%
25.	2.05%	59.57%	40.43%
26.	2.05%	58.35%	42.65%
27.	2.05%	57.15%	42.85%
28.	2.05%	55.98%	44.02%
29.	2.05%	54.8%	45.205
30.	2.05%	53.7%	46.30%
31.	2.05%	52.59%	47.41%
32.	2.05%	51.53%	48.47%
33.	2.05%	**50.46%**	**49.54%**

So, we come to the bottom line. Brother Bob had nearly a 50-50 chance of making it through his 50 missions, or 33 trips. Flying combat missions was a hazardous business. Death, injury, or capture became more and more of a certainty as the number of missions increased. An explanatory statistical note: The foregoing table represents an individual's chances of not returning from a mission. Not returning means missing in action, death, or being taken prisoner of war, or internment by a neutral nation. The foregoing table represents those chances as they look to a crewman on the first mission. As a new crew member began his 50 mission tally, that crewman had a fifty-fifty chance of making it through those 50 missions safely. But if that crewman got through the 16th mission safely, the 16th mission being an approximate halfway mark, then that crewman's chances of getting through the 50 missions safely increased greatly. The crewman who needed one more mission to complete 50 missions had a 97.95% chance of completing that last mission safely and thus his whole quota of 50 missions. Each mission he completed safely improved his chances of completing his quota of 50 missions because he had to risk his life fewer times. The more times he went out, the more likely were his chances of not coming back.

<u>   Another statistical note</u>. As the war continued, each mission, on average, became less hazardous toward the end of the war. The statistical table presented on the previous page does not reflect that change.

We can only guess what the average crewman was thinking as he went through his missions. Maybe it was this. I wonder if will complete my 50 missions and get back to the states and into the arms of my wife and family. I hope I can get home safely and be home by Christmas time so I can eat Christmas dinner with my wife, parents, sisters and brothers. I might get show down on the next mission, but maybe I will get through it and the other missions safely. I can do it if I avoid all the hazards.

I can get home safely…

> - If the pilot is careful and takes off properly and we have no mishaps on takeoff.

> - If we do not have an air-to-air collision while the planes are forming up for the mission.

> - If we do not have a failure of the electrical system that

heats our suits and we freeze to death.

- If our navigator gets us to the right target without getting lost

- If something does not go wrong with one of the engines on the way to the target and we have to turn around and and go home and not have the trip count as a mission.

- If we do not run into clouds and have a mid-air collision while we are flying blindly in the clouds

- If enemy fighters do not attack us on the way to the target and shoot us down.

- If the enemy flak is not so heavy that our plane is damaged and we have to bail out.

  - Or, the flak causes our plane to crash and none of the crew survives.

  - Or, we get to the target and the plane above us drops their bombs on us.

  - If we suffer flak damage that causes us to be a straggler and we get picked off by enemy fighters.

- If we do not crash land after we have managed to get .close to home base.

Chapter 15 - Aces: Enlisted Gunners and Officer Pilots

During World War II those airmen who had shot down five or more planes were designated as aces. This honor, for the most part, was bestowed on officers. There were however, a few enlisted aces. The reason that most of the aces were officers rather than enlisted men was related to the fact that they each performed different jobs and is not necessarily related to the distinction between officers and enlisted men.

Nations involved in World War II kept track of the number of planes that pilots shot down and called those pilots aces if they shot down at least five enemy planes. As we will see later, there were numerous aces and the Americans were not necessarily dominant in this area.

So, why the large number of officer aces and why were there so few enlisted aces. There are a number of feasible explanations. First of all there is a broad general reason that accounts for much of the difference in the number of kills. One must consider the differences in the roles of officer fighter pilots and the roles of the enlisted aerial gunners. The role, or assignment of the aerial gunner, is to defend the bomber from attacks by enemy fighter planes. There is little of the offensive concept in the duties of the aerial gunner. They did not go out on mission for the primary purpose of shooting down enemy fighters. They went on a mission in a bomber for the purpose of bombing enemy factories, refineries and other war-related targets. As part of that mission, they defended the capability of the bomber to complete its mission. They defended the bomber in two ways one of which was passive and the other was active. The passive role was simply to be there and make the enemy fighters fearful, cautious and reluctant. Their presence contributed to the safety of the plane. The other role was active and critical. They fired their 50 caliber machine guns at any enemy fighter plane in the vicinity.

Fighter pilots, on the other hand, were more offensively oriented. On some missions, in the latter part of the war, they actively sought combat with enemy fighters. "The best defense was a good offense." The fighter pilots had many other types of mission assignments other than escorting bombers. While the typical gunner on a bomber flew only one sortie per day, the fighter pilots commonly flew multiple missions in a single day thus having many more opportunities to engage in combat with enemy planes. Those missions were nearly always offensively oriented and the fighter pilot was likely to be actively opposed. This meant there would be aerial combat where one side or the other would score a kill.

Then there was the matter of training. Fighter pilots were much more

highly trained than aerial gunners. It might take a year or more to train a
fighter pilot while the aerial gunnery school was about five weeks long.
The guns on the fighter planes were usually larger than the 50 caliber
machine guns on a B-17 and likely to cause more damage to an enemy
plane.

There were other very specific reasons for fighter pilots achieving more
kills. It was relatively easy for the fighter pilot to verify his kills and very
difficult for the enlisted aerial gunner to get his kills verified. An important
difference was that most fighter planes had gun cameras installed on their
planes. The camera operated synchronically with the machine guns or the
cannons in the plane. If a cowardly pilot wanted to avoid fighting situations,
he might go off on a mission and fire his guns into the air. Examination of
the film after such a mission would reveal that there were no targets. The
gun cameras kept pilots honest. In actuality, pilots as a group, were very
brave. Some might have been conservative, but few were cowardly. If the
pilot shot at something, the camera recorded it. At the end of the mission,
the film was developed and the results of that pilot's mission were
recorded. The gun cameras had other purposes other than keeping track of
how many planes a pilot had shot down. It could provide useful feedback
about the pilots aim and the pilot could learn what he needed to do to
correct his aim. The Germans, who were short of ammunition, used gun
cameras to determine whether or not the pilot was opening fire too soon and
thus wasting ammunition. Fighter planes often went on tactical missions
where they strafed enemy convoys or freight trains. Sometimes strafing a
target was more effective that dropping bombs on the target. The fighter
pilot could get close to the target and could see his target more clearly than
a bomber at 25,000 feet. Operations and Intelligence officers used the film
from strafing missions to determine the effectiveness of such missions.

Recording and verifying claimed kills was an important function of the
gun camera. When the film was shown, it showed the bullets, some of
which were tracers, entering the enemy plane; it might show the plane
catching fire and spiraling downward. Often two or more pilots claimed the
same kill of an enemy plane. Careful scrutiny of film could sort out some of
the conflicting claims. One solution to conflicting claims was to credit each
of two pilots with half a kill. Thus, records often show fractional numbers
of kills such 7.5 kills.

Thus it was that officers who flew fighter planes had a fairly good and
verifiable record of their victories. After every mission, there was a formal
debriefing session with all pilots present. The other pilots could help to
verify claims of planes shot down by their comrades. The verification of

claimed kills was moderately accurate, but was not always exact. Airfields were frequent targets of fighter missions. How to count planes on the ground that were strafed in a raid on an airfield? How to count a claim by pilot that he had finished off an already crippled plane? Give credit for shooting down an unarmed observation plane? Give more credit for shooting down a four engine bomber than a single engine fighter? It was not an exact science.

. If determining the exact number of planes shot down by an officer pilot in a fighter plane was less than completely exact, the determination of planes shot down by gunners in a bomber was even less exact. The difference was analogous to the difference between a scientist measuring with a caliper or micrometer and a farmer measuring his field using strides.

Why was the assessment of gunners' kills such a problem? There are a number of answers.

The B-17 had thirteen 50 caliber machine guns. Some of its guns were in pairs: the ball turret, the top turret., the tail, and the chin. The location of the machine guns meant that most of time in a combat situation two or more gunners fired at attacking fighter planes. Suppose that a fighter attacked the B-17 from the front, a common tactic. Initially, nose, chin and top turret and ball turret gunners would fire at the attacker. After it passed over or under the bomber, the top turret or the ball turret and the tail gunners would fire at the attacking plane. If it passed to the side, then the waist gunners fired at the attacking fighter. Thus in the course of one fighter attacking one bomber, it is possible that six of seven gunners fired at the attacking plane. If the attacking fighter went down, which of the six or seven gunners should receive credit for the kill? It was not an easy decision to make.

The aforementioned situation is simple - seldom did a single fighter attack a single bomber. More commonly, a large group of fighter planes attacked a large formation of bombers and the air was full of bullets. More gunners firing meant more bullets flying and the entire situation got more and more complicated. Determining which single gunner, in the midst of a combat melee, was successful in shooting down a fighter, was indeed difficult to determine.

Complicating the matter still further was the fact that many planes in a bomber formation fired at attacking fighters; it was not possible to know from which bomber came the bullets that downed a fighter.

Still another problem was the fact that the gunners on a B-17 fired 50 caliber machine guns. These were good weapons, but not likely to impose an immediate spectacular result that a fighter plane might achieve with its cannons that were more powerful weapons and more effective at killing and achieving spectacular effects. .

Still another consideration, the gunners on bombers did not have gun cameras. That meant that verification was difficult. There was no film to run and re-run to verify claimed kills. Sometimes another gunner in the same plane could verify that the tail gunner had been the one who was firing at the Bf109 and responsible for the kill. Verifications from gunners in other planes were difficult.

Perhaps the most important factor in the tallying of kills by fighter pilots and tallying kills by enlisted gunners was the fact that the Army Air Force had no official system in place to keep track of kills by gunners but they did have an official system for keeping track of kills by fighter pilots. It is not quite accurate to say that the Army Air Force had no system for keeping records of the kills by enlisted gunners. They had no overall, official system, but various agencies or people did keep records. There are records of enlisted gunners receiving official citations for a certain number of kills. Researching the achievements of gunners at a later date means reliance on second hand accounts of crew members whose memory may have faded or whose accounts are uncertain.

We can get a partial idea of the difficulty by looking at what Brother Bob said about several of his encounters with enemy fighters.

On his mission to Vienna on 26 June 1944, his first mission that counted for credit, Brother Bob says, *"I shot abut 20 rounds or so at enemy fighters. I saw quite a few but out of range".*

On his next mission on the 27th of June in 1944 Bob went on a mission to Brod, Hungary, he says, *"(Saw) some enemy fighters - took a pot shot at a 109. Never got him but a P-38 was sure on his tail. He was sure a brave guy - he attacked middle ship in element back and below us."*

On 30 June 1944 Brother Bob went on a mission to Budapest, Hungary. He says, *"Saw a few fighters, but they stayed out of our range. We saw P-38s giving them a rather rough time."*

On 7 July 1944 bob went on a mission to Blechhammer, Germany. He says, *"We saw a B-17 get shot down. It salvoed its bombs - couldn't keep up with formation and it was attacked by 4 or 5 Me110s. After attack they came in under and behind our ship. I took a potshot at them of 30 or 40 rounds but they were 1000 or so yards out so I couldn't hit them."*

The foregoing experiences of Brother Bob are probably typical of the combat experience of a gunner. Bob did not think that he had made any kills, but was not certain. It was possible that one of his rounds hit a fuel line or shorted out an electrical system that caused the enemy fighter to crash before he got home. However, it illustrates the uncertainty of claiming a kill by a gunner in a B-17.

Nevertheless, gunners did shoot down fighter planes and there are records and narratives to support the claims of gunners. In source (15-1) EugeneYarger says, "We would fly through two three hours of concentrated flak. As the Germans retreated, their anti-aircraft fire became more concentrated. So did their fighters. One day in April 1945, our turret gunner shot down two German planes and one of them was a jet."

If the report that the turret gunner shot down a jet is correct, then it was a notable event. The Germans developed a jet fighter plane late in the war that was a very effective weapon. Shooting down an ordinary fighter plane was an important accomplishment, but shooting down a jet fighter was indeed a great combat feat.

Colonel O'Bannon who flew with the 461st Bombardment Group of the 15th AAF tells of a mission to Budapest Hungary. (From source 15-2) He went on a mission where B-24 Liberators bombed the Duna Repologepger Aircraft factory in the Budapest, Hungary vicinity. On this raid they used a new radar-like device which they called, "Mickey." This device enabled them to drop bombs even though the target hidden by clouds or hidden by smoke. On a later raid on the 25th of July, the 461st Bombardment Group went on a mission to bomb the Herman Goering tank factory in Austria. A very large group of German fighters challenged the bombers so as to protect the factory. On this mission aerial gunners claimed to have shot down 35 enemy aircraft. The crew of one particular B-24 bomber named the "All American" claimed 14 enemy aircraft destroyed. The bomber, " All American" had the reputation of shooting down the most enemy aircraft in a single mission - more than any other bomber had ever shot down

.   On another mission a single gunner was credited with shooting down four enemy aircraft on a single mission. These were remarkable achievements. If the AAF had kept official records or even good unofficial records then such achievements could have been verified.

Confirmation of kills was always a problem. Thomas Hansbury, flying in the 8th AAF in1942, discusses this problem. (15-3)

He begins by saying that the life of gunner was very difficult and it was hard for someone who has not been there and done that to understand the difficulty of the situation. This is what Hansbury has to say about the confirmation of kills. "The roughest thing about combat is trying to get an enemy plane confirmed. Even if you shoot one down, even if you see him blow up in mid-air doesn't mean you get credit for him. ... At least two other men on your crew or any other crew must also see you get him. Nine times out of ten they are shooting at one the same time that you are getting yours. Even so it is hard to get them to say that you got him." …"after you come back and get to the interrogation officer you must be able to convince him. This is a very hard thing to do. All the claims are sent to Wing Headquarters and they are the ones who decide whether or not you shot down a German fighter. Many times two or three gunners shoot down a fighter and do not claim it. … "On some of the raids forty planes are claimed but only fifteen or twenty are confirmed."

Hansbury, in spite of the difficulty in getting claims confirmed, got a FW109 in a raid on the 20th of December, 1942. On the same raid the ball turret gunner got one and one of the waist gunners also shot down a fighter. In a tremendously large fight the Americans claimed 44 German fighters shot down in the air and another 50 were destroyed on the ground with a loss of seven B-17s. A few days later Hansbury says that helped bring down a FW109.

On another raid on the 3 of January, 1943 Hansbury says that four members of his crew shot down enemy aircraft. Later in April of 1943 Hansbury received DFC, The Distinguished Flying Cross, for his achievements.

Not only enlisted gunners got credit for kills but officer gunners sometimes got credit for kills. The navigator and the bombardier manned 50 caliber machine guns when not doing their navigational and bombing duties. The following material is taken from a report of the 70th Historical Society. (15-4) Lt Sebby (the bombardier) delivered his bombs in relative calm, reporting that it appeared 40% of our load found the target. On the way out of the target area several FW190s found us and began to work us over. Lt. Sebby flamed a 190 coming at us from twelve high - his fifth kill as well!

The following material is from (15-5). Perhaps the most remarkable single feat ever credited to an enlisted gunner was the shooting down of on one of Germany's top Aces. Adolf Galland was a famous German ace Galland was quite well known in Germany and was a friend of the top brass in the Luftwaffe.

Galland personally knew both Goering, the head of the Luftwaffe, and Adolph Hitler. Galland, at one time, had a picture of Mickey Mouse painted on his fighter plane hoping that it would discourage American pilots and gunners from shooting at him. Since Galland was one of the top ranked fighter pilots, he was given one of the new and most advanced German planes, the Messerschmidit 262.

The American gunner was Henry Dietz. The event occurred in the last days of the war. Dietz was flying in a B-26, a medium bomber. His group was stationed in Dijon France. On a bombing mission Henry Dietz got his first glimpse of a German jet plane which he had never seen before. The jet plane was the Messerschmidt 262. Before it came into Dietz's gunsights, it had just shot down one and possibly two B-26s. The Messerchmidt 262 attacked the American B-26 formation and Dietz fired his guns at the attacking Messerschmidt 262 and was pleased to see that he had hit the plane and he and other crew members saw the jet go down near an autobahn. Dietz was given credit for the kill and was most proud that he had shot down one of Germany's newest and best planes. The Messerschmidt 262. Dietz had no idea who the pilot of the plane was.

Fifty years went by and the incident, though not forgotten, was just one of Dietz's war stories and memorable mostly for that fact that he had shot down a jet fighter. Over in Germany, Adolph Galland, retired and in poor health, prepared his autobiography, The First and the Last.

In the Autobiography Galland described his experiences in detail and included the mission where he had been shot down and landed next to an autobahn. An American, Donald Edelen, read the autobiography and noted that the incident described by Galland was identical to the one where one of his crew mates, Henry Dietz, had shot down a German jet plane. He communicated the information to Dietz. Henry Dietz and Galland started a series of communications and concluded that it was probably Henry Dietz who had shot down the famous German ace, Adolph Galland. In one of the letters Galland told Dietz that he still had a splinter in one of his knees that belonged to the US Government.

Records and stories of kills by enlisted gunners vary greatly in credibility. The story of John Foley falls in the middle of the credibility spectrum. (material from 15-6) John Foley enlisted in the Air Force and was assigned to the South Pacific theater. He, like Dietz, flew on B-26 bombers. his heroics are memorialized in a song popular during World War II. The title of the song was "Johnny Zero." The song told of boy who scored zeros on school tests but excelled at shooting down Japanese fighter planes called Zeros. One line of the song says, "Johnny got another Zero today." John Foley apparently had a natural talent for aerial gunnery. He did not go to a gunnery school; the Air Force assigned him to do repair and maintenance work on machine guns. At some point a regular gunner had been injured and was not available for duty The Air Force gave John Foley an orientation and he flew one practice session. After that he flew missions as an aerial gunner. Two days later John Foley shot down his first Zero. Several weeks later he shot down two Japanese Zeros. A war correspondent coined the name, Johnny Zero and America, looking for real war heroes, embraced the man, the name, and the song.

Before John Foley came down with malaria he had flown 32 missions and had scored seven confirmed kills. John Foley was sent home to recover his health. When his health improved, he went on a speaking tour of the United States and taught aerial gunnery for the AAF. Later in the war he volunteered for combat duty in the European Theater and ended the war as a B-24 gunner in the European Theater.

One rather well-documented and reliable story of enlisted aces is the story of Sergeant Benjamin Warmer. Warmer flew with the 99th Bombardment Group of the 15th AAF. Brother Bob also was in the 99th Bombardment Group of the 15th AAF, but he flew at a later time. Sergeant Warmer's record is recounted in a book by Charles Watry and Duane Hall. (15-7) Warmer flew with the 15th AAF during the invasion of Italy. The book credits him with a total of nine kills. Two of the kills came on a bombing mission over Naples. Warmer got seven more kills on a raid on German air fields in Sicily. Of all of the aerial gunners who have claimed ace status, the information on Sergeant Warmer seems to have the best documentation.

Watry and Hall appear to be serious researchers. They name two more candidates as possible or probable aces. One candidate is T/Sgt Arthur Benko who may have downed nine planes. Watry and Hall say that T/Sgt George Gouldthrite may have shot down five planes. There was a Sergeant Quinlan who was the tail gunner on the famous B-17, The Memphis Belle. Quinlan may have had five kills but the record seems not to be official.

A review of the enlisted aerial gunner aces should include the name of Michael Arooth. Some sources credit him with 17 kills. It is very difficult to make a judgment about this gunner. Perhaps it is true that he was the king of the enlisted gunners, but data and verification of his kills seems to be missing.

In the last few paragraphs there are numerous instances of uncertainty, ambivalence and irresolution. Discussion of enlisted aerial gunner aces is difficult and fraught with the possibility of praising a self-promoter; not giving due credit to a genuine hero; omission of worthy deeds; making an incorrect appraisal of gunner because of his fame or making an incorrect appraisal of gunner who never gained fame; and failure to give due credit for respectable performance.

Next we shall consider the performance of fighter pilots who by their high level skills became identified as aces. This area is better documented and the information on fighter pilots is more reliable.

Several factors deserve consideration in identifying the best fighter pilots. One factor to consider was how long a fighter pilot's nation was involved in a war. For example, France was actively engaged in World War II for only about eight months. The fighter pilots who fought for France did not have years in which to build up their totals. they may have had the good planes and good pilots but were not in the war long enough to score high numbers of kills. The same may be said of the Dutch and Belgian pilots. Germany and the Soviet Union were engaged in the war for about four years. Germany, in the period between World Wars had sent pilots to Spain and these pilots gained experience in flying German planes in combat. After these pilots came back to Germany, they were employed as instructors by the Luftwaffe. This gave Germany an advantage in the early war with Britain. Germany had a pool of combat-experienced pilots and a pool of pilots trained by pilots with combat experience. In the "Battle of Britain" German and British pilots engaged in deadly combat for an extended period of time. By the time Germany attacked the Soviet Union, it had an experienced, well-trained and well-equipped air force. It was an air force much superior to the Soviet Air Force.

A second factor was that the status of some nations changed during the course of the war. Italy as an example dropped out of active war participation in the middle of the war. Finland's status changed several times during the course of the war. As some nations such as Hungary and Rumania were occupied by the Soviets, then their active participation ceased. Early in the war when Germany was gaining control of nearly all of continental Europe, a scattering of pilots migrated to Great Britain to continue the fight for another country Some sources list Norwegian fighter aces, but it is not clear on which side these pilots fought.

Another factor, one most critical, was the quality of the planes that the aces flew. The Germans. Americans and British all produced very good planes. Late in the war the Americans built two excellent fighters - the P-51 and the P-38. The Germans, at the very end of the war began production of the Me262 which was probably the best fighter of World War II. However it came into the war so late and in relatively small numbers that it had little effect on the outcome of the war.   The British had some excellent planes and the Spitfire is an example of their high quality planes. Other fighters and bombers were not so good. As an example, the planes made in the Soviet Union were probably not as high in quality as the German, American and British planes.

Another determinant appears to have made the Germans successful was their system of honoring and glorifying individual aces. The Germans meticulously kept track of the scores of individual aces and the scores were widely publicized. The highest scoring aces were showered with awards and honors. They became public heroes. The role of fighter pilot was a high status role in German military and civilian society.

German society and Soviet society were very different. The Soviet Communist system tended to glorify the accomplishments of groups of individuals while the German Fascist system glorified the accomplishments of individuals.

The quality of opponents was another factor that affected the number of kills that a pilot could make. If a pilot consistently flew against poorly trained opponents, then it was easy to become an ace. When Germany went to war against the Soviet Union, it had a substantial cadre of pilots who had fought in the Spanish Civil War and an even larger cadre of pilots who had participated in the "Battle of Britain" The Soviets went into the war with no cadre of experienced pilots and very average planes. Near the end of the war, the situation reversed. Due to extreme losses of pilots and due to a shortage of fuel, the German pilots were poorly trained and relatively easy marks for the better trained British and American pilots.

Still another factor concerned strategy and tactics, and motivation. If a nation was in a do or die situation where its continued existence depended on the performance of its air force - think of Britain during the "Battle of Britain" as an example. In that situation, the air force commanders may have had to order extreme tactics and extreme missions of great danger which resulted in high casualty rates. In an emergency situation such as the "Battle of Britain" there many opportunities to score kills and many chances of being killed. The Soviet Union also asked for maximum effort and lost many planes and pilots because of the severity of its situation. Another aspect of this situation is that of living to fight another day. If an air force command repeatedly put its best pilots in jeopardy, then it would not be long before all of its aces were dead.

So, in interaction, all of the factors mentioned had an effect on the number of kills that a pilot might score. Following is a summary of the best aces from the major participants in World War II. Be sure to consider the factors in evaluating the number of kills.

Table of Top Five Scoring Aces
Major Participants in World War II

Germany	Italy	Japan
352 - Erich Hartmann	26 - Anthony Visconti	113 – H. Nishisawa
301 - Gerhard Barkhorn	22 - Teresio Marinolli	80 - Tetsuzo Iwanoto
274 - Gunther Rall	21 - Franco Lucchini	70 - Shoichi Sugita
267 - Otto Kittel	21 - Leonardo Ferulli	64 - Saburo Sakai
258 - Gunther Nowotny	19 - Franco Bisleri	60 - Junichi Sasai

United States	Great Britain	Soviet Union
40 – Richard Bong	37 – James E. Johnson	62 – Ivan N. Kozuhedub
38 – Thomas McGuire	32 – Brendan Finucane	59 – A. Pokryshkin
34 – D. McCampbell	29 – Bob Braham	58 – Gregori Rechkalov
28 – Francis Gabreski	29 – Robert S. Tuck	57 – Nikolai Gulayev
28 – Robert S. Johnson	28 – F.R. Casey	52 – Arsenii Vorozhekin

France	Finland	Canada
26 - Pierre Closterman	94 - Eino Juutilainen	31 – George Beurling
23 - Marcel Albert	75 - Hans Wind	21 – V. Woodward
21 - Jean Demozay	56 - Eino Luukkanen	21 - H.W. McLeod
20 - Edmond Marin	57 - Nikolai Gulayev	17 – Robert McNair
20 - Pierre LeGoan	44 - Oiva Tuominen	17 - George Wittman

Data on the number of kills for fighter pilots is more definite. Rules and systems were in place to verify the number of kills and so the data in the foregoing table is fairly reliable. There are a few confounding factors in the presentation of the data. Example: In 1936 there was a civil war in Spain. There were two factions. One was a Socialist/Communist faction supported by the Soviet Union. The other faction was a Fascist faction supported by Germany. Germany sent planes and pilots to support the Fascist faction. Those kills that the German pilots made while serving in Spain are counted in their total kills. As an example, Werner Moulders scored 14 kills during the Spanish Civil War that were included in his total of 115 total kills. In a similar situation a few of the kills by American aces include kills made later during the Korean War.

Another possible confounding factor was credit given for fractional kills. The Germans did not record fractional number of kills. The Americans credited half and even one fourth kills.

Great Britain was in the war for a long time but seems not to have a large number of aces. One should remember that the British Empire or Commonwealth was still in existence during the second World War and Commonwealth members fought alongside the British. Examples: Australia, New Zealand, and Canada.

There are some amazing pieces of information supplied by the full tabulation from which the previously mentioned chart was constructed. The full information is not presented here but you can find the full tabulation at this citation. (15-8)

One surprising statistic is that Germany had about 400 aces who made more kills than the top American ace, Richard Bong.

There are other surprising statistics. The German Luftwaffe had more than 850 aces. However, there were more American aces than German aces. There were more than 1200 American aces. When one examines the lists for Germany and America one finds that there were a tremendous number of American aces who scored five, six, or seven kills. The number of German aces with smaller numbers of kills is much less.

One of the amazing pieces of information is that the top German ace, Erich Hartmann scored an astonishing 352 kills. No other nation had an ace that even approached that number of kills. Erich Hartmann had more than eight times as many kills as the foremost American ace, Richard Bong.

Erich Hartmann's record is really amazing. He was the world's foremost ace in all of history. His record was unequaled and will likely never be equaled. He is an important wartime figure and it is worthwhile to analyze his accomplishment in terms of skill, luck, nature of opponents, and the nature of the weapons of his opponents.

The following material is based on these citations (15-9) (15-10)

Hartmann was born in 1922 and joined the Luftwaffe in in 1941 when he was 19 years old. In October of 1942 he was assigned to *Jagdeschwader* 52 on the Eastern front. The highly individualistic Hartmann did not immediately become an expert fighter pilot, but he had some good instructors and leaders. In his first encounter with Soviet airmen he had his Bf 109 badly shot up and was barely able to survive a belly landing. In November of 1942 Hartmann got his first aerial victory but got shot down in the process. He received punishment for not following the rules during his engagement. Hartmann had flown as a wingman to a more experienced pilot and had failed to follow established protocol.

Hartmann kept flying and had only limited success. His superior urged Hartmann to get close before opening fire. It took some time for Hartmann to absorb and practice this advice, but he finally did so and began to score victories. In early 1943 Hartmann flew as wingman to a pilot named Krupinski who was sometimes called the "wild man." Krupinski recklessly sought combat wherever he could find it regardless of the odds. Hartmann's life was put at risk, but both Krupinski and Hartmann began to score a high number of kills. In the course of aerial combat alongside the "wild man" Hartmann was shot down several times.

In May of 1943 Hartmann went down for the fifth time. On this occasion he was rammed by a Soviet plane. Hartmann survived but had a nervous breakdown. He was sent to his home and recovered and by June of 1943 was back in combat.

By this time Hartmann had mastered the art of aerial combat and began to score a great number of kills. In 20 days of August 1943 he went on 54 combat sorties and shot down 49 Soviet aircraft. On the 20th of August he was shot down and returned to combat that same day. On his second sortie of the day, he was shot down in Soviet territory, captured, but managed to escape.

Hartmann received multiple decorations for his achievements. He received the "Knights Cross to the Iron Cross with Oak Leaves, Swords and Diamonds." Only two other Luftwaffe personnel received higher awards: Herman Goering the head of the Luftwaffe and a dive bomber pilot named Hans Rudel.

Hartmann had great success against the Soviet Stormovik, an aircraft an airplane designed as an armor support plane. The Stormovik was excellent as an armor support plane but not so good when matched against a Bf109. Hartmann also shot down a number of Airacobras. The P-39 Airacobra was an American built plane that America sent to help the Soviets. Half of American production of this plane went to the Soviet Union.

As the war continued, the Soviet forces pushed the Germans forces back, but Hartmann continued to score victories. At the end of the war, fearful lest he be taken prisoner by the Soviets, he flew to west so as to avoid capture by the Soviets. The Allies captured Hartmann and later handed him over to the custody of the Soviet Union. He remained a prisoner of the Soviet Union for the next ten years.

There is no doubt that Hartmann was a courageous and skilled pilot. He had some great advantages: the advantage of a natural ability; the advantage of training by some expert pilots; the advantage of flying against Soviet planes that were not as good as German planes; the advantage of an extraordinary amount of courage. All of these factors helped Hartmann to score his amazing number of kills.

There was another element that helped Hartmann and other German pilots. Stalin wanted volume in all things. He wanted lots of pilots and lots of planes and he wanted them in a hurry. He was less concerned about the training of pilots and he was not much concerned about the quality of planes produced. He wanted quantity and he got quantity at the expense of quality. Stalin's obsession with quantity contributed to the success of German aces, but it may also have helped the Soviet Union to win the war.

The top American ace of World War II was Richard I Bong. Bong was born in Superior, Wisconsin in 1922. He was the son of Carl T. Bong who had immigrated to America from Sweden at the age of seven. Material from (15-11)

Bong showed great interest in aviation from a young age. After graduation from Superior High School, he attended Wisconsin State Teacher's College. There he participated in the Government sponsored Civilian Pilot Training Program. He did not graduate but collected enough college hours to enlist in the Army as an Aviation Cadet. He trained as a pilot first at Gardner Field in California and later at Luke Field in Arizona. Bong flew the relatively new P-38 and became expert at flying the new plane. He showed great talent and great promise as a trainee. He was expert and liked to "show off" his flying skills. He received a reprimand from General George C. Kenny for his antics, but General Kenny recognized his talent.

In late 1942 the Army sent Bong overseas to the Pacific theater. He was an immediate success and by January of 1943 he had achieved five victories and became an ace. Bong, like the German ace, Erich Hartmann, liked to get in close to his prey. When he had equaled the 26 kills of the American World War I ace, Eddie Rickenbacker, Bong remained in an overseas combat region but was reassigned to training duties. In spite of the assignment, Bong managed to shoot down an additional 13 planes.

For his accomplishments Bong received the Congressional Medal of Honor, the nation's highest award. In addition he received almost every award possible for a pilot to receive.

After Bong had achieved 40 kills, General Kenny pulled him out of combat and sent him back to the United States so that Bong could get married. Bong went home and married his long time sweetheart, Marge Vattendahl.

Bong's next assignment after his marriage was as a test pilot in Burbank, California. His assignment was to test one of the new jet planes, the P-80, Shooting Star. Just a few weeks before the war against Japan ended, Bong was killed when the jet stalled on takeoff and he had to bail out at a low altitude and was killed.

In the Mediterranean Theater of Operations where Brother Bob served, the top American ace in the theater was John Voll. Material on John Voll taken from (15-12) (15-13)

John Voll was a native of Goshen, Ohio and had been trained as a teacher prior to his service in the AAF. He came to the war rather late and did not complete pilot training until January of 1944 at which time he was commissioned as a 2nd Lieutenant in the AAF. The AAF assigned him to the 31st Fighter Group, a part of the 15th AAF. Before Voll's arrival in Italy the 31st Fighter Group had participated in the invasion of North Africa and in the invasion of Sicily as well as the mainland of Italy. Lieutenant Voll arrived at his assignment with the 31st Fighter Group in Italy in the spring of 1944. Prior to this time the 31st Fighter Group had flown British Spitfires and at the time of his arrival were reluctantly changing over to the P-51 Mustangs. Voll, the new man, did not have a problem with the transition.

By July of 1944 Voll had scored his 5th kill and became an ace. Voll had named his plane "American Beauty." Voll had his best day and achieved some spectacular results because of an unusual set of circumstances. On the 16th of November in 1944 Voll was flying escort to bombers headed for Munich, Germany. He had some electrical problems and decided he could not continue on his mission and turned for home. As he proceeded on his way home, he saw a German plane, a Ju88 near Udine, Italy. When the German saw Voll, he headed in the direction of Germany. As Voll chased the Ju88, he was attacked by 12 Me 109s and FW-190s. Voll hurriedly shot down the Ju88 and turned to deal with attacking German fighters. A convoluted melee followed with Voll swirling, diving, and attacking amidst the German fighters who were trying to get a bead on the elusive Voll. The fight ended with two FW-190s shot down, one Me-109 destroyed, two more probable kills and two German planes damaged.

By the time these kills were added to Voll's total, he had a total of 21 kills. He was the leading American ace in the Mediterranean Theater of Operations. His commanding officer decided that Voll had done his part in the combat operations of the war. The AAF re-assigned Voll the non-combat duty in China where he served until the end of the war. In 1948 the Air Force recalled Voll to active duty and he remained in the Air Force serving in both the Korean War and the war in Vietnam. He retired as a colonel in 1968.

Chapter 16 - Letters Home

Throughout his career in the Army Air Force, Bob wrote letters to the home folks. Following are selections from those letters home. Most of the letters reproduced here were letters written while he was serving as a gunner and was based near Foggia, Italy. Several are from his early experiences in the AAF. During the time that Bob was in the service, his parents, Arthur and Bessie Ekwall, were farming and raising six children. Most of his letters home were written to his parents but some were written to other family members. Arlene, his oldest sister was working in Lincoln, Nebraska. His other sister Norma was living at home and teaching in a rural school. His brother, next younger than Bob, was Dick who, during the time that Bob was in the service, finished high school and soon after enlisted in the US Marines. His next younger brother, Ralph was in high school and his youngest brother Edward was attending a local rural school.

Soon after entering the Army Air Force he was temporarily at a base near Salt Lake City, Utah. He has some ordinary and expected comments. He writes to his younger brother: *"Well, Ralph, tomorrow I'm on guard duty and will report for duty at 7:00 AM I will be on duty for 6 hours and then off for 18 hours. This is the second time I've had guard duty since I've been in the Army. Today, I was on a detail where I had to clean up several tents and polish a glass case at the post engineers.*

Bob soon left the base near Salt Lake City and was sent to an AAF base near San Antonio, Texas. Some letters may be missing from the collection, but it appears from his letters sent home from San Antonio that he is no longer an Aviation Cadet. In a letter to his parents, he refers to his status as a G.D.O. (ground duty officer?) Bob is struggling to adjust to life in the military.

We had inspection of personal dress and appearance here on Saturday. From what I hear there is personal inspection in the Army and Army Air Corps every Saturday. Boy it is plenty tough in my opinion. I got called for not having my shoes shined good enough and for having my collar flaps turned up slightly. I had to buy a collar brace and some liquid shoe polish besides my paste polish. We have inspection of quarters about every day. We have to be prepared for it at least. Your bed had to be made just so. The closet and shelves must have clothes arranged in only one way: the right way. If you don't, you will be liable for a gig. When you do a gig, you walk the ramp for certain length of time or else sit on the very edge of a chair for a good long time - say about six hours. I guess they quit doing that so much because several soldiers got their spines displaced or hurt their back or spinal cord. You must sit erect with shoulders back with eyes straight ahead.

Bob provides more information concerning his status and future in the AAF in his next letter to his parents.

It's likely that I won't be her more than a week or 15 days. I don't know where I'll go; if I did I'm not supposed to write you of it till I get there and I am settled. I had an interview with Captain Brown yesterday. I did not get much satisfaction. I found out that radio, communications and meteorology all require three years of college. The AAF does not need any more glider pilots. Well, after that interview, I decided to go wherever the Army sends me. So, I may be an enlisted man. Perhaps that means that my training will be less difficult than pilot training. I learned that one should not join the Air Corps unless you're awful sure you can pass a rigid mental and physical exam. That's for you Dick; stick to your idea of joining the Marines.

It appears that Bob stayed in Hondo for Army Air Force basic training. After he completed basic, the AAF sent him to Goldsboro, NC for aircraft mechanic training. This was a fairly long course and Bob does not tell much concerning the content of the training. He is, however, adjusting to the military. He says -*We've got a new commanding officer in our squadron. He is a little tougher than the previous one. We had personal inspection again on Saturday. I didn't get reprimanded for anything this time. They might make a soldier out of me yet.*

Months later, in October of 1943, Bob has finished aircraft mechanic training and has been sent to Fort Myers, Florida for gunnery training.

He writes to his parents - *Pretty nice weather down here. It is cool at night sometimes as low as 45 degrees... Many of my friends from school in North Carolina were sent down here for gunnery training... It's too bad that Ralph can't get any shotgun shells for pheasant hunting...It will be tough on Dick if he cannot get a furlough after basic training. I thought sure he would as soon as he finished boot camp... Guess I never told you that I went to chapel service here last Sunday....Quite a few WACs in church. They have some nice looking ones here. Those in North Carolina all seemed pretty old - yeah, and pretty fat too.*

The letter reflects news items that had been in his parent's letters to him. His brother Dick had finished high school the previous spring and after the summer had enlisted in the Marines. Dick had been trained to be a Marine engineer and learned to operate heavy construction equipment. He did not get a furlough after Boot Camp. The Marines badly needed engineers. There were shortages of many things in civilian life. His brother Ralph is complaining that he cannot buy shotgun shells.

Bob's next assignment after finishing gunnery school is crew training at Ardmore, Oklahoma where he trained with the same crew that he would go overseas with and fly with in combat. He says in a letter home.

Monday night our crew went on a high altitude practice bombing mission. The bombing target is on a range about 20-30 miles from here. We went up to around 20,000 feet. The temperature there was 10 degrees below zero. We only stayed at that altitude for an hour as oxygen got low on one side of ship and we had to come down to about 8000 feet. We only got to drop only one bomb. We carry 24 of the 100 lb bombs in the bomb bay. The armoror on our crew had trouble with his ears so I had the job this time of putting pins back in the fuses when we could not drop the bombs. I rode in a new B-17G this time. So Dick has moved again. I wouldn't doubt but that he has finished training and is moving to the combat zone.

The bombs carried a safety pin device to ensure safety. When on a bombing mission the pins were removed. If the plane did not drop the bombs, the pins had to be replaced - a tricky and dangerous business.

After crew training at Ardmore, Bob gets some leave and his next letter home is from Kearney, Nebraska. It is his last letter home before going overseas.

He says, *Suppose you got the card with my APO number. That number will be my overseas address along with New York, New York. You can still send mail here for the present. I had an allotment made out of $50.00 a month. It will be sent to Dad. I would like him to deposit it to my account. I made out the allotment because I figured that there would not be much to spend money on when I was overseas... I also made out a power of attorney for Dad. I suppose he has gotten it by now. Thus he can endorse checks for me in the U.S. or other business if any in the U.S. while I am overseas. I had to so some processing on Sunday, so I did not get to chapel. That is it for now.*

Bob has taken care of some important business before going overseas. Behind his matter-of-fact statements is the reason for appointing and giving his father the power of attorney. The reason is the real possibility that he would not come home and the AAF wanted to tidy up that piece of legal business before Bob went overseas.

When Bob writes again he has shipped overseas and had gone to North Africa and then to Foggia, Italy. This is his station for his entire tour of overseas duty. His letter home is dated 21 June 1944.

Bob's first letter home was short and very general in nature and contained very little specific information. It probably reflects his sensitivity to the fact that his mail was being censored. Generally speaking all mail that officers was not censored, but there were some exceptions.

There were several reasons for the censorship. The main reason was to
keep information out of the hands of the enemy. However, for many
soldiers such as Brother Bob there was little danger of mail being
intercepted by the enemy. In other theaters of war and in other situations the
danger was greater. In a military unit one officer was assigned the duty of
censoring letters. It was not considered an important job. It would not help
an officer to get promoted. Often the censors were chaplains or dentists
assigned censorship as an extra duty. In some commands where security
was a major consideration, WAC officers were assigned to full-time duty as
censors and developed a high level of skills.

Another reason for censorship was to allow the commanders to
determine the level of morale of their men. The censor was in a very good
position to supply this information to the commanding officers.

Soldiers and their families sometimes tried various methods of avoiding
censorship. A soldier might write some information on the inside flap of an
envelope. Sometimes arrangements were made for soldiers to appeal to a
higher level if they felt their letters were being unreasonably censored.

If a soldier had a friend that was going home, he could ask that friend to
call, or write to parents, wife or friends with messages as to his assignment
and whereabouts.

Some of the American soldiers were the sons of immigrants who had a
good command of a foreign language such as Polish, Italian, or Czech. If
they wrote a letter home in that language, the censor would probably
confiscate the letter. The soldier would wonder why his letters were not
being delivered. It was not an effective method of avoiding censorship.

In Bob's family they knew were Bob was, but they often did not know
where their Marine son, Dick, was. They devised a system to find out some
information. Mail sent to soldiers was not censored; only mail going out
was censored. So the Ekwall family, reading the newspapers and listening
to radio reports guessed that perhaps Dick's latest move was to the
Marianas Islands. So, they sent him a letter saying," We think you are in the
Marianas Islands. If you are, please start your next letter like this - Dear
Mom, Dad and brothers." So when the Ekwall family got a letter with that
exact salutation, they knew where Dick was. It was not very informative but
provided a small amount of information.

Sometimes the degree of censorship varied. When the invasion of
Europe was planned, security and censorship was very strict. Whenever any
important event was planned, then censorship and security were tight.

If a soldier violated the rules of censorship, he generally would receive a reprimand. It was not considered a serious offense.

Bob's letter home says, *The Red Cross has a pretty good place here in this town. There is a writing room, game room and a barber shop. The natives give us a little music now and then. They have guitars and mandolins - anyway I guess that is what they call them. They have a snack bar too. I've completed three missions now. I have not seen any boys from my home area. I don't know what else I can tell you - so I guess it is so long for now.*

In his next letter home Bob writes, " *it's the Fourth of July - what a way to spend the 4th. Yes, it is quite different this year for me. I have completed six missions now. I got the Signal,(his hometown weekly newspaper) and saw the story in it about Bob Witte. Guess you saw in the Signal about Bob Newman. His accomplishment is expected of me.*

I and my buddy honored the citizens of the local city with a visit again the other day. There is not much to do in town. We went to the beach yesterday. We got a Dago to give us a long ride on sailboat. It was fun. It cost 50 Liras or 50 cents American. I got Arlene's letter yesterday from Omaha written about the 16th of May.
The weather here is disagreeable here lately. It is like Nebraska during the middle of July in the worst years.

Well so long for now. I bet you think my letters are beating Dick's when it comes to brevity. You remember the old saying 'brevity is the soul of wit.'"

Bob's letter shows his attempts to avoid the scissors of the censor. He tells his folks back home that some of his friends have been killed by noting that the story in Signal tells about the death of a home town boy. He says that the same thing has happened to some of his friends. He refers to the return home of an Air Force veteran who has completed 50 missions and says that the same will be expected of him. Bob may have been being unnecessarily careful and sly.

In his next letter home on 16 July Bob writes in generalities and gives little specific information. He notes that he has not gotten any mail for the last three months. This, no doubt, was due to the fact that he was traveling overseas during that time.

He begins his next letter home on the 28th of July by saying that he had gotten his mother's letter written on the 16th of July. So, his mail was now getting through to him. He says later in the letter, " *Yes, mother I guess that it is a good thing that I do not have a dear girl friend or wife. My buddy in my tent writes and receives a letter nearly every day. Another fellow in my crew has got only two letters from his wife since he came overseas. He got married while we were in Oklahoma. I am pretty sure his wife is having a good time and running around with other boys or service men. He is sucker if you ask me. Besides his allotment to her, he sends her most of what he gets here.*

In a 3 August letter home to his youngest brother, Edward, He says that he has been promoted to staff sergeant. He notes that he now has completed 21 missions.

In a letter to his mother on the 7th of August he comments on something that his brother Ralph must have written to him, or perhaps his mother wrote that Ralph had made a prediction that the war would be over before the end of the year.

Here is Bob's response. Ralph is an optimistic prophet. Personally, I think that Ralph has rocks in his head, or perhaps bats in his belfry. Maybe he should have his head examined. y buddy and I went to town yesterday and saw a fellow who used to be the preacher in my buddy's church. We heard him preach in the morning and it was a good sermon. He is a young chaplain who has already been overseas for a long time. He can speak Italian like a native. He took us to an Italian home and got a meal for us. It was served by a middle-aged Italian lady and a young woman of about 21. It was a good meal. Boy, those Italians like spaghetti! When we were there, they dropped a loaf of bread on the floor and I thought it was going to crack that stone floor. I managed to eat a slice of it and it was pretty good.

Quite a number of Italians have visited America, but their English is still not very good.

At the end of the letter he says, *I may be wrong but I still think that Ralph must have rocks in his head.*

In Bob's letter of 17 August, Bob asks his mother to read the article in the Readers Digest for June. He says it is pretty true to life. A guess about the contents of that article is that it dealt with the daily life of bomber crew much like Bob's.

The next letter home on 16 August features some printed stationery with Bob's new rank and his APO address. He writes, *How do you like this stationery. I got a Dago to print this up for me. His machine is a little cruder than some in America, but does a good job. I figured that since I was a staff sergeant, nothing but the best for me. Sunday my buddy and I went to nearby town and I heard my friend's chaplain preach again. I do keep some good company once in a while.*

Bob writes to his sister, Norma, on the 29th of August. Norma has an Air Force boy friend who is in pilot training. (She later marries him.) *I am glad to hear that your boy friend George will be flying P-38s they are the best. They are some of the best pals I've got.*

*Yes I know that Dick Wagner (*a home town friend of Bob's*) is over here somewhere close. He flies in B-24s. The Post Office won't tell me the location of units so it is hard to find out exactly where he is. I am making progress. To date I have completed 42 missions.*

On the 31st of August Bob writes that he has completed 44 missions over enemy territory. He tells of a "romance" that an acquaintance had. *A fellow I know had aspirations of marrying a girl from a French refugee family in a nearby town, but it was a "no go." He must wait till the eldest got married. His girl was the second eldest. ... We got paid today. We get Allied invasion money. There are no coins over here. If you want something for 5 or 10 lires, you pull out a 5 or 10 lire note. Those notes are almost as big as our dollar bill.*

*I got a letter from Irene Gruenhage (*a former teacher of Bob's*) She is married and must have married an older man. She said he was overseas for 22 months in the first war.*

We hear lots of rumors - some are good and others not so good.

On 14 September Bob writes, *Guess it high time I wrote again.... Recently I spent a week at an Air Force rest camp on a nearby island. I really enjoyed myself. All of our crew went together. I went swimming quite a lot but I also went on several boat trips. The food and quarters were very good at the rest camp. We even had an Italian maid to make beds and perform other room services. And what about this: I actually ate from a plate and drank from a regular home-like cup! They had good silverware too! I bought a few souvenirs. I plan to keep them and bring them back whenever that is. It was really a beautiful place at that rest camp. I will try to tell you more whenever I see you.*

I recently visited the city of Naples. It is a big city, but the war has certainly left its marks on the city, but it could have been completely destroyed.

I have now completed 46 missions. I had a letter from Dick. He said he had been on Saipan and Guam and now Tinian. This was the first time he had ever named islands. I guess life is not exactly easy for him.

Bob did not tell where he had gone for the one week of rest and relaxation. He went to the Isle of Capri a world famous resort before and after the war. During this part of the war the Armed services used it as a rest area.

On the 23rd of September Bob writes, *I got several more copies of the Signal. I see that lots of boys from Fillmore County are serving overseas.*

There have been a lot of them who have been killed. My tent buddy gets a paper from his home town in Massachusetts and there are lots of soldiers from there who have been killed. ...To date I have completed 48 missions.

On the 30th of September Bob writes, *The Italians are plowing with a walking plow and a team of horses, mules or oxen. They can surely plow a straight furrow using a walking plow. ..The answer to your important question is yes, I hope.*

Bob answers a question posed by his sister and question almost certainly was "Will you be home for Christmas?"

Bob sends some long awaited and very welcome news in his next letter of 9 October. *To date I've completed 50 missions... Don't write any more letters to me at this address because of circumstances that are going to rise to prevent me from getting them for some time.... I will continue my correspondence but it will be limited.*

Even in his last letters home Bob is cautious about saying that he is going home, but rather mentions changing circumstances. It was probably quite clear to the home folks that he was coming home since they knew he had completed his 50 missions and they could put it all together. Bob actually did make it home for Christmas that year.

Bob sent one more letter home after the one with the really great news. He writes this on 15 October. *Recently I visited the city of Bari. There are a few peculiarities over here that one notices. When you walk through the streets, the streets are very dark. There are very few if any lights except on main street where lights may shine through windows. I get a creepy feeling walking through these streets. As you know in America stores usually have glass fronts. Here the fronts are very small and they have a steel plated door that they can pull down over the window. At home fruit and vegetables are displayed in store windows, but not here in Italy. Here they have a block that is just an open space where sellers have their goods displayed. Some of it is on boxes or tables or sometimes it is just laid out on the ground. It is a very crowded, noisy and dirty place. People haggle and argue over the price of a few tomatoes, grapes or what have you.*

We are getting a few apples here now, but they are inferior to most American apples.

Today is Sunday and I am getting ready to go to Church. I have not been to a morning service since I left the states. Over here Sunday is just another day as far as duties go. It has to be that way in wartime I suppose.

That ended Bob's correspondence from Italy. Bob came home for Christmas and after leave there was sent to California for reassignment. He was sent to Amarillo, Texas where he had some easy duty working as an aircraft mechanic. He had another opportunity to enter the Aviation Cadet program, but Bob declined. He had had enough of the military and was looking forward to a civilian life.

One letter home is quite interesting. It was written on the 14th of April in 1945 and almost all of the content of the letter concerns the death of President Roosevelt. *Yes, mother, the President Roosevelt died and we are sure hearing lots about it.*

All Army personnel cannot attend bars, beer halls, movie houses or any place of entertainment from Friday afternoon till Monday morning. I guess it is no more than right. Tomorrow morning (Sunday) we have formation at 9:00 AM. It regards rites for the president I guess. Personally I think that is going a little too far. It is alright to request men to attend memorial service but compulsory, well I don't know about that. Since I have been in this Army, I have developed one thought or ideas stronger than ever. Maybe it it is good and maybe it is bad. In this Army, one thing about it stands out. There is no such thing as an irreplaceable man. If one fellow dies, somebody takes his place and the world goes on just the same. Overseas, at times some thought that only one or two crews could fly lead positions yet someone else was always able to take over and did amazingly well. When a crew got a one-way ticket to Hitler's fatherland, some other crew or crews completed their missions.

All in all, plenty of bally-hoo over the death of a president if you ask me. Mother, I trust that this doesn't sound too harsh, but these are my sentiments. Enough of this for now.

Bob's Army Air Force experience taught him that no man is irreplaceable. He had a good deal of very dangerous experience to help him formulate that opinion.

Chapter 17 - Fighter Planes: Friends and Foes

From the first combat mission to the last mission those men who rode in the heavy bombers during World War II were profoundly concerned with fighter planes - the friendly escort planes and the enemy fighter planes. They developed a high level of expertise in the identification of all types of planes. They knew which enemy planes were deadly and which enemy planes were not so fearful. They knew which of the escorting fighter planes offered them the most protection and which planes offered lesser amounts of protection. Events in the earlier part of the war showed that bombing raids without escorting fighters were so dangerous that an airman could expect to live through only two or three raids. Fighter planes were an essential part of the life or death game that airmen were forced to play.

Oil related targets were perhaps the most fiercely defended of all targets. Brother Bob tells about a raid on the oil refineries at Budapest. On this raid Bob flew in #436, Vicious Vixen. He describes the flak as heavy, intense, accurate and tracking. He writes that they got 15-20 flak holes in the Vicious Vixen. Bob writes that it looked like they did a good job and were successful in the bombing mission. It was a tough trip. Several factors combined to make the raid very difficult. Somehow, some of the oxygen hoses got tangled up and one of the crew members passed out from the lack of oxygen at just the time they were over the target. They managed to get the unconscious gunner to the radio room and administered some emergency oxygen and revived the gunner. The problem was that the oxygen supply lines to the different gun positions were tangled and no oxygen got through. Only two of the gun positions were operative due to the lack of oxygen. That meant that the Vicious Vixen was nearly defenseless and vulnerable to attack by enemy fighters. Bob says that P-38s flew with them after they had finished their bomb run. In his diary Bob writes, "I *indeed can say as another gunner of 50 missions said,' God Bless America and the P-38s."*

Another WWII veteran, Robert Shorts in citation (17-1) flew on a very hazardous mission over Germany and has this to say of his appreciation of escorting fighters. "We were always glad to see the P-47s come in. A lot of Germans were lined up to come at us. Even if there were only four P-47s, they would tear right into the German formation of 12 or 15 planes and shoot about half of them down before they knew what was happening. After the mission the P-47s flew over our station and waved their wings at us."

Another Veteran, Keilman, (17-2) tells of a dangerous mission where they had a gasoline leak that compounded their hazard. A group of German fighters began to work themselves into position for an attack on Keilman's bomber. Keilman called for fighter support, afraid that the fighter support would come too late. He began to mentally prepare himself for a fatal attack. Then, at the very last second - "Two P-38s dived from 'nowhere' right into the gaggle of German fighters. The German fighters scattered like frightened sparrows - and we were saved."

Whether every last detail in the foregoing accounts is accurate it difficult to know. What is certain is the bomber crews admired the escorting fighter pilots and appreciated their courage and dedication to the task of bringing the bombers home safely.

We will discuss the missions of the men who flew the fighter planes and then briefly characterize the men who flew the escort planes and then describe in detail the kinds of planes flown by friends and by foes.

We begin by discussing the missions of the pilots. The men who flew the fighter planes were called on to do all sorts of assignments in addition to the requirement of protecting the bombers when they left on a raid over enemy territory. The terms tactical and strategic are adjectives to describe the missions assigned to pilots. Sometimes the adjectives were used to describe AAF units. Strategic missions were larger in scope and usually concerned long term goals such as destroying the enemy's capability to produce fighter planes; or destroying the enemy's capability of producing petroleum products. Most of the missions flown by the heavy bombers were strategic missions. Fighter pilots often escorted bombers on strategic missions and since the bombers mission was strategic it is rational to say that the mission of the fighter escorts was also strategic. However, the role of the fighter pilots was varied and they were called on to perform a wide variety of assignments.

Fighter pilots flew both tactical missions and strategic missions. For many of their missions, it is difficult to specify missions as either tactical or strategic. In some instances they flew over enemy territory for the express purpose of engaging in combat with enemy fighter planes. This was more likely to happen near the end of the war when enemy fighter pilots were poorly trained and unlikely to win in a single one-on-one combat. Such missions had the effect of showing who had control of the airspace over any given area. Fighter pilots were sometimes ordered to strafe enemy truck convoys, enemy freight and passenger trains. The term "strafe" refers to an aerial attack by a fighter plane on a smaller target on the ground. The target might be either stationery or in motion. Such attacks were usually made from a low altitude with the pilot flying downward and in the same direction as the moving target while firing machine guns. Some fighters were equipped with rockets which the pilot released during the attack.

Another very important tactical mission was the support of ground troops. Fighter planes might be ordered to attack enemy fortifications preliminary to an infantry attack. The might be ordered to attack convoys bringing supplies to front-line enemy troops. Allied troops felt more certain of victory when they knew that Allied air forces controlled the air space over the area where they were fighting.

Reconnaissance was another tactical mission of the fighter pilots. Some of these missions were performed by smaller planes. The smaller planes were poorly armed and some were unarmed. If reconnaissance missions went over territory where enemy fire was likely to be encountered, then a fighter plane would be the most appropriate plane for the mission.

The men who flew the fighter planes were highly qualified. In the first part of the war the Army only accepted men for pilot training who had completed at least two years of college. Later in the war, the demand for pilots was so great that the Army used tests to determine which of the applicants for pilot training were sufficiently knowledgeable and adequately skilled to complete pilot training. Not only did all applicants have to be intelligent, they also had to be excellent physical specimens. They had to have excellent eyesight and they had to be well coordinated. Only those with the highest physical and mental capabilities were qualified for pilot training.

There was an economic element in the selection of men for pilot training. The AAF had only limited facilities for training pilots so they wanted to be certain that men selected for pilot training would successfully complete the pilot training. The AAF did not want to waste time, money and facilities to train men who could not make the grade.

In spite of the high standards, not every trainee made it through the program. The AAF recruited some of those who failed pilot training as bombardiers and navigators.

The job of fighter pilot was an exclusively male job. There were no female fighter pilots. However, the AAF did train a number of women for pilot positions. These women pilots were used in various non-combat positions. One job in particular was often assigned to the ladies. That was the job of ferrying planes from one place to another. For example, a woman ferry pilot might fly a brand new bomber, or fighter plane, to an AAF training facility for use in training pilots.

Another group of men made history in World War II. Following is the story of that group of pilots. Those pilots were known as the Redtails because the tails of the fighter planes were painted red. The story of the success of the Redtails is taken from the following material: (17-3) Beginning in July, and through October of 1944, the Redtails flew numerous missions, usually bomber escorts. Sometimes they shot down German aircraft, and began to build a respectable Group tally. Less often, they lost one of their own; but they never lost a bomber. …The bomber pilots began to appreciate the Redtails. In <u>Mustang Aces of the 9th and 15th Air Forces</u>, one B-24 pilot recalled, "The P-38s always stayed too far out. Some of the Mustang group stayed in too close… The Redtails were always out there where we wanted them to be… We had no idea they were Black; it was the Army's best kept secret."

Before the second World War, it was AAF policy not to use Blacks in any capacity. However, that policy was voided by President Franklin Roosevelt who ordered the development of an all Black unit, the 99th Pursuit Squadron. The Army selected an all-Black college in Tuskegee, Alabama as the site for the development of the training program. Subsequently, the unit and the graduates were often called the "Tuskegee Airmen."

By May of 1943, the 99th had arrived overseas in the Mediterranean Theater of Operations. The AAF in the Mediterranean Theater did not immediately welcome the 99th. It took the AAF some time to get used to the fact that the 99th pilots were highly skilled and highly trained pilots with skills equal to that of white pilots. As time went by the 99th flew more and more missions and completed their assigned missions with skill and courage. They gained an initial grudging acceptance and later full acceptance for their competence. Before the war was over the 99th and the other black units had developed an excellent record.

Brother Bob never mentioned the fact that some of the pilots escorting the B-17s were Black. He may not have known.

To better understand the situation in Brother Bob's War, it is useful to know more about the fighter planes that escorted the B-17s and the fighter planes that attacked the B-17s. We will describe a number of fighter planes, but give special attention to those that helped to guard Brother Bob and those planes that attacked his B-17.

First we will consider some of the qualities of fighter planes so as to provide a vocabulary of qualities used to describe fighter planes.

Speed was a critical quality of fighter planes, but it certainly was not the only critical quality. Being faster that one's opponent was highly desirable. As an example suppose that an Allied pilot is engaged in a one-to-one dogfight with a German fighter plane. Suppose that the Allied pilot runs out of ammunition. If he has the faster plane, he can run for home and escape his attacking foe. Speed had the advantage in attack; if the enemy fighter is the one out of ammunition, then the Allied pilot can overtake the German fighter and shoot him down. Speed is strongly related to the ability to catch-up or to run away. There is some use in the speed quality in the ability to get some place in a hurry if a fighter plane is needed to be in some place at once -or sooner.

Climb rate is another desirable quality in a fighter plane. Perhaps it is not as important as speed, but it is very important. A plane with superior climbing ability can sometimes climb out of trouble. It is related to, but not synonymous with, speed. A fast plane is not necessarily a fast climbing plane. The ability to climb is related to complex design features such as the amount of wing surface.

Maneuverability is a critically important feature of the fighter plane. It refers to the ability of a plane to perform maneuvers in a hurry - to turn sharply, to reverse direction, and to dive rapidly and safely.   A one-on-one dogfight was largely a contest of maneuverability. Each pilot tried to maneuver his plane out of harms way; each pilot tried to maneuver his plane into a favorable attack position. Maneuverability was closely related to the skill of the pilot. A plane with great maneuverability was no advantage unless the pilot had a high level of skill in the use of a plane's maneuverability.

Power was still another important quality. This quality was related to the speed of an airplane. However, if it took a fighter plane a long period of time to attain its maximum speed, then the speed advantage was largely lost. If a pilot ran out of ammunition and had to make a run for home, he had to get his plane up to top speed in big hurry. If his plane could travel fast but it took a long time to attain that top speed, then that pilot might be dead before he could get his plane up to top speed. Power was also related to the load that a plane could carry. A low-powered plane could carry less gasoline, bombs, and ammunition and was thus handicapped in its overall performance if it lacked sufficient power.

Range was another critically important quality. The best fighter in the world - one that had great speed, climb, maneuverability, power, armament, ceiling and survivability was of little value unless it had the range to get to where it was needed. In the early part of the war fighter planes often lacked the range to escort the bombers to distant targets and so the bombers had to go it alone over the target. Just when the fighters were needed the most, they were not available to help escort the bombers.

The ceiling of a plane referred to the altitude that a plane could attain and still be able to perform the functions of a fighter plane. Most Allied bombers flew on missions of 25,000 feet give or take 5000 feet. Yet there were some fighter planes that could not climb to that height. Their ceiling was 10,000 to 15,000 feet. A fighter with such a low ceiling was worthless to a bomber scheduled to conduct a bombing raid at 25, 000 feet. The American fighter plane, the P-39, was in other ways quite a good fighter but it ceiling was such that precluded it from being used in high-level bombing raids. The P-39 and other planes with low ceilings were well adapted for use in support of ground troops even if they could not escort bombers.

The armament that a plane carried was, in one sense, the very purpose of having a fighter plane. A fighter plane's fundamental function is to fight. To do this the fighter had to be equipped with the necessary ordnance. It must not be so heavy as to overload the plane; it must not be so light as to lose its potency. There was a large area in the middle of the spectrum that was useful. In the early years, fighter planes had smaller weapons such as 30 caliber machine guns. However, 30 caliber machine guns were not sufficiently deadly for the work that fighter planes performed. The next step up was the 50 caliber machine gun. It was much better, but still not sufficiently deadly. As the war progressed most fighter planes were equipped with guns larger than 50 caliber. Usually these weapons are called cannons. There was a limit to the size of cannons. If the cannons were too large, they added too much weight to the plane. The cannons were heavy; the ammunition was heavy. Designers and armorers experimented with different sizes of cannons. In some instances fighter planes were equipped with both machine guns and cannons for use in different combat conditions.

Aerodynamics is a difficult quality to quantify, but it made a difference in the performance of planes. A major portion of this quality was streamlining. A plane designed so as to offer the least amount of air resistance will accelerate and fly faster than a poorly designed plane. To some degree the aerodynamics of fighter planes was determined by the type engine that was available for use in the plane. The engine was always placed in the front of the plane and if the engine was bulky, it was difficult to construct an aerodynamic design around such an engine.

The last quality for consideration was survivability or toughness. This referred to the ability of a plane to take punishment without going down in flames. A large plane such as the B-17 was very tough - it could take a great deal of punishment and keep on flying. Some fighters were better at taking punishment than others. In the following material the vulnerability of liquid cooled engines is cited as an example of poor survivability.

Previously, we have discussed the qualities that made a fighter plane good. Next, a consideration of what we shall call factors. Another term that can be used is design elements. A plane's design qualities did not necessarily make a fighter better or worse, but factors sometimes were important considerations in the evaluation of fighter planes.

Aircraft engines in the early part of the war were usually either air-cooled or liquid cooled. Generally speaking liquid-cooled did not a;ways mean water cooled. The liquid cooled engines had a serious vulnerability. If any part of the liquid cooling system was damaged, such as a hose being punctured by a 50 caliber bullet, then that plane was doomed to a very short period of flying time. What might be a minor problem in another plane would be a disaster in a liquid cooled engine. The air-cooled engines were better and replaced the liquid cooled engines later in the war.

Another factor to consider was comfort. Pilots had to fly for long periods of time and if the plane was uncomfortable the degree of pilot discomfort and pilot fatigue might make the plane and the pilot more vulnerable.

Another factor was the supercharger. This was related to the ceiling of a plane. At high altitudes the air gets thin and the engine does not function well because of a shortage of air. The supercharger is a device that pumps extra air into the fuel mixture so that the engine functions nearly as well as at ground level. The P-39 mentioned earlier was never fitted with a supercharger and that was the reason for its low ceiling.

There were several other factors. Some planes were easy to fly and other required constant attention to fuel gages, fuel mixtures, and so on. A plane that required a lot of attention to fly put the pilot in danger. A pilot in a dogfight, or about to engage in a dogfight should give his full attention to the dogfight and not to the fuel mixture. Some planes were easy to land and some were hard to land.

A final word on the qualities and factors. The skill of the pilot was probably the most critical characteristic. An experienced and skilled pilot could overcome many of the undesirable qualities of planes by his experience and skill. A novice pilot in the very best plane might meet disaster on his first sortie.

It is difficult to compare the different fighter planes because the design of the planes was not constant. Some authors make comparisons according to periods of the war, or according theaters of the war. If the design of a plane remained static, then it gradually became inferior to the planes on the other side. Therefore time was an element that had to be considered. The best fighter plane in 1940 might be tenth best plane in 1944. Some qualities were important in certain theaters of the war, but less important in other theaters. The Spitfire with a relatively short range was invaluable in the Battle of Britain and not handicapped by its short range. Planes used in the

Pacific theater had to be long-range in order to be useful.

There are a number of references to the qualities of different fighter planes in the material that follows.(17-4) (17-5) (17-6) (17-7) (17-8) (17-9)

First on the list for consideration, but not necessarily the best, is the Messerschmidt Bf 109. Sometimes this plane has been referred to as the Me109. With one exception, more Me109s were produced than any other fighter plane used in the second World War. The production figure often used is 33,000. The fighter plane that may have exceeded the Me109 in production is the Soviet "Sturmovik" which had a production of 37,000.

Chuck Hawks, who has made a study of the best of the World War II fighters, rated the Bf109 as one of the best of all fighter planes. The Germans first produced the Me 109 in 1936. Willy Messerschmidt, a German designer designed the Me109. Chuck Hawks says that Willy Messerschmidt built the smallest aircraft possible around the biggest engine. His concept was successful. After the plane came out in 1936, Willy Messerschmidt changed and modernized the design of the plane a number of times. Each of the new models was an improvement over the previous model. Part of its excellence was the result of constant correction and improvement of the newer models.

A specific element in the program of corrections and improvements in the Me109 concerned the Civil War in Spain. During that Civil War, the German government gave a substantial amount of help to the Fascist government of Francisco Franco who was fighting against substantial Communist rebel forces. In the air war portion of that war, the Franco forces were coming out second best fighting against the Communists who were flying Soviet planes supplied by the Soviet Union. The Germans came to the aid of the Franco government. Part of that help consisted of sending German planes manned by German pilots to assist the Franco government. The specific plane that the Germans sent was the Me109. In spite of a problem of armament which the Germans corrected the Me109 was successful in combat against the Soviet supplied fighter planes. The German government was able to work the "bugs" out of the Me109 before it had to be used in a war intended to conquer all of Europe and maybe the entire world.

The Me109 was obviously an excellent plane. Two of the top German aces, Erich Hartman (352 victories) and Gerhard Barkhorn (301 victories) Hartmann and Barkhorn were top-notch pilots but probably could never have achieved such totals unless they had first-rate fighter planes.

In the war with France, Belgium and Netherlands in 1939-1940 the principal German fighter plane was the Me109 and the German Air Force quickly established air superiority over their opponents. None of the French, Belgian, or Dutch planes could match the Me109.

The Me109 had a number of qualities that made it an excellent fighter plane. It was one of the fastest planes on either the Axis or Allied sides. It had an excellent rate of climb. The Me109 had a fuel injection system rather than a carburetion system. In a carburetion system the engine cannot get fuel if the plane is experiencing negative gravity, or if it was flying upside down. This meant that the Me109 had a greater range of maneuverability than planes with carburetion systems.

In summary the Me109 was an excellent fighter plane that benefited from a number of changes, revisions and improvements that made it better than some Allied fighter planes and the equal of many other fighter planes. By the latter part of World War II, both the German designers and Allied designers had developed planes that were at least marginally better than the Me109. The Germans developed a jet fighter that was definitely superior to the Me109. The Americans developed the P-38 and the P-51 fighters which were at least equal and possibly superior to the Me109.

The other very important German fighter plane was the Focke-Wulf190, or FW190. It was known for several excellent qualities. It was easy to fly and the pilots liked to fly the FW190. It was heavily armed and had two 20mm cannon in addition to its machine guns. It was a fast plane with a speed of 395-405 and up to a max speed of 436 miles per hour. It also had an extraordinary range - 820 miles. That long range made it possible to give it assignments for long distance flights at a time when few fighter had such a long range. Its ceiling was extraordinarily high with a ceiling of 37,000 feet. The total production figure for FW190 was 19,000

The Spitfire was one of two premiere British fighter planes - the other being the Hawker Hurricane. The British developed the Spitfire fighter plane in the mid 1930s at about the same time that the Germans developed the Me109. They experimented with various versions using different engines. The British did not have the opportunity to "war test" the Spitfire in the same way that the Germans had "war tested" the Me109 in Spain. The Spitfire scored high on aerodynamics and it was easy to fly and hence loved by pilots. The two top British pilots flew the Spitfire. Johnny Johnson was the leading British ace with 38 victories and Douglas Bader who flew with two artificial legs scored 9 of his 20 kills from a Spitfire. By some standards the Spitfire was not as heavily armed as some fighters. It carried eight 30 caliber machine guns - not especially lethal weapons, but there were a lot of them. Later in the war it was sometimes fitted with two 20 mm cannons. Still later in the war there were four 20 mm cannons. The Spitfire was in many ways close to the Me109 in performance and other qualities. A major problem with the Spitfire was its lack of range. The Spitfire was marginally faster and maneuvered better than the Me109, but the Me109 could dive faster. The Spitfire had an engine with carburetion rather than fuel injection. This meant that the engines would quit for lack of fuel if the plane flew upside down or in negative gravity situations. Later in the war the British improved the carburetion system. The real tribute to the Spitfire was its contribution in winning the "Battle of Britain."

Since the "Battle of Britain was fought in the skies over Britain, the fact that the Spitfire had a limited range did not make much difference.

The British also had another good fighter plane, the Hurricane, which did its part in the "Battle of Britain." The British built more than 14,000 of these planes and that in itself is a tribute to their importance. Several notable British aces such as Douglas Bader flew the Hurricane although he also flew the Spitfire. After the war, research showed that the Hurricane was responsible for shooting down more enemy planes than any other fighter plane. They shot down more German fighter than the air defense forces did and they shot down more German planes than both Spitfires and air defense combined. This was an exceptional tribute to this plane.

The Hurricane was not as fast as the Spitfire nor was it as fast as the Me109, but it was extremely maneuverable and that quality made up for its lack of speed. It was easy to fly and easy to handle on the ground. Unlike some of the other fighters, the design of the Hurricane remained the same throughout the entire war.

The Americans produced a number of excellent fighter planes. The P-40 was much produced (14,000 planes) and much used, but it was not the equal of the better German and Japanese fighter planes. This is not a blanket condemnation because it served the United States well until better fighter planes came along. Later in the war better fighter planes replaced the P-40s or relegated them to lesser missions.

Among American fighter planes the P-47 Thunderbolt was one of the most produced planes. Republic Aviation produced more than 15,000 of these planes. It had a number of good qualities. It was fast at 424 mph and it had a long range at 950 miles. It carried either six or eight 50 caliber machine guns so it was well-armed. I could also carry bombs or be fitted to carry rockets which added to its versatility. It had a ceiling around 40,000 feet so it was suited for escorting high lever bombing missions.

Some who have studied and compared the different American, German, Japanese, Russian and British planes think that the American P-38 was the best fighter plane of World War II. The one exception might have been the

Messerschmidt 262, but it was produced in such low numbers and came into use so late in the war that it had little or no effect on the outcome of the war.

The P-38 was a revolutionary design; it had two engines and twin tails. Enemy fighter pilots sometimes called it the "Fork-Tailed Devil." One useful element in its design was that the central section, where the pilot flew the plane, offered excellent visibility. The P-38, if fitted with additional fuel tanks, could operate in range as far as 2600 miles. This long range made it especially valuable in the Pacific Theater of Operations where long-distance missions were common. There was another very positive factor and that was the fact that guns could be mounted on the central pod that did not have to have fire through the propeller. That was a common feature on most fighter planes and required a complex mechanism. The P-38 armament could be simpler and lighter. Lockheed did not produce a large number of these planes and they did not come into use until later in the war. One possible reason for the lower production figure is that the revolutionary design of the P-38 caused some problems and these problems had to be solved before it went into mass production.

An expert who actually flew American fighter in the war, and some of the enemy's fighters at a later time argues that the P-38 was the best all-around fighter. This man is C.C. Jordan. These are his six arguments for citing the P-38 as the best. 1. Its tricycle landing gear made landing and taking off easier and safer. 2. It had two engines; if one failed or was damaged by enemy fire, the other could get the pilot home. 3. It had a very long range which increased the number of things it could do. 4. Its engines turned in opposite directions; one turned clockwise and the other counterclockwise. This made the plane more balanced and stable. 5. Placing the pilot in the middle pod where he could see well and aim the guns well. Jordan says that this gave the pilot capability to get close to the enemy before opening fire. 6. Some explanation is necessary to understand the value of the 6th favorable quality of the P-38. By the time Lockheed developed the P-38 it along with other planes were able to dive at speeds approaching the speed of sound. Some airplanes experienced great vibration and some broke up as such high speeds. To overcome this problem Lockheed developed a dive brake so slow the fast diving speeds to a safe diving speed.

Lockheed produced and delivered about 9900 P-38s. Therefore it was certainly not one of the most used fighter planes in World War II. If it was not the best, it certainly was among the best.

The other outstanding Allied fighter plane of World War II was the P-51 Mustang. A number of outstanding aces flew the P-51. Some of the aces:

Captain John Gentile with 35 kills; Captain John Godfrey with 31 kills and Colonel Donald Blakeslee with 15 kills.

North American Aviation built the first P-51s for the British according to their specifications. This happened in 1940 before America became involved in the war in Europe. North American produced planes in approximately equal quantity for both the British and American Air Forces. The designer experimented and produced production models with different engines. They finally settled on a Packard/Merlin engine which enabled the P-51 to fly as fast 445 mph - a very fast airplane. In addition to its high speed the P-51 was noted for it maneuverability and its ease of handling. Most of the Mustang models were armed with four 50 caliber machine guns. Near the end of the war an even more powerful Packard/Merlin engine was installed as standard equipment. At that same time the designers increased the armament so that the P-51 carried six 50 caliber machine guns. These final design improvements pushed the ceiling to 41,000 feet and the top speed to 486 mph.

Many of the bombers and fighters used in World War II were discontinued shortly after the war, but the P-51 was good enough for use in the Korean War from 1950-1953 - a tribute to its excellence.

Among other important fighter planes there are at least three worthy of discussion: the Japanese Zero, the American P-39 and the Soviet Sturmovik.

The Japanese Zero, at the beginning of World War II was better than any available, mass production American fighter plane. The adjective, available, indicates that America had some good designs for fighter planes that they were testing, but not yet in production. They had some good planes in the first stages of production, but production was insufficient. In 1940 and 1941 the main American fighter available to oppose the P-40. The Japanese Zero was a better fighter plane.

The top Japanese aces flew the Zero. Saburo Sakai had 64 kills. Other high scoring Japanese aces were Shoichi Sugita, Tadashi Nakima and Naoishi Kanno.

One of the great positive qualities of the Zero was its long range. Range was a most important quality in the Pacific where targets were distant and hard to get to. An appropriate adjective to describe the Zero was *agile.* In addition to range it was highly maneuverable, a fast climber and a high top speed. It lacked protective armor and did not perform well at high altitudes, but overall, it was an excellent fighter plane.

One must consider the time factor in judging the worth of the Japanese Zero. In the first part of the war it was the best fighter in the theater. Near the end of the war when America had developed the P-51s and P-38s, it was no longer superior.

The American P-39 or Airacobra was unusual in that half of the production of this plane went to the Soviet Union. Total production was about 10,000. This fighter had some limitations such as a low ceiling and so was not able to fight at high altitudes. Its armament was good and it was able to absorb a great deal of punishment. The Soviets often used the P-39 as a ground support aircraft; the Soviet pilots who flew the plane liked it and the plane made an important contribution to the Soviet war effort.

The Soviet Sturmovik was probably the most produced fighter in World War II. The Soviets produced more than 37,000 of these planes. However, it was a fighter/bomber rather than a fighter plane. Neither the Sturmovik nor the P-39 was an adequate match for the German Me109 or the FW190 flown by expert German pilots. Some of the extremely high totals of German aces were achieved on the Eastern Front where experienced German pilots flying their high quality fighters were matched against poorly trained Soviet pilots flying planes inferior to those of the German Luftwaffe. Near the end of the war the volume of Soviet planes began to have a telling effect; there were simply too many Soviet planes for the Germans to combat successfully. Quantity triumphed over quality.

This discussion of fighter planes is not comprehensive. Many other nations such as France, Finland and Rumania produced fighter planes some of which were anywhere from average to good. Planes such as these did not greatly affect the outcome of the air war.

Chapter 18 - Routes

You can best follow this discussion of routes by referring to the map of Europe in the Appendix. This map shows the routes that Brother Bob would have taken on some of his missions. It does not represent all of his missions. He had multiple missions to some targets such as Ploesti.

When Brother Bob left on a bombing mission, he might go to the northwest if the mission required hitting targets in France. If the mission called for hitting targets in Germany the planes flew in a nearly straight northerly direction. Targets in Hungary and Rumania required northeasterly heading. On a mission to Greece the direction was southeast. There was one direction that they avoided. They did not go in a direction that took them over Switzerland.

Switzerland was a neutral country and both Axis nations and Allied nations recognized its neutrality. For Allied mission planner and bomber pilots, it meant that no mission routes went over Swiss air space. The same rule applied to the other side. Apparently, the rule was generally observed. A look at the map will show that Switzerland was not located on an obvious route to targets that the Allies planned to bomb. Bob mentions that they could see Switzerland as they flew by. However the routes of Allied pilots never intentionally took them over Swiss territory.

Nonetheless there were at least 1500 American airmen who were interned in Switzerland during the war. The status of an internee is difficult to describe. They were not held in prisons unless they misbehaved. Often they were put up in hotels and apparently the Swiss fed them. Some sort of arrangements were made to give some monetary allowances to the internees and they seem to have paid for their food. An interesting aspect of their situation was that there were Germans present in the same cities where the Americans were held. Neither the Germans nor the Americans were armed, but there was some conflict between them. For example, some American internees stole a big German swastika that was in front of the German consulate and there was a good deal of trouble about that. If either side created too much trouble, they were sent to a prison camp. One internee tells of attending a dance where the Swiss girls had the choice of dancing either with Americans or Germans.

The Germans routinely sent officers to Switzerland for rest and recuperation. They stayed in hotels and did whatever they could to relax and enjoy themselves. Interaction between those officers and American internees was possible.

Switzerland suffered from food shortages as did all European countries.

They had a system of rationing like almost every country in Europe. So, food was adequate for internees, but there were no feasts. The internees probably suffered from boredom.

Many of the missions that the Fifteenth Air Force flew required them to fly over the Adriatic Sea. Therefore it quite often happened that a plane would be damaged and they had to go home by way of the Adriatic Sea. That was not a pleasant prospect, but one that was often faced by the crews of Fifteenth Air Force bombers. If the plane had problems and the pilot decided to ditch over water, then that action presented one hazardous set of options. In some instances where the plane was barely able to continue over water, then the crew would start throwing things out of the plane to lighten the load. Sometimes this worked and sometimes they had to ditch in the Adriatic Sea. If they were over land, then the pilot might crash land, or perhaps the crew would bail out. The degree of difficulty or danger of the different options depended, to some extent, on the route taken. Targets in different countries or areas presented different dangers   Some held multiple hazards and some held fewer hazards.

Prior to, and during the invasion of southern France, Brother Bob participated in missions to Montpelier and Toulon. The first part of the trip would have taken them over the central part of Italy and perhaps over the city of Rome. In one mission Brother Bob mentions seeing ships that had taken part in another invasion of Italy at Anzio, not far south of Rome. Then the route required them to cross a portion of the Mediterranean Sea and they may have flown over the island of Corsica. They certainly encountered anti-aircraft fire when they bombed targets at Montpelier, Cannes and Toulon. If they had to ditch on the return trip, they would have had to ditch in the Mediterranean. Generally speaking this body of water was controlled by the Allies. The B-17 was equipped with life rafts and other survival gear for use in ditching over water. Therefore, if crew members were successful in inflating life rafts, they might get picked up by a friendly ship. If the plane had gone down over water the USAAF and the Navy would have done a search for survivors.

Route problems on bombing missions to Germany such as those that Brother Bob participated in to Memmingen and Munich, were much more hazardous. Suppose the plane had to crash land or bail out over German territory. Even if the parachutists landed safely or even if the crash landing was successful the crew members were not necessarily safe. A digression is necessary here to explain why.

By 1944 Germany had been at war for five years. During that time Germany had bombed our British allies frequently, but had never bombed the United States because they had no bombers with sufficient range to bomb the United States. The Germans had been bombed by the RAF from bases in Britain since 1939. There had been periods where there were fewer raids and there were periods of intense bombing. When the United States got into the war, another air force was formed and based in Great Britain. This was the mighty 8th Air Force which was a very large Air Force and approximately equivalent in size to the RAF. For a complex set of reasons the RAF and the 8th Air Force had come to an agreement. They agreed that the RAF would do night bombing and the 8th Air Force would do the daylight bombing. So, the RAF had been bombing the Germans for five years by 1944.

The 8th Air Force had been active since 1942 and by 1943 and 1944 the intensity had grown considerably. By 1944 there was still another AAF, the Fifteenth, to add to the distress of the German population. The Germans, quite naturally, feared and hated the bombing and the people who did the bombing. In some instances the German populace was extremely hostile to crew members who appeared in their midst. It was an opportunity for the German populace to take action against crew members. Stories vary, but on some occasions crew members were killed by the German populace. In some instances the crew members were physically assaulted. If German police or military members were in the area where crew members came down, then they would take the crew members into custody. Crew members taken into custody and later to prisoner of war camps fared better at the hands of officialdom than other crew members.

When passing over or going on bombing missions to Austria the problems were nearly the same as for those missions over Germany.

On missions to Czechoslovakia, Hungary and Poland, the planes flew over countries that had not been as intensively bombed as Germany. The populace was perhaps less hostile to crew members that suddenly appeared in their midst. The same was true for Rumania except for those areas around the oil fields and refineries at Ploesti.

An examination of the map shows that many of the routes to Austria, Czechoslovakia, Hungary, and Rumania required the planes to pass over Yugoslavia. This was a special situation. Officially, the Germans occupied Yugoslavia and were in control of the country. Yugoslavia is a mountainous country and Germany had never been able to completely control all of the areas in Yugoslavia. There were partisans, or guerillas, operating in many sections of the country. If crewmen had to bail out over Yugoslavia, or if they had to crash land in Yugoslavia, they had a fairly good chance of being greeted by some of the partisans who were anti-German. These partisan groups had some communication and received some assistance from the Allies. Therefore, they sometimes collected allied airmen and arranged for those airmen to be returned. There are a group of islands along the west coast of Yugoslavia. These islands are known collectively as Dalmacia. Some of these islands were controlled by the partisans under Tito. At least one of the islands had a landing strip where it might be possible to make a landing. However, it was only about half as long as necessary to make a safe landing, and all landings were crash landings. Most planes that landed there crashed in some fashion. The runway was not long enough for a bomber t take-off. Hence it was a point of no return for the big bomber. If the crew got out safely, then the partisans sent a radio message to Foggia and a DC-7 would come and pick up the crew. The DC7 could land and take off on a much shorter runway.

From the standpoint of routes, the trips to Germany were probably the most hazardous. The route would have taken them over northern Italy which was, at that time, still occupied by Germany. It would have taken them over both Austria and Germany and both were dangerous. The route also went over the Adriatic Sea. All in all, it was a very hazardous route.

The remainder of the routes all had hazardous aspects. All routes were dangerous; some were less so.

The members of the RAF and the 8th Air Force had some of the same problems as the 15th Air Force. Overall, the RAF and the 8th Air Force bombed more targets in Germany that did the 15th Air Force. They had to fly relatively long distances over Germany and from that standpoint their route hazards were different from those of the 15th Air Force. If the RAF or 8th Air Force personnel had to bail out or crash land over Belgium or Netherlands, the populace might treat them better, but there were few places to hide in a small, flat country like Belgium or Netherlands.

There were at least a few aircrews based in England, the US 8th and the RAF, who, after bombing raids on Berlin, could not make it home to England and landed in Sweden to be interned there.

Chapter 19 - Counting Down

As veterans approached the end of their tour of duty, they sometimes counted the days until that they would reach that magic day. They worried even more than they had earlier. They were by no means certain, that having finished more than half of their tour of duty; they could safely finish the last part. Wherever, and however possible, they tried to keep themselves safe. They did not want to do anything foolish or take any unnecessary chances in the final part of their tour of duty. But in the case of airmen, there was little they could do to avoid danger. For the most part it was out of their hands - out of their ability to make themselves safe. The hazards of the last mission might be as great as the hazards of the first mission.

There were some changes going on in the war that Bob may not have known anything about, or he might have had only partial knowledge of these events that affected his safety as he flew his missions.

As the year 1944 went on, the Russians had continued their advance eastward. They had driven the Germans and their allies out of most of the Soviet Union. (Russia) By August of 1944. The Russians had begun their advance into Rumania. At that time Rumania decided to get out of the war. They changed sides and became part of the Allied Powers. This probably had only a minor effect on the outcome of the war. However, when the Russian armies approached the oil fields and refineries in Rumania, it changed the bombing strategy of the 15th AAF. When the Russians gained control of the Ploesti area by the end of August, it meant that the 15th AAF would no longer go on bombing raids to Ploesti. For Brother Bob it meant that his raid on Ploesti on the 18th of August would be his last trip to that fearful target.

Intensive Allied raids on German targets had weakened many parts of the German war machine. One of the major targets had always been aircraft factories and that meant that the production of fighter airplanes was cut drastically. The Germans were no longer able to replace fighter aircraft lost in action. To Brother Bob that meant that there might be fewer German fighter planes to oppose the 15th AAF bombing missions.

A very long war that had been going on in one form or another for five years had depleted German resources. One of those resources was German manpower. Germany had, at the beginning of the war a large pool of manpower. Some of the German infantry and air force units in the first part of the war were excellent. But the five years of the war had taken a toll. Many of those skilled infantrymen, submariners, and pilots got killed during the course of five years of war. The replacements were fewer and younger and unskilled and less capable than those in the early part of the war. The result for Brother Bob was that there were fewer fighter pilots to man the planes that opposed the B-17s.

The damage done to Ploesti and other German petroleum producing facilities had its effect. There was less fuel to use in training new pilots and the quality and length of their training suffered. They had fewer hours of flying time and were less skilled than pilots of earlier times. So, the shortage of petroleum meant that there were fewer fighter planes, and the fewer planes were manned by poorly trained pilots.

The men who fired the flak guns had less ammunition available to use and so there was less flak in the air. The men who manned the guns were sometimes very good as Brother Bob noted from time to time. However, some of those who manned the guns were men that the Germans held as prisoners of war. The Germans gave these men some better food and other inducements to work as flak gunners. One wonders if they always did their best to bring down American and British bombers.

As the months went by there were fewer fighter planes that came up to oppose the B-17s. There were fewer, but they were still there often enough to make life miserable and dangerous for the men who flew in the B-17s. The flak may have been slightly less intensive or less accurate, but it was still there.

The statisticians and historians who analyzed the losses incurred at different periods of the war could chart a gradual decrease in the percentage of losses as the war went on. During the time that Brother Bob flew the average loss per mission was in the general range from 2% to 4%. In some missions there were no losses and in some missions the losses were greater than 4%. Generally speaking, the losses at the beginning of Bob's tour of duty were averaging close to 4% and at the end of his tour the average was going down to close to 2%. That may not sound very dangerous, but a statistical table presented in the Chapter14, Hazards, shows that Bob had only about a 50% chance of finishing his tour safely.

Bob was about to make his third and last raid on Ploesti. On 18 August he was assigned to a mission to Ploesti. Here is his account: *Flew in "855" and carried 500 lb. Bombs and hit oil fields at Ploesti again. Flew with our crew except Bones who had a minor nervous breakdown. No fighters were encountered or seen at all. The ship, "286"* (Bob flew in "286" on his previous mission to Ploesti.) *came back with engine no.2 feathered; it got hit with flak pretty bad. We had no really bad hits scored on us; just a few dime sized holes. I'm not afraid to say I did some hard praying this time though. The radio operator of "286" had a piece of flak come through the ship as he was leaning over the table - just clipped his headset wire, narrowly missing his head - yes a lucky boy - bet he'll sweat out every mission from now on. The war may be over according to some American optimists, but over here, we are still fighting a war.*

The official 15th AAF account has this report of the raid on Ploesti: *370(sic) fighter escorted B-17s and B-24s bomb 5 oil refineries around Ploesti, Rumania; 89 B-24s with fighter cover bomb Alibunos Airfield, Yugoslavia. The detachment of the 94th Fighter Squadron, 1st Fighter Group, operating out of Aghione, Corsica with P-38s returns to base at Salsola, Italy.*

Bob had made some previous mention of the absence of one of the regular crew members. On the last mission to Ploesti, his mental condition was such that he was not able to go on the mission. Some of the casualties were not physical and bleeding; some casualties were mental but crippling.

Two days later Bob was flying another mission this one to Krakow, Poland or as listed officially to Osweicim, Poland. He says, Flew *with Blackman's crew in "570" "Achtung. "* (The plane's name, "achtung" means attention or be careful in German.) *We carried 500 lb. Bombs. We hit a synthetic oil and rubber plant at Krakow, Poland. A very long double mission it was. We took off at 0625 and returned at 1430. Flak was intense, accurate and tracking - one gunner was definitely followed our ship "570" for nearly four minutes - the flak was right close to us and only about 50 yards away. That gunner was not just shooting upward at a formation of B-17s, he was shooting at* <u>Us</u> *old* <u>"570"</u> <u>Achtung.</u> *I really sweated it out for a while. However, our ship got only a few minor hits. Hawksley (another pilot) flew "370" with another crew and came home on 3 engines. They got a hole through the stabilizer that you could stick your foot through. For the first time in quite a few missions the Luftwaffe put in an appearance. I saw three FW190s about 600 yards out, but by the time I figured out that they were enemies, I was not able to get a potshot at them. Tailgunner with Bud's crew got the ear cover of his helmet blown off - also piece went through bombardier's pants and heated suit and bruised his leg a little.*

The 15th AAF report: *460(sic) B-24s and B-17s, some fighter escorted, bomb the airfields and marshalling yard at Szolnok, Hungary and oil refineries at Dubova, Czechoslovakia, and Czechrice and Auschwitz, Poland.*

On his next mission, Bob again flew with a different crew. There were several very interesting events that made this mission notable. Here is the story.

Flew with Burke's crew in "064" on a mission to Vienna. The flak was heavy, intense and tracking but not as bad as in previous raids. We hit south industrial area of city. Out of our group there were five feathered engines. When we were coming back home we noticed a group of our bombers flying on our left maybe 500 yards away. One plane had an engine feathered. Part of the engine fell off and the plane heaved to and fro and went into a spin, but the pilot pulled out of the spin after it had gone down several thousand feet. The pilot called on Command(a communication circuit of other bombers) *and asked if we saw any of his crew bail out. We told him that some had bailed out because we had seen them go. The pilot, on his own plane's interphone, received no reply on the interphone and thought that his plane's interphone was out. He put the plane on autopilot and started throwing things out: ammunition, flak suits, and armor plate. As he did this he discovered that every member of his crew had bailed out! Those boys are either prisoners of war or walking back from Yugoslavia.*

Today a waist gunner in the 347th *Squadron got killed. A piece of flak through his helmet and head. We taxied past his ship, "023" just after they had taken him out. Well, somebody had to get it once in a while. I guess we have to expect some trouble in comba*t.

The official report from 15th AAF: *In Austria 472 B-24s and B-17s supported by P-51s bomb the industrial area of Vienna, the Wiener-Neudorf aircraft factory, Vossendorf oil refinery, and Markersdorf Airfield, and attack targets Ferrara, Italy, missing a river bridge but hitting a synthetic rubber factory.*

A reading of Bob's account of the pilot who had his entire crew bail out and was left alone is rather confusing, but Brother Bob tended to be somewhat cryptic and often wrote in a series of sentence fragments. Some additional research by the author revealed more information concerning this interesting anecdote. There are two additional reports

The historian of the 99th Bomb Group, Dick _____ ?, has provided some additional information. Bob's account of how and when the crew bailed out is confusing and perhaps unreliable because he may have had no first hand knowledge. The 99th Bomb Group historian affirms that the crew bailed out and the pilot stayed with the place. The pilot was Warren Christianson. (Christiansen?) He ordered the crew to bail out. Christianson lost the use of another engine, but managed to bring the ship back to its base. The plane was refitted and continued in use until the war ended. The crew members were "rescued" by Yugoslav partisans and returned to Italy on 29 August just six days after they bailed out. The historian does not say how they got home so quickly but one can guess that perhaps the AAF sent in a plane to Yugoslavia to bring them out. There are numerous examples of cooperation between Yugoslav partisans and the Allied Forces.

George ____?, who was a member of the 99th Bomb Group, supplies this account from his own knowledge of the incident. It may differ in a few details from Brother Bob's account. He says, *"On August 23rd 1944 "282" and crew were to bomb a German aircraft factory in the industrial area of Vienna, Austria. The crew makeup was this: 1st Lt. Warren C. Christianson - pilot, 2nd Lt Richard P Anderson - co-pilot, 2nd Lt Norris J Domangue Jr. - Navigator, 1st Lt James M Parrish - Bombardier, T/ Sgt John H Rice Jr.- Radio Operator, T/Sgt William J Hornik - Engineer, S/Sgt Edward D Remas - Asst Engineer, S/Sgt Laurie T McGowan - Asst Radio Operator, S/Sgt Anthony T Canty - Waist Gunner, S/Sgt William H Williamson - Tail Gunner, Sgt Francis H English - Photographer.*

Flak at the target was heavy and accurate at 28,000 ft. The no.4 engine out and #1 had an oil line damaged and was losing oil pressure. The oxygen system was damaged to the extent that Remas and English passed out. Rice and Canty used walk around bottles to revive them. There were numerous holes throughout the fuselage and shell had passed through the vertical and left horizontal stabilizers. As the plane pulled off target they dropped out of formation and fell behind the group. The crew jettisoned guns and ammo in an attempt to lighten the plane at this time. The navigator informed the crew they were over Yugoslavia and the pilot ordered everyone to the waist and to prepare to bail out. When the bail out bell rang the crew was being tossed about inside the plane and it required a determined effort to jump clear of the ship.
Ten of the crew parachuted safely and were ;picked up Tito's Partisans on the ground and were eventually able to rejoin their unit Tortorella.

As for the pilot, Christianson had both hands full of a wounded B-17 and as the last of the crew jumped he was able to gain control of the errant plane and made for home. Word got back to Portobello that a B-17 was coming in with only one man on board and men gathered in numbers to watch the landing. Christianson made a very good landing by accounts and was awarded the DSC for his efforts of that day. The "282" was repaired, survived the war and was eventually salvaged at Walnut Ridge AR according to Freeman and Osborne's The B-17 Flying Fortress Story.

To the best of my knowledge Andersen, Domangue, and English are still with us. Mr. English clarified a few points on this story within the last week and his version is exactly as it was reported 61 years ago.

MACR(Missing Air Crew Report) 7989 does not mention any engines separating from the aircraft nor have I heard mention of any by the crew and witnesses.

James Parrish tells this story "Bail Out Over Yugoslavia" in the book The Diamondback, the History of the 99th Bomb Group.

Brother Bob's next mission was to Pardibuce, Czechoslovakia and it was an uneventful mission. He probably appreciated a relatively quiet mission in between two missions that were dangerous and memorable. The second of those two dangerous missions was the mission to Blechhammer, Germany on the 27th of August. Here is his account.

Flew with Delp and Sibley, a mixed crew in "182." The flak was heavy. We straggled just before the target. Our bomb altitude was supposed to be 28,000 feet, but we only got to 26,000 feet. We saw ship "570" go down. There were several gunners that I knew on that ship, but no close friends. Reports seem to indicate that 10 chutes got out. I guess it was a good thing that we did not get to altitude as were 2000 feet below and never got any holes of any consequence. (Maybe Bob means that his plane was alone 2000 feet lower and the main targets of the flak were 2000 feet higher and the flak gunners aimed at the formations at a higher altitude.) We caught up with the formation after the target. In the ship "055" they had several casualties. The tail gunner in "055" got hit rather badly in the arm and the waist gunner got a scratched ankle with a piece of flak; the ship had lots of holes in the wing. (Bob had flown 4 missions in "055.")

The official report from the 15th AAF: *530+ fighter escorted bombers attack targets in Germany and Italy; the B-17s hit an oil refinery in Blechhammer, Germany; the B-24s also hit an oil refinery in Blechhammer and in Italy a railroad bridge at Ferrara, and viaducts at Avisie, Venzone, and Borovnica.*

Bob was counting down and he had a number of moderately easy missions but even so they were not without hazards. He mentions seeing a German fighter, something rarely seen at this time of the war. He tells of a B-17 having a mechanical failure and watching as all 10 airmen get out safely, but the ship crashes over Yugoslavia. As he flew his 46th mission over Genoa, Italy, he had a piece of flak hit his ball turret and broke through the glass on his ball turret. Bob was uninjured. (late note: Blechhammer was in Poland)

Bob's next mission took him to an area where he had not flown before: Athens, Greece.

We flew in "435(The Adventuress) with our crew except for Lt.White, our navigator who had gone to Russia to bring back an airplane. We hit an airdrome and we carried frags. (fragmentation bombs). We saw several

*planes burning on the ground. Since this was a radar ship I flew as a
waist gunner. This is the first mission in that position. I had flown 44
missions as a ball turret gunner. Our squadron bombed from 28,000 feet.
It was the highest I've ever been in combat. The flak was heavy but off to
the side. I don't believe any hits were scored on our squadron. One group
lost four planes according to some rather reliable reports. We saw no
enemy fighters.*

The 15th AAF report says, *In Greece 276 B-17s and B-24s bomb Tatui,
Eleusis and Kalamaki airfields and Salomis submarine base; P-38s and P-
47s fly escort; target cover and sweep target areas; the attacks are aimed at
hampering the withdrawal of enemy forces from the area. 53 B-24s begin
evacuating aircrews formerly imprisoned in Bulgaria from Cairo Egypt to
Bari, Italy.*

The bombing raid and the official operations report reflect the advance
of Russian and Allied forces. Bulgaria was a former Axis partner, but by
this time Russian troops had occupied Bulgaria. When that happened,
American troops who had been held captive there could be returned. The
report says that one of the reasons for the raid was to hamper German
withdrawal from Greece; the Germans were pulling back their forces or
retreating. In Bob's narrative he notes that LT White had gone to Russia to
help bring a plane back. This was probably a plane that not made it back
home after a bombing raid but had landed in territory occupied by the
Russians.

Bob mentions that he flew as a waist gunner since the ship was a radar
ship. Some of the B-17s were fitted out with special radar jamming devices
designed to frustrate enemy radar systems. To install the radar device the
ball turret was removed and the device was installed in the place where the
ball turret had been hence there was no need for a ball turret gunner.

At this point Bob's record keeping regarding his missions ends. He did
fly two more times to complete his 50 missions. He flew as waist gunner
again on a mission to Szob, Hungary and as a top turret gunner/engineer on
a last mission to Munich, Germany. Bob had finally counted down to fifty.

Bob did not record his feelings after completing his last mission. A few
days later he has a few words to say. The Army Air Force assigned him to
duty as an aircraft mechanic and he mentions the fact that members of his
crew had just returned from a bombing mission. Bob did not miss going on
the mission; he was glad to be working as a mechanic.

We can only imagine his feelings on the last mission. On the last mission
he flew as top turret gunner and got a view of the formations of planes from
a very different point of view. Since his view was out of the top of the

plane, he did not see the bombs drop as he always had as a ball turret gunner. He had a different view on his final flight.

As his plane completed the final bomb run and turned for home, he must have felt that a great burden had been lifted from him. He was going to live through the war. He was going to go home. He had a whole civilian life in front of him. He could dream and plan of a new and different life. For the immediate future he may have turned over some thoughts about his life in months to come. What would the Air Force do with him at the completion of 50 missions? How soon would he get to go home? Would he be home for Christmas? What assignments after that? How long before he would again be a civilian?

Chapter 20- Home Again

Bob has left little record of his trip home. He had abandoned his diary even before he got word that he was going home. We can be quite sure that he went home in much the same way that he had first traveled overseas - on a Liberty Ship. He now had some experience at sea and we can guess that he did not suffer from seasickness, but likely suffered from boredom. Liberty ships are not very interesting.

There was much happiness in the Ekwall household in that December of 1944. There was a big Christmas dinner with roast chicken and all the fixings that went with a big holiday meal. There was a Christmas tree with gifts. The Ekwall family exchanged gifts on Christmas Eve. Bob and his family attended the local rural church and he was greeted with affection by the members of the Martland Church.

During World War II soldiers were required to wear their uniforms when on leave. So, when Brother Bob went to town, he was immediately identified as a returning veteran and received thanks and congratulations on his safe return. World War II veterans who returned home received a very warm welcome.

When Bob and other veterans returned home on leave, they had to get acquainted with some of the changes that had occurred in civilian life. America, unlike the European nations, had not been scarred by bombs, artillery or any other weapons of war. Pearl Harbor, on the island of Oahu was the almost the only exception. America suffered no serious shortages of food and clothing and other necessities. A nationwide system of rationing was in effect. Some items were not rationed but in short supply. Many food and clothing items were rationed. Meat, butter, gasoline, shoes, sugar and other items had been rationed. The returning veterans did not always come home to a sumptuous feast, but the home folks did their best based on the food and raw materials available. They saved their ration stamps so they could buy butter and meat for homecoming meals. The homecoming soldiers found it a little strange that there was a shortage of some food items. In stateside mess halls there was no food shortage. There was plenty of butter, meat and other foods that were in short supply at home. However, the quality of preparation was not up to mother's standards.

Bob came home to a farm home where rationing did not create serious eating problems. Bob's parents, like most farm families, had most of their own supply of meat, butter, eggs. Therefore, rationing had a lesser effect on their diet. They did, however, feel the shortage of sugar, gasoline, shoes and other rationed items that they could not supply for themselves.

Wartime America was a different place from peacetime America. Many of the popular songs reflected wartime romances: separation of lovers, wives missing their husbands, remembrance of idyllic peacetime love affairs, or the difficulty of waiting for the return of a loved one. Although a few of the songs were funny and related to fighting the war, the mass of the songs were sad and sentimental.

The War had created an imbalance between the sexes. A huge majority of the young men between the ages of 18 to 35 were in the military service. Only a small number of women joined the Women's Army Corps. (WAC). That meant that there were lots of young ladies without dance partners, dates, or boy friends. One popular song of this period said that the men were "Either Too Young or Too Old." Soldiers coming home on leave had no trouble getting dates.

World War II was a letter writing time. Soldiers wrote home to their home folks and the home folks kept the soldiers informed about happenings at home. Wives wrote to their husbands and vice versa. Soldiers generally did not have to pay postage, but home folks did.

America needed iron and steel and other metals so, during the war, they had scrap iron drives where citizens collected all sorts of old cars, old machinery and other scrap metal for use to make tanks, and other war equipment.

World War II was a period when everyone was interested in the war news. They assiduously listened to the war news. They learned the times of newscasts and they learned the names of the newscasters and the war correspondents. Citizens bought maps to find out where their sons and brothers were. The whole nation improved their geographic IQ. By the time the war began, radio broadcasting had improved to the place where, in some cases, such as the bombing of London, the listeners got reports of world events as they were happening. Americans became aware of the world leaders and the generals who led the American Armies. Patton, MacArthur, Eisenhower, Montgomery and Marshall were names known to all.

Brother Bob came home that Christmas of 1944 to a nation that had changed greatly. It was still his home, but not exactly the same place he had left.

For Brother Bob, on completing his furlough and returning to active service, it was almost as if the war were over. Bob and any other observer could tell that the Axis ;powers were already beaten. It was only a matter of time. The rest of the war which would have been from January of 1945 to May of 1945 for the European Theater, was being won by the Allies. The territory held by the Allies increased as the Allied armies continued their advance. The Axis resistance lessened, but the Germans continued the fight.

The Army Air Force assigned Brother Bob to duties at an Airbase near Amarillo, Texas. It was not a difficult assignment. He worked there as an aircraft mechanic. He served there until he was discharged from the AAF in October of 1945.

<u>Chapter 21 - Later Life</u>

In many ways the later life of Brother Bob was typical of many other veterans of World War II. They began to blend into the mass of the civilian population. Some continued their education through the GI Bill of Rights. Some apprenticed to learn a trade. Others set up their own business. Many of them went back to doing what they had done before they entered the service. Many of them struggled for a while to find the thing that they wanted to do. Bob was one of those.

Bob was discharged from the service in early October, 1945. He decided to continue his education but with a little different emphasis. His work at Wayne State Teachers' College had been in pre-engineering, but he decided that he wanted to attend the College of Agriculture at the University of Nebraska. He stayed at home with the home folks for only one day and then went off to Lincoln to enroll at the University of Nebraska. He enrolled several weeks after the semester had begun, but the University was generous in bending its rules to accommodate returning veterans. Bob was dissatisfied with the course work and dis-enrolled after only a few days. The late enrollment may not have been a very good idea. He may have made a hasty decision on that particular matter. Bob was like many returning soldiers searching for a spot in society that fit his talents. In spite of his dis-enrollment at the College of Agriculture, Bob was still interested in agriculture. His next move was to enter a GI Bill sponsored apprentice program where he worked for a farmer and learned the practical side of agriculture. He continued this work for several months and he began to suffer health problems which proved to be an allergy to agricultural crops. So, that meant an end to plan to work in the field of agriculture.

Then Bob found his spot in the civilian world. He had always been good at mechanical work and had been trained as an aircraft mechanic. He entered a GI Bill sponsored apprentice training in auto-body repair in Lincoln, Nebraska. He worked through an apprenticeship period of several years and completed the program.

After the completion of his apprenticeship, he returned to his home town, Geneva, Nebraska and worked as an auto-body repairman for the local Chevrolet garage. He continued this work for several years and then opened up his own shop, Bob's Body Shop.

During this period of time he had at least one moderately important romance. Perhaps Bob did not pursue his romantic interest with enough vigor. At any rate nothing came of it.

Bob worked at his own body shop for a number of years and took in a partner. His partner had a growing family and may have had greater financial needs than Bob who lived with his parents. At any rate the body shop was closed down and Bob moved to Lincoln at worked at several places including a Chevrolet dealership in Lincoln.

At long last he found a romantic interest in Lincoln. In his 40s married Marilyn and together they started a family. They had three children: Carla, Lisa and Kirby. Bob and Marilyn were like many other newly married couples; they had to struggle to get along. They bought a home in Lincoln and were active in church work. Earlier in his life Bob had been interested in veteran's affairs, but after his marriage he apparently was less active in veterans' affairs.

During the time that Bob worked in his body shop and later in while he was married and working in Lincoln, Bob continued his interest in hunting. At the beginning of the hunting season, he would meet with his three brothers, usually at the home of his parents, and hunt pheasants.

Bob had been stationed in Amarillo, Texas during the last months that he was in the service. He liked Texas and he liked the absence of long, cold winters. He had always had it in the back of his mind that he wanted to live in Texas. So it was that he took off several days from work and went to Texas to find out if there were jobs for an auto-body repair man. He found that he could easily find work in that field. He sold his house and moved his wife and three children to Waco, Texas and began work as an auto-body repairman

He continued to work in Waco as his three children grew to be adults. Texas had long, hot summers but the winters were mild. Bob like the mild winters and was glad to escape the snow and frigid weather in Nebraska.

He was very active in Church work and made many friends in the religious community.

After a lifetime where he had enjoyed average or above average health. Bob discovered that he had prostate cancer. Even with this affliction he continued to be active up until shortly before his death. He died in 1991. .

Bob was a good man - a patriot who had served his country well. He worked hard at an honest trade. He was a good husband and father. What better epitaph for any man?

Chapter 22 – An Officer's Story

Bob Winstead and Brother Bob were both members of the same crew. Lt. Winstead was the co-pilot. In this section we will identify him by his last name. Later in life, Winstead decided to prepare an account of some of the things that he remembered about his time in the US Army Air Force. His remembrances were the basis for the following material.

Winstead, a southerner, was born in 1922.   He grew up on a tobacco farm in Wilson County in North Carolina. His family lived in a rural area where as he says, "there were very few airplanes and not many cars." He had an interest in flying even as a boy. It may have begun when his father told him of an airplane ride with a barnstorming pilot. When Winstead was 10 years old both he and his twin brother were thrilled by the chance to ride in a Ford Tri-motor airplane. The plane landed in a runway that the locals called a cow pasture. Winstead's father paid two dollars so each of the twin brothers could go for a ride. That ride changed his life; at that time he made up his mind that he would become a pilot.

He continued his interest in aviation by building model airplanes and by reading about World War I aces such as Eddie Rickenbacker.

Even before the Japanese attacked Pearl Harbor on 7 December of 1941, Winstead had already begun to prepare to enter the Army Air Force as a pilot. At that time the Army Air Force required two years of college training as a prerequisite for entering training. (Later that requirement was dropped.) He attended Atlantic Christian College and collected some of the required college hours. In 1942 he applied for acceptance into the Aviation Cadet Pilot Training Program. In September of 1942 Winstead received notice of his acceptance into the program.

He was called to active duty and reported first to Nashville, TN for induction and from there he went to Maxwell Field in Montgomery, AL for nine weeks of pre-flight training. He, and other entering cadets, rode the train from Nashville to Maxwell Field.

Winstead received an eye-opening welcome to the world of the Army Air Force. When he stepped off the train, they were met by a group of upper classmen from the school. They were dressed in dazzling full dress uniforms with sabers. The upper classmen immediately began the process of hazing the new cadets into the program. The upper classmen went at the hazing with vigor and enthusiasm. New cadets had to follow strict discipline. If asked a question, they could only reply "yes sir" or "no sir" or "no excuse sir." The hazing was so severe that some of the new cadets requested transfer out of the program. Winstead said that the cadets new to the Army Air Force endured the hazing better than some old time, regular Army Air Force personnel. Fortunately, after a few weeks the hazing let up as new classes of incoming cadets became the targets of the hazing. The cadets in Winstead's group began to have some time off and things got easier.

During this time Winstead had a good friend who introduced him to a college student, Lois Harper. It was love at first sight. When he returned from overseas in 1945, they were married. The marriage endured.

The next stop for Winstead was primary flight training at an air base in Douglas, Georgia. He learned to fly in a two wing plane with open cockpits. Winstead enjoyed every minute of it.

His next training session was at Cochran Field at Macon, Georgia. There he flew a more modern plane, the BT13 Vultee. Winstead noted that the plane was called the "vibrator" for a good reason: it vibrated. At Cochran field he learned some more advanced flying skills. He tells of an interesting incident. They were taken to an auxiliary field where they would then fly a night mission and return to the same auxiliary field.. Everything went well until he had nearly completed his flight. He heard another plane call to the base. That pilot said, "My controls will not work." Shortly after that, Winstead saw a crash and the crashed plane caught fire. Winstead had to fly in a holding pattern until the runway was cleared. When he landed, he learned that his good friend had been killed in the crash landing. This was not the end of his hair-raising experience. He was told to take off and return to the home base at Cochran Field. When he took off his engine started missing; he thought he would have to bail out. That was not a feasible option because he lacked the altitude to bail out safely. He tried to gain altitude while at the same time making adjustments on the carburetion. Then, miraculously, the engine resumed normal operation. His troubles were still not ended. As he approached what he thought to be his home field, it did not look familiar so Winstead took off and flew around and decided that yes, that was the home field. It was. Winstead was so distressed that he considered dropping out of the program. After further consideration and some sleep, he decided to continue.

During the remainder of his time at Cochran Field, Winstead learned how to do instrument flying, night flying, and formation landing.

Winstead's next station was at Moody Field in Valdosta, Georgia. There he learned how to fly twin engine planes. He flew a plane called the A-10 which was made mostly of wood. They practiced navigation and something called "flying the beam." This was a navigational system that used radio signals as a method of navigation. Winstead felt that by time he had gotten to be fairly good pilot. Near the end of 1943 Winstead got his wings and a commission as a 2nd Lieutenant.

Shortly after this, Winstead had to report for training at Ardmore, Oklahoma. Here he first piloted a B-17. At Ardmore Winstead was assigned to a crew that he would train with and stay with until he returned from overseas. Training at Ardmore was crew training so each crew main got training in their specialty.

While Winstead was at Ardmore he had the mumps and had to go to the hospital. However, he recovered in time to avoid reassignment.

In April Winstead's crew was shipped to Salt Lake City to pick up their B-17 to fly to Europe. Jay Weese was the pilot and Bob Winstead was the co-pilot. Crews were assigned in alphabetical order keyed to the last name of the pilot. When they got down the alphabet to the Ws, there were no more planes to fly. Instead of flying they went by train to Virginia and then by Liberty ship to Oran and then by ocean liner to Foggia for assignment to the 99th bomb group and the 346th Squadron.

In Foggia they were assigned to tents. Four officers were assigned to one tent and six enlisted men were assigned to a tent. The tents were not comfortable; they were cold when the weather was cold and hot when the weather was hot. The toilet facilities were primitive: a two hole outhouse tent.

Lt. Winstead began flying his missions. Earlier in his training, he had learned to fly in formation. That was a critical skill and he tells of a pilot who had failed to master that skill. His narration of the consequences: " We had dropped our bombs and were on our way back and still over enemy territory. The planes were all in formation - a typical nine plane box formation. This formation requires the pilot to continually adjust to maintain his position in relation to other planes in the formation. One plane drifted back and came in contact with the following plane. That plane went down and I do not know how many, if any, of the crew were able to bail out." Fatal accidents could occur due to a pilot's inattention or error. Formation flying required constant attention or the results could be fatal.

Winstead tells of his first experience with German fighter planes. He says he had been on a mission to southern France. Their target was a railroad yard. When they finished the bomb run, they were met with a sudden and unexpected head on attack by German fighters: FW-190s. Winstead could see the flashing guns of the attacking fighter and he heard the response of the top turret gunner. The attack ended as quickly as it had begun. He says his plane did not get hit and he guesses that the attacking fighter was not shot down.

He tells of another interesting mission. The mission was one of the oil fields either Ploesti or Vienna. The target was defended by at least five hundred 88mm and 105mm anti-aircraft guns. On this mission they had a direct hit on one of the engines. The shell came up and completely penetrated the engine - coming out the top of the engine. The engine caught fire, but at that altitude there was little oxygen and the fire soon went out. The engine was inoperative and they could not keep up with the formation. They straggled home behind the formation. Fortunately, a P-51 fighter was nearby and it escorted them home. All was well for that day.

On a mission to bomb airfields at Munich, he tells of running into a heavy cloud cover and explains the difficulty of flying in formation in cloud cover. It was very hard to maintain proper position in a formation when the other planes were not visible, or only occasionally visible. Apparently, he could see the lead plane in the formation from time to time and thus, tenuously, was able to maintain his position in the formation. After they broke out of the clouds and into the clear, Winstead saw his first German jet plane, a Me 262. There was a formation of B-24s off to Winstead's side and the Me 262 flew through the formation of B-24s and shot down two B-24s. The Me 262 then flew in front of Winstead's B-17 at an extraordinarily high rate of speed. He flew so fast that the nose gunner was not able to track the jet.

Winstead flew in support of the invasion of southern France. There were huge formations of B-17s, B-24s, and other bombers plus lots of fighter planes. They started out on the mission in the middle of the night. The greatest hazard was keeping out of the way of other planes. He tells of seeing a collision of two bombers. He said that a B-24, apparently lost, joined their squadron of B-17s. The whole sky was full of planes of every description. He made the bomb run successfully and encountered little if any enemy fire. Formation collisions were the greatest danger on that day.

His last mission, on 3 December, 1944 was to Blechhammer, Germany. This was a double count mission with extremely heavy flak over the target area. It was also his longest mission in the air: 9 hours. On his return from that mission he had completed 51 missions and had completed his tour and was ready to go home.

Winstead summarizes his achievements and the hazards that he encountered. He flew on 39 missions. He flew 27 single count and 12 double count missions. He completed his tour of duty with a total of 51 missions. He enumerates damages that happened during his missions: an engine shot out, an oxygen tank destroyed, bomb bay doors that locked and had to be cranked up by hand, and flak damage on almost every mission.

Before the end of his tour, he had qualified as a pilot and had been promoted to First Lieutenant.

Winstead is still amazed at what he was able to accomplish as a very young officer, turning 22 in August of 1944. He says that he slept well during the time that he flew his missions. Only after he had completed his missions did he have trouble sleeping.

Winstead felt that the Air Force extensive training program did a good job of preparing him for an arduous and dangerous job.

He returned home, married and returned to the civilian world.

Chapter 23 - Tribute

As the European war clouds gathered, Americans began a reluctant and partial preparation for a war they hoped to avoid. World conditions had become so hazardous that America had little choice but to make war preparations.

Congress instituted a draft requiring one year of service for young single men. The men reported for the one year of service with a marked lack of enthusiasm. The war was being fought on the other side of the world; American was safe behind two oceans and unwilling to get involved in other nation's conflicts..

The broad Pacific Ocean separated America from the Japanese aggressions in Korea, Mongolia and China. America felt sympathy for the Chinese as the Japanese Army won victory after victory in China but America did little to help the Chinese. Americans looked on the Asian countries as highly populated countries with a culture that differed greatly from the American norm. They were unwilling to make a major effort to help the Chinese.

The Atlantic Ocean separated America from the aggressive intentions of the Germans and the Italians. During the period before the actual outbreak of war Americans had a hard time identifying the enemy. The Communist system in the Soviet Union was an anathema to American capitalism and democracy. The Fascist systems of Italy and France seemed to be aggressive and imperialistic, but the criminality and depravity of the Nazi government was barely known to the American public.

Americans reacted with awe and apprehension as the German war machine occupied European countries; defeated the French and drove the British back to their island. After driving the British out of Europe the German Army plunged ahead to attack the Soviet Union. At that point the British gained an ally, albeit an uncomfortable ally. The Germans seemed unstoppable and the casualty figures mounted to almost unbelievable figures. American sympathy favored the Soviet Union, but the sympathy was weak. They opposed the Communist system and saw the Soviet Union as only marginally better than the German Reich.

The Americans stood on the sidelines and watched as the Axis powers won battle after battle and encroached on more and more neutral and Allied territory.

Then on December 7th 1941 the Japanese made a surprise and devastating attack on the American naval facility at Pearl Harbor on the American island of Oahu. The damage to American naval power was substantial. America's view of world politics underwent a sudden and tremendous change. America was galvanized into immediate action. President Roosevelt and the American Congress immediately went to war with Japan. Germany and Italy declared war on the United States and we reciprocated.

In a matter of days America was transformed into a nation at war. A powerful wave of patriotism engulfed the nation. Americans arose to the challenge of the Axis attack with a declaration of war. On the Monday after the Sunday attack on Pearl Harbor the nation's recruiting offices could not accommodate the influx of American young men trying to enlist in the armed services.

After the nation's recruiting offices had absorbed the huge initial influx of volunteers, the voluntary enlistment rate continued to be high throughout the war. America's need for men was great. It had two wars to fight: one in the Far Eastern theater and another in Europe. They also needed to be assured that the homeland was safe. The manpower needs were tremendous. To get all of the manpower needed the nation resorted to a draft when the volunteers could not fill the need for manpower. The volunteers and draftees alike were patriotic. There were few foot draggers or reluctant warriors. The draftees reported for induction as a patriotic duty.

They came from all corners of America. There were coal miners from the hollows of West Virginia; there were ranch hands from Wyoming; newspapermen from New York, farm boys from Nebraska. steel workers from Ohio, auto makers from Michigan, cotton farmers from Mississippi; lumberjacks from Minnesota, longshoremen from California, and college students from Connecticut.

They all came together in a great unifying experience. They had a common motivation. In spite of the great economic and cultural differences that might have separated them in different circumstances, they came together for a common purpose: preparation for the defense of the United States of America. They prepared by entering basic training in the Army, Navy or Marine Corps. .

They entered as civilians and came out of basic training as soldiers with the skills needed to fight a war. They learned many needed military skills. In basic training they learned, first and foremost, how to handle, clean, fire and use the M1 rifle. They learned to use the 45 Colt semiautomatic pistol, the Browning Automatic Rifle (BAR) and other basic weapons.

Other sailors, marines, soldiers and other military men learned more extraordinary and unique skills. They learned to manage, aim, load and fire the huge 16 inch guns on Navy battleships; they learned the discipline of the submariners life; they learned how to operate bulldozers, cranes and all manner of heavy construction equipment; they learned the skills of land, sea, and aerial navigation; they learned to pilot bombers, fighters and transport planes; they learned to decipher codes; they learned to treat battle wounds; they learned the skills of emergency life-saving; they learned how to drive tanks and other armored and tracked vehicles; they learned to operate ball turrets; and all other manner of extraordinary but critical skills.

In actual combat they learned things not in the instructional manuals. They made emergency repairs on equipment that was not in the instructional manuals. They learned to make do, get along without, and somehow get the job done.

They developed qualities of character that they did not know they had. If it was already a part of their personality, it developed to a greater degree. They learned the quality of courage. They learned that their life depended on the courage and endurance of their comrades. In turn their own personal safety existed only when they could depend on their comrades. They learned and exhibited the qualities of courage, forbearance, integrity, endurance and fortitude.

They were sent to many uncomfortable and distant places. Some experienced the frigidity of Alaska winters, or the steaming heat of Pacific islands, mud and rain in Europe. They were exposed to the elements; they could not seek warmth; they could not seek the cool shade; they suffered from excess of rain, from excess of sunshine, from excess of snow, from excess of aridity and a general excess of discomfort. Some were as far away from their home as it was possible to be. Even those whose duty assignment was in the United States did not always find the weather and living conditions to be comfortable.

They were sent to many dangerous places. They fought the war in dangerous places. They fought in the Phillipines and at Wake Island, Okinawa, Saipan and Tinian and many other unnamed islands They fought in North Africa, at Monte Casino in Italy. They took part in the invasion of Europe; they fought at the Battle of the Bulge. They fought in France, Belgium and finally in Germany; they continued until they met the Russians in mid-Germany. They flew in countless hazardous bombing missions to Tokyo, Blechhammer, Ploesti and Berlin.

They missed their mothers' home-cooked meals and learned to live on K-rations, C-rations, spam, cold food, lukewarm water, poorly prepared food, and sometime no food at all.

More and more as the war progressed; they began to prevail. Their training, courage, perseverance and patriotism was enhanced by good equipment, good weapons and their skill in the use of those weapons. Their morale was enhanced by Allied successes in the different theaters of the war.

They served our country well; they were unremarkable men who accomplished remarkable triumphs. They gave up the prime years of their lives to perform a patriotic service. All Americans owe them a continuing and monumental debt of gratitude. Shall we ever see their like again?

Appendix I - A BRIEF HISTORY OF THE SECOND WORLD WAR

1. Background Information: World War I. To better understand the causes of World War II, it is useful briefly review the history of World War I because there is a strong relationship between the two wars. Therefore we present this information on World War I. The causes of the First World War are fairly easy to state, but difficult to justify or explain why a single event caused such a long, bloody, and costly conflict. Data sources: (A-1) (A-2)

First of all it is important to know that, in the early 20th Century, in Europe and in other parts of the world many nations had entered into agreements, also called alliances, with nations friendly to them. If two nations had an alliance it obligated the first nation to come to the aid of the second nation if some other nation attacked or declared war. In Europe, in the early 20th Century many nations had entered into alliances. This gave them a feeling of safety and security because they knew that if they got into a war, they would have one or more nations that were obligated to help them. As we will see it was not helpful and in fact contributed to the onset of World War I.

Prior to the First World War, Austria-Hungary was an important country in central and southeast Europe. Its area comprised most of what is now the two nations of Austria and Hungary plus some additional territory. Its neighbor on the southeast was the nation of Serbia. Officially Serbia was an independent nation, but in fact it was at least partially under the control of Austria-Hungary. At least some of the people of Serbia resented the influence of Austria-Hungary. In June of 1914, Franz Ferdinand, the heir to the throne of Austria-Hungary, and his wife were making an official visit to Serbia. A Serbian nationalist who opposed the Austria-Hungary influence in Serbia shot and killed Franz Ferdinand. This assassination set off a series of events that led to the First World War

Austria-Hungary issued a demand to Serbia that required that the assassin be brought to justice. It also made other demands that infringed on the sovereignty of Serbia. Before Austria-Hungary made their demands, they made sure that their demands would be backed by their ally, Germany, and the Germans agreed to back Austria-Hungary.

Austria-Hungary was not satisfied with the Serbian response and declared war on Serbia. However, Serbia and Russia had an alliance that required the Russians to help the Serbians in event of war. Germany was likewise bound by a treaty with Austria-Hungary and declared war on

Serbia and Russia. France had a treaty to come to the aid of Russia and honored the treaty by declaring war on Germany. Britain had an agreement with France to come to her aid and so joined the war on the side of France.

Thus the long bloody First World War was fought between these two sides:
 The Central Powers: Serbia, Austria-Hungary, and Germany
The Allies: France, Great Britain, Russia, Italy, and at a later date, the United States.

The First World War lasted more than four years. In 1917 Russia had an internal revolution that caused that nation to drop out of the war and make a peace treaty that favored the Central Powers. In 1917 the United States entered the war on the side of the Allied Powers. The First World War ended in November of 1918.

   2. **Causes of World War II.** The peace treaty that ended World War I was the Versailles Treaty. It was named for suburb of Paris where representatives of the Central Powers and the Allied Powers met and signed the treaty in 1919. The winning Allies imposed a harsh treaty designed to punish the Central Powers and eliminate future German imperial ambitions. The Versailles Treaty made many important changes. The treaty redrew the map of Europe so that Germany lost some territory. The treaty created several new states. The treaty broke up the old Austria-Hungarian Empire divided the empire into independent component states: Austria, Rumania, Hungary and Bulgaria.

As another result, the treaty reconstituted Poland as a state. To give Poland an outlet to the sea, the treaty established *a Polish Corridor* between East Prussia and the rest of Germany. The Germans did not like this separation and it became a factor of contention..

The Treaty of Versailles imposed other burdens on the Germans. It required Germany to make cash payments, reparations, to the victorious Allies. It limited the size of their military establishment.. The treaty required Germany to demilitarize land along the Rhine River next to France.

 The Germans were unhappy with the stern provisions of the Versailles treaty and found it nearly impossible to comply with all of the requirements. The reparations payments were especially onerous.

World War I had been a bloody conflict and casualties were extremely high on both sides and this left a residue of bitterness. In the United States, American casualties were not nearly as high as those suffered by the

French, British and Germans. The Americans had the advantage of being separated from the Europeans by the Atlantic Ocean, and the Americans began to develop a policy of avoiding interaction with the European powers. This policy was called, " *Isolationism.*" -

Russia had made a separate peace with the Central Powers in 1917 more than a year before the war ended. Russia was on the verge of collapse and in the middle of a revolution. The Communists in Russia started a revolt against the government of Russia. Russia was not able to fight a revolution and continue the war against Germany. Therefore they signed a peace treaty with the Germans. The treaty that the Germans imposed on Russia was harsh. The Russian territorial losses were substantial. In Russia a Communist revolution was in progress at the time that Russia got out of the war.

From 1917 until much later Russia was ruled by a Communist government, and the country was known as the Soviet Union up until 1991.

When the war ended, the Soviet Union got some of its territory back as a result of the treaty of Versailles, but some of its territory was incorporated into the new state of Poland. Poland had existed off and on over many years and was reconstituted at the end of the war.

In summary, World War I had bled much of Europe dry. All nations were war weary. America preferred to remain isolated from European affairs. Britain and France were war weary. Germany was impoverished, bitter and vengeful. The Allies had said that World War I was " a war to end wars." However it was not so. World War I set the stage for World War II.

3. **Events between the wars**. One of the provisions of the Treaty of Versailles established the League of Nations. Member nations set up this organization to act as an international peacekeeping institution where nations could settle disputes without resorting to war. The United States, with an isolationist mindset, opted not to join this international organization.

France built an elaborate and expensive defensive line between itself and Germany called the Maginot Line. The French designed it to protect their country from a German attack. Later events proved that the Maginot Line was not an effective protective barrier. France built a line to protect itself from a 1914 war and it turned out to ineffective in a 1940 war.

America rapidly disarmed and turned its attention to affairs within the United States. There was a strong body of public opinion that America would be better off by having nothing to do with European affairs.

Russia, now the Soviet Union, concentrated in remaking itself as a Communist state and, to some extent, was also isolationist.

Britain tried to build up alliances with France and some other European nations so that it would not face another war alone.

Germany found it difficult to recover from the effects of the war because of territorial losses and the burden of reparations. Germany was a breeding ground for radical ideas of all kinds.

In Italy, Benito Mussolini came to power in 1922. He called his system of government *Fascism*. Some adjectives that describe fascism: super-patriotic, undemocratic, and authoritarian. It was a capitalist system attached to an authoritarian state: a corporate state. Later when Hitler came to power in Germany, he may have used Mussolini's system as model for his Nazi government.

Italy changed its alignment in the inter-war period. In 1936 the governments of Italy and Germany signed an alliance and trade agreement called the Rome-Berlin Axis.

In the following year Japan joined.. All three countries were not satisfied with the Versailles Treaty and all three countries were undemocratic and authoritarian.

4. **Inching towards war.** The people of Germany considered the Versailles treaty to be unfair and burdensome. They were unhappy with the Treaty and its harsh provisions. In Russia, afterwards called the Soviet Union, the Communist Party had gained control of the government and was in the process of installing a Communist system. Joseph Stalin, the ruler of the Soviet Union and his Communist Party tried to promote Communist systems in other countries. He encouraged Communist efforts in other countries and gave aid, comfort and money to Communist parties. In Germany a movement that included Communists and their allies gained strength.

Adolf Hitler, a corporal in World War I, emerged as a minor leader of a party that later became the National Socialist Party. His National Socialist party, later called the *Nazi* Party, was anti-communist and definitely not an ally of the other socialist parties. In 1923 Hitler failed in an attempt to take power in Germany and was sent to prison. In prison he wrote a book, Mein Kempf. In this book Hitler explained his ideas. He blamed Germany's troubles on the Versailles Treaty, the Communist parties and their allies, and he also blamed the Jews for the problems that Germany encountered.

In a few years Hitler was out of prison and into politics again. In 1933 the Nazi party received the most votes and Hitler was chancellor of Germany. There was never another major election in Germany until after the death of Hitler.

In the next few years Hitler took a number of actions, many of which violated the terms of the Versailles Treaty. Before the year 1933 was out Hitler had withdrawn from a disarmament conference. In that same year Hitler took Germany out of the League of Nations. He began a conscription program to enlarge the German army. In direct violation of the Versailles Treaty, Germany re-occupied the Rhineland, an area between France and Germany. Hitler took actions to build the bigger and better air force. He encouraged the building of an armored force with the latest equipment. Germany had many skilled engineers and scientists and Hitler put them to work creating new and better weapons systems. He enlarged and improved the German Army so that it may have been the best army in Europe.

Hitler was able to gain support from the people of Germany. He constantly complained about the terms of the Versailles Treaty. He blamed Germany's troubles on the Jews and the Communists. He talked of a "Greater Germany" to be constructed from territory Germany had lost in World War I. He planned to bring other European areas under German control.

In March of 1938 German armed forces moved into Austria and annexed it as part of what Hitler called the *Third Reich.* Apparently, there was little opposition to Hitler's action, but Austria was a small country with little capability of resistance.

In 1938 Czechoslovakia became the next country whose territory Hitler wanted to absorb. His initial claim was on the *Sudetenland,* a small border area between Germany and Czechoslovakia. Hitler wanted to annex this area. His excuse was that there were a large number of Germans living in this area. Hitler's intentions created an international crisis. Hitler, the German chancellor; Mussolini, the dictator of Italy; Neville Chamberlain, the prime minister of Great Britain; and Edouard Daladier, the premier of France; met in Munich to decide what should be done about Hitler's demands. Chamberlain and Daladier gave in to Hitler's demands. Hitler said that the *Sudetenland* was his last territorial claim in Europe. Chamberlain returned home and said he brought, " peace in our time."

In March of 1939 Hitler's armed forces completed the occupation of Czechoslovakia and Hitler said that Czechoslovakia had ceased to exist.

Poland was the next country to be threatened by Germany. Both Great Britain and France had guaranteed that they would protect Poland in event of war. Hitler wanted to invade Poland but feared that if he attacked Poland, France and Great Britain would declare war. Another aspect of the problem that faced Hitler was what the Soviet Union would do if Germany declared war on Poland. Hitler did not want to fight a war on two fronts: one in the east against the Soviet Union and one in the west against France and Great Britain.

In spite of Hitler's hatred of the Soviet Union and Communism, he temporarily laid aside his revulsion for his immediate political purposes. In August of 1939 Germany and the Soviet Union signed a non-aggression pact. A secret section of the pact said that if Germany attacked Poland, then the Soviet Union could occupy the eastern part of Poland. This agreement with the Soviet Union allowed Hitler to make plans to invade Poland.

5. **The war begins**. On September 1st 1939 Hitler's forces invaded Poland. They made rapid progress against an overmatched Polish army that was used horse-mounted cavalry against German tanks. The German armies used a new warfare system they had developed, *Blitzkreig* or lightning war. It was very effective against the poorly prepared Polish army. By the 3rd of September, France and Great Britain had declared war on Germany. Many historians use this date as the beginning of the Second World War. Before the end of the month the Polish army had been defeated. On the eastern side of Poland, the Soviet Union moved in to occupy eastern Poland and Poland ceased to exist as an independent nation.

Hitler concentrated his armed forces against Poland and made little effort to move against France. The French thought they were safe behind their Maginot line. The British moved troops into France to help the French. From September until the following spring there was little fighting along the French and German border. This period of the war has sometimes been called *the Phony War*.

The United States, though sympathetic to the French and British, decided not to enter the war, but did give some help to both countries. Canada supplied some troops to the British.

The *Phony War* continued until the spring of 1940. In early April, Hitler's armed forces moved in to occupy Denmark and Norway.. In May Hitler's forces attacked in the west and moved into Belgium, Netherlands, and Luxembourg. In attacking these three countries Hitler did not have to directly attack the French Maginot line. Once again the German army used the *Blitzkreig*" system with a high proportion of armor supported by the German air force to beat both the French and the British. By some measure of luck the British were able to extract most of their army to fight another day.

The French surrendered to the Germans and the Germans conducted a victory parade down the main Paris avenue, Champs Elysees. According to the terms of the peace agreement between France and Germany, Germany occupied about one half of the nation.

Nearly all of Europe had fallen under Nazi control. The British stood alone in opposition to the German Army which stood poised on the French side of the channel for the invasion of Britain. Hitler began an air war against Great Britain designed to complete his domination of Europe. Hitler, in order to invade Britain had to control the air over the English Channel and over Britain so that his forces could cross the channel and invade the mainland of Britain. To do this he had to control the air over Britain and the channel. This meant that he had to destroy the British Air Force. Thus began the Battle of Britain a war that was fought exclusively in the air. This battle was tremendously costly in lives and planes for both the British and the Germans. The Battle of Britain was not a decisive battle. Neither nation won, but the British persevered, prevented the invasion of Britain and their Air Force, Army and Navy survived to fight another day.

As the spring 1940 phase of the war ended, Germany stood triumphant in Europe. The table below shows the status of the major European countries.

Country	Status
Germany	-
Austria	Incorporated into Germany
Poland	Germany occupied the western half
Switzerland	Neutral
Sweden	Neutral
Italy	An ally of Germany
Rumania	An ally of Germany
Bulgaria	An ally of Germany
Greece	Defeated and occupied by Germany
Yugoslavia	Defeated and occupied by Germany, but some parts continued to resist
Albania	Annexed by Italy

Finland	Changed sides ; German ally at the end of the war
Norway	Occupied by Germany
Estonia	Incorporated into the Soviet Union
Latvia	Incorporated into the Soviet Union
Lithuania	Incorporated into the Soviet Union
Spain	Friendly to Germany, but non-combatant
Portugal	Friendly to Germany, but non-combatant
Soviet Union	In 1940, the Soviet Union was friendly to Germany. Later, one of the Allies.
Great Britain	At war with the Axis powers
France	Defeated by the Axis powers - partially occupied
Belgium	Defeated and occupied by Axis powers
Netherlands	Defeated and occupied by Axis powers

9. **The United States enters the war**. The sympathies of the people of the United States had always been on the side of the British and French. Americans opposed Hitler and his Nazis. They disliked all of the Axis regimes: Germany, Italy and Japan. However, much of the old isolation remained. The people of the United States did not want to get involved in another war. President Franklin Roosevelt was able to convince congress and the American people to give some assistance to the British.

It was an Asian situation that caused the United States to be involved in the war. Japan was a small nation with a large population and few natural resources. Japan felt that it needed more territory and more natural resources. Japan had occupied Korea for many years and in the 1930s was engaged in a war against China. It felt that it needed to control more territory that contained needed resources such as petroleum and iron ore. They believed they could get the desired territory and raw material from these areas: the Philippine Islands, then an American possession; the Dutch East Indies, a Dutch possession; Indo-China a French colony (Now Laos, Cambodia and Vietnam) and other island areas in southeast Asia.

There were at least two forces that had kept the Japanese from acting on their policy of expansionism. One was the British fleet. However, as the British home island faced a possible German invasion, the first priority of its fleet was to protect the island kingdom. It had few ships to spare to patrol southeastern Asian waters. The American fleet was present in the

Pacific and with the American fleet intact, the Japanese could not safely follow through on their expansionist policies.

The Japanese decided to launch an attack on Pearl Harbor, the primary American naval base in the Pacific, and thus destroy the American fleet. The American action that may have triggered the attack was the decision to quit selling scrap iron and petroleum to the Japanese. The Japanese launched their surprise attack on December 7, 1941. Many American ships were destroyed and overall American losses were great. Many of the largest American battleships were destroyed in the attack. By a stroke of luck the American aircraft carriers were at sea and were not lost in the Japanese raid.

The war against Japan was different from earlier wars. The battleship was no longer the dominant weapon in sea war. Instead, the aircraft carrier was the dominant weapon. The Japanese attack had missed the American aircraft carriers.

America and Japan declared war on each other. Germany and Italy honored their alliance with Japan and declared war on America. America declared war on Germany and Italy.

The United States was not well prepared for a war. It immediately increased the number of men drafted into the armed forces. It trained infantrymen, pilots, sailors and every kind of serviceman. It stopped unneeded civilian production and switched to war production of tanks, guns and planes. As rapidly as possible it prepared to actively take part in the war.

Since the Soviet Union was fighting the Germans, the United States, perhaps reluctantly, began to treat it as an ally. The United States sent large quantities of materials to help the Soviets fight the Germans.

The United States immediately became involved what could be called two separate wars. One was a Pacific Ocean war. It consisted of naval battles that often involved carrier based airplanes. The other part was a land war that often involved battles over islands. Soon after the war began, the Japanese invaded the Philippine Islands, then an American possession. By May of 1942 the Philippines had fallen to the Japanese. The Japanese also occupied the islands of the Dutch East Indies, now the nation of Indonesia. Other smaller, and almost unknown islands became important battlegrounds in the Pacific Ocean war.

10. **American involvement in the European Theater**. The United States did not immediately become involved in the European war. We did however, immediately increase all kinds of help and assistance to the

British. We also sent aid to our new allies, the Soviet Union. American Army Air Force planes and crews were sent to Great Britain in 1942, but the first American raid on Germany did not occur until January of 1943.

In November of 1942, American forces participated in the invasion of North Africa. General Erwin Rommel, commanding the German Afrika Corps, had been fighting a see-saw battle with General Montgomery, who commanded the British forces. The invasion of North Africa was the first American participation in the European phase of World War II. Inexperienced American troops, with no experience in desert warfare, did not do well in their first encounters with German fighting forces who were hardened veterans of desert warfare.

The British and the Americans had one great advantage in the North African War. The British, with their powerful navy, controlled the Mediterranean Sea and were able to limit the amount of supplies that Germany could send to Rommel's Afrika Corps. By February of 1943 Allied forces began to gain the upper hand over Rommel. Rommel suffered from a lack of supplies and reinforcements. American soldiers and officers gained experience in desert fighting.

By June of 1943 the Axis forces in North Africa had been defeated. Rommel escaped back to Germany to fight another day. Allied forces controlled all of North Africa.

In Italy, the regime of Mussolini was faltering. Italy had been successful in expansionist actions only when they were unopposed or opposed by substandard armed forces. The quality of their fighting forces was far below that of their major ally, Germany.

Within a month of defeating the Germans in North Africa, on the 9th of July, the Allied forces began an invasion of the island of Sicily which was part of Italy. On the 25th of July Mussolini was removed from office and replaced by Pietro Badoglio. By the 16th of August 1943 the Allied conquest of Sicily was complete.

On September 3rd and 9th Allied forces landed on the Italian mainland. On the 8th of September Italy made peace with the Allies. From that time forward, Italy was not an active participant in the war. The Germans sent troops to Italy so that all of Italy did not fall to the Allies. Italy, a mountainous country, Made German defensive actions easier. By the 1st of October the Allies had captured Naples and began a long, difficult movement northward.

The conquest and control of Italy, particularly the southern part of Italy, was an important Allied goal. American and British generals and air force planners saw the existing air force bases in southern Italy as strategically important. In southern Italy there were airfields in the vicinity of Foggia. If the Allies could capture these facilities, it would make it easier for Allied planes to bomb targets that were out of range, or nearly out of range for bombers based in England. (See map in Appendix) One target was of special interest. A main source of German petroleum was the Ploesti oil fields in Rumania. Rumania was a close ally of Germany. Bombers based in Foggia could get to targets such as Ploesti because of the proximity factor. Vienna was another important target closer to Foggia. Other southern German and northern Italian targets could also be bombed from Foggia.

11. **Germany and the Soviet Union.** To a great extent, the war between the Soviet Union and Germany was affected by the seasonal changes. The summer months were favorable for the Germans. The roads were better and German armored vehicles and transport could move rapidly and with comparative ease. The winter months favored the Soviet Union. The Soviets were used to cold weather and had generations of experience in coping with bad weather. The German advance into the Soviet Union had been rapid and the Germans were not always able to control all of the areas through which they passed. Communist led guerilla forces were not limited by availability of roads and vehicles. They went on foot and often struck at night and ran away. While such raids were not strategically critical, it was an important irritant and damaged German morale.

The summer and autumn of 1942 saw the greatest German penetration into Soviet territory. By late 1942 the German had gotten as far as Stalingrad(now Volgograd) and had captured a portion of the city. During the late months of 1942 the Germans and Soviets fought a bitter and costly battle for control of the city but neither could prevail.

The Germans had made a deep penetration into the Soviet Union to attack Stalingrad. In doing so they had left their flanks exposed and vulnerable to a flank attack. On the northern German flank some of the positions were held by Rumanian forces. The Rumanian forces were not as dedicated to the war as were the Germans.

The Soviets planned a tremendous offensive. They made a last ditch stand at Stalingrad and began to build up forces for a flank attack from the north and from the south so as to isolate Stalingrad.

The Soviets launched this attack in late autumn. From the north, they attacked south against the positions held by the Rumanians. Soviet forces in the south attacked in a northerly direction. In just a matter of a few days the two forces met. Thus the entire German 6th Army was isolated in Stalingrad and the area around Stalingrad. When the two Soviet forces met, the land communication and transportation between German rear supply bases and Stalingrad was cut. The German 6th Army in Stalingrad could not be reinforced, resupplied or helped. Herman Goering promised Hitler that he could resupply the 6th Army by means of air supply drops. Only a few supplies were flown in and as time went by even that source of help diminished. General Paulus had wanted to fight his way out of Stalingrad, but Hitler had forbidden him to do so.

The situation in Stalingrad became desperate. General Paulus was, by long distance order, promoted to Field Marshall. No German Field Marshall had ever surrendered. Hitler expected Paulus and the 6th Army to fight to the last man. However, the 6th Army was in no position to fight to the last man. Soldiers lacked cold weather gear; they had almost no rations and were short of every kind of equipment. Shortly after the first of the year, 1943, Paulus bowed to the inevitable and surrendered the entire 6th Army to the Soviets.

The German surge to Stalingrad marked the maximum of German advance into the Soviet Union. It is reasonable to call it the turning point of the War. The Germans had some success in the summer of 1943, but for the rest of the war the front in the Soviet Union moved westward as the Soviets regained their territory and the Germans lost conquered territory.

12. **Allied Conferences.** Allied leaders met in a number of conferences. Only three of these conferences are briefly discussed here. The purpose of these conferences was to develop and improve cooperative strategies for winning the war. The later conferences made plans for the structure of the post-war world.

The conference at Casablanca was the first of the major meetings. Originally this conference was to be a "Big Three" conference, but Stalin did not attend. Roosevelt and Churchill met in Casablanca in January of 1943. The main decision was to determine the major priority after the conquest of North Africa. There was discussion of several options. Would it be best to make the invasion of Italy the main Allied thrust, or, should the Allies follow through on the cross channel invasion as the main effort. The Allies decided that the cross channel invasion would be the main thrust.

. In late 1943, Roosevelt, Churchill and Stalin met at Tehran. The main topic of discussion was the planned cross channel invasion where Allied

forces in Britain would invade the European mainland. Churchill was
reluctant to agree to this huge undertaking; he preferred to exploit the
situation in Italy and possible make landings in the Balkans. However, he
was outvoted by Roosevelt and Stalin. The code name given to the cross
channel invasion was *Overlord.* An American general, Dwight Eisenhower,
was given overall command of the planned invasion.

A later conference dealt with the planned shape of the post-war world.
The Allies held a third conference at Yalta in February of 1945. By this
time the Allies were certain of victory and the conference dealt with plans
for the immediate and long range plans for a post-war Europe.

13. **Allied decision to demand Unconditional Surrender**. Roosevelt
broached the idea of unconditional surrender at the Casablanca conference
and the other Allied leaders agreed to this policy. There were pros and cons
to this decision. A negative aspect was that the demand for unconditional
surrender might lengthen the war because many German officials and
officers feared the consequences of actions they had taken while serving
the Nazi Party. This also might have been true of enlisted men and low level
officials. They might have chosen to fight to the last man.

From the Allied point of view there were many positive aspects of
unconditional surrender. An unconditional surrender meant the Germans
would have little or no say about the terms of peace. It meant that Adolf
Hitler would face prosecution for war crimes after the war was over. They
could arrest and try German officers and officials responsible for the mass
slaughter of Jews and other national groups. It meant that the Allies could
control a post-war Germany and construct a new, democratic Germany
without a trace of its Nazi past.

14. **The Air War in Europe - The RAF and the 8th Air Force.**. An
important early action of the air war in Europe was the Battle of Britain.
After Britain had established control of the skies over Britain and the
English Channel, The RAF(Royal Air Force) undertook bombing raids on
Germany. These early raids were only partially successful and RAF losses
were severe. General Harris, who commanded the RAF decided that RAF
losses in daylight raids were unsupportable. He decided to begin a
campaign of night bombing that targeted a general area of interest rather
than a specific target. These bombing raids were somewhat more
successful, but resulted in many civilian casualties and were somewhat
controversial.

In 1942 the United States began to send Army Air Force personnel and planes to Britain. The men and planes formed the basis of a separate American Army Air Force, The Eighth Air Force. It grew and became the largest American Air Force and was approximately equal in size to the RAF. The American 8th Air Force had some advanced navigational and bombing equipment designed for daylight use. The 8th Air Force believed that their B-17 bombers were best for daylight use. So, the "round the clock" bombing campaign started with the American 8th Air Force bombing during the daytime and the British RAF bombing during nighttime hours.

Both the RAF and the 8th Air Force were designated as strategic Air Forces. That meant they were used for larger, overall purposes such as damaging German civilian morale, destroying the German oil industry, or German aircraft production. One overall, strategic principle was to prepare for the upcoming invasion of Europe. Tactical Air Forces performed smaller scale actions in support of troops, or escorting bombers, or other smaller scale, but critically important missions. For example in the invasion of North Africa and the invasion of Sicily and Italy, the tactical Air Forces supported the landing forces by strafing missions, and by reconnaissance missions.

In 1943 The 8th Army Air Force and the British RAF planners conceived what they thought was a brilliant plan. About half of all German ball bearing production was concentrated in the German cities of Schweinfurt and Regensburg. The planners thought that they could destroy most of German ball-bearing production with a large scale, well planned raid. They believed they could cripple German industry because they would no longer have a supply of ball-bearings. The Allies made two raids on ball-bearing plants in the two cities. They made the first raid in August and the second in October. Losses were extremely heavy.

Subsequent data showed that ball bearing production was slowed for several months but the Germans had sufficient inventory and capacity in other places so that the raid did not achieve its strategic objective.

Repeated attacks on German aircraft plants slowed production, but only temporarily. Allied attacks on rail yards and marshalling yards caused inconvenience, but such damage was of short durations and repairs could be made without causing major problems.

In one area of strategic bombing, The Allies had great success. Germany had only a small amount of petroleum and depended on two sources for petroleum. Its ally, Rumania, produced large amount of oil from its oil fields in the areas around Ploesti, Rumania. This was a major source of German natural petroleum. Germany also had a number of synthetic petroleum production plants. The American and British raids on the German oil production crippled the German petroleum industry and many other industries that depended on petroleum. The consequences proved to be disastrous to the Germans.

15. **The Fifteenth Air Force**. After the Allied forces landed in southern Italy in September of 1943. They began a slow drive northward to drive the Germans out of Italy. Before the invasion of Italy, American air forces had used bases in North Africa to bomb targets on the European continent. In November of 1943, in Tunisia, two existing American army air forces, the 9th and the 12th were combined into a single force, The Fifteenth Army Air Force. By the first of December, Allied forces had pushed the Germans far enough to the north so that it was safe to establish the Fifteenth Army Air Force to the Italian mainland. The first location was near Bari on the Adriatic Sea on what might be called the "heel" of Italy. A short time later the Fifteenth Army Air Force was relocated to the Foggia, Italy area. Some of the units that made up the Fifteenth Army Air Force were as follows: two kinds of heavy bomber units - six B-17 units and fifteen B-24 units; there were mid-sized bomber units - two B-25 units and three B-26 units; there were fighter escorts units - 3 P-38 units, one P-47 unit and 3 P-51 units.(Foregoing data was the strength at the end of the war.) (Information from the History of the Fifteenth Air Force by Gary Leiser.)

The overall strategic function of the Fifteenth Army Air Force was to weaken the German defenses on the mainland of Europe and thus support the Allied invasion of Europe. The location of the Fifteenth Army Air Force at Foggia, Italy was such that raids on critical German oil supply centers such as Ploesti were much easier to reach from Foggia than from bases in England. Other critical centers were oil refineries in the area of Vienna and German factories in the southern part of Germany. In addition the Fifteenth Army Air Force could supply tactical and strategic support to the Allied forces fighting in Italy.

The Allied forces invaded the European continent on 6th of June in 1944. This effort was supported by the 8th Army Air Force and the RAF. On the 15th of August of 1944 Allied forces invaded the European continent a third time. This time on the south coast of France. The Fifteenth Army Air Force was on hand to support these landings.

By the time of the invasion of southern France, the Allied picture had brightened considerably. From the German point of view, things were getting really bad. They were fighting the Soviets in the east; they were fighting the Allies in Italy; they were trying to stop the Allies in northern Europe; and last but not least, they were trying to oppose the Allied landings in southern France.

In the first part of the air war, it was difficult to protect bombers by providing them with fighter escorts. The basis of the problem was that fighter planes had shorter ranges than bombers and it was not always possible for fighter planes to provide fighter support throughout bombing missions. Several things helped this situation. Locating the 15th Army Air Force in location closer to targets improved the degree of fighter escort protection. A second factor was the production of better fighter planes, such as the P-38 and the P-51 that had greater ranges and could provide fighter escort for all of the dangerous parts of bombing missions.

16. **The Home Front.**   America in the 1930s had gone through a long and deep depression. Unemployment had been a serious problem all through the decade of the 1930s. American mid-western farmers had suffered from a severe drought. Many American farmers had lost their farms to foreclosure in that decade.

In 1939 America watched as war came to Europe. America, finally aware of the dangers of living in a world endangered by aggressive Axis powers began to awake from its isolationist torpor. America, under the leadership of Franklin Roosevelt began to take steps to build up their armed services. They began to produce some needed war equipment and passed a draft law requiring compulsory military service.

Perhaps the Great Depression had been ending, but the initial, limited, wartime preparations put more people to work and by the beginning of the decade of the 1940s the worst of the Great Depression was over. After the war began, American experienced a great industrial boom created by the huge demand for war equipment to fight the war.

By the end of 1941 everyone had something to do. Unemployment disappeared. Those who were in the armed services actively participated in the fighting. The soldiers fought in the battlefields of Europe. The airmen flew on bombing raids over Germany. The Marines landed and fought on Pacific islands. The Navy fought at sea against the Japanese. These were the active, front line fighters of the Second World War.

But ordinary Americans at home supported and supplied the fighting men. The workers in shipyards built the needed warships and transport ships required by the Navy. The workers in aircraft plants built the airplanes that the Army Air Force needed. The workers in ordnance plants built the M-1 rifle needed by the infantrymen. The auto workers who had built autos before the war now built Jeeps and trucks. The American economy shifted direction and increased its capacity. Women and older workers replaced those men who had been called to the armed services.

The US Government caused a whole new set of offices to be set up. There were ration boards to distribute equitably the goods in short supply. The Government rationed sugar, gasoline, meat, butter, shoes, farm equipment and other items.

There were draft boards to decide which people to take into the Armed Services. Single men in their late teens and early twenties were taken first. Those designated for early entry into the service were classified as 1A. Others such as married men with children received a lower classification and were not taken until later when needs became greater. Some men with critical skills were not drafted.

Civilians of every kind made every effort to support the troops. The US Government sold war bonds to support the war effort. For example they sold a $25.00 War Bond for $18.75 and they sold a $100.00 War Bond for $75.00. In ten years the purchaser could cash in the bond for the larger price; cash in the $100.00 and get the full price for a bond that had cost $75.00 The Government sold bonds of larger denominations. This was one of the methods used to raise the money to fight the war.

There was a shortage of iron and steel; the industries could not easily supply the tremendous need for iron and steel to build rifles, Jeeps, tanks, ships and all the other materials needed to fight a war. So, all over America there were "scrap iron drives" to collect and recycle old cars, old machinery, old implements and anything made of iron or steel for recycling into war materials.

There was a shortage of many kinds of food: sugar, coffee, butter, meat and other foods were rationed. The US Government urged the farmers to increase food production. Brother Bob's parents responded. The increased demand increased farm prices and farm production. The farmers prospered along with the rest of the country.

The war created a new mobility. Many of the jobs were in places far from home. For example on the west coast of the United States there were many shipyards that needed laborers. People from the Midwest migrated to the west coast areas to work in the shipyards. Rural people moved to cities where war factories needed laborers.

The civilian population was extensively involved in the war. They eagerly listened to radio newscasts about battles in places they had never heard of before. They eagerly searched maps to find the places that radio newscasters told them about: Midway, Solomon Islands, Sicily, Normandy, Anzio, Caen, and Foggia. They listened to stories of bombing raids on: Ploesti, Vienna, Schweinfurt, Montpelier, Berlin, and Blechhammer.

Civilians learned the ranks of the Army and Navy and learned many new words and became familiar with military terminology. The learned about: night bombing, Blitzkrieg, Liberty Ships, platoons, Norden bombsights, radar, battalions, aces, divisions, Browning Automatic Rifles, Landing Ships of various kinds, flak, missions, sorties, bomb shelters, and many other terms.

The war changed every aspect of civilian life. Even the popular music of the 1940s reflected the fact that men were away from home engaged in fighting a war and their wives and girl friends were home doing whatever patriotic things they could to help win the war. Some of the popular songs were about air force pilots and other wartime exploits. Others recognized the loneliness of the soldier away from home, and away from his wife or girl friend. Other songs were about the loneliness of the ladies left at home who waited for the return of their men.

16. **Victory in sight.** By the late summer of 1944 the Soviets had pushed the Germans back so far that the Soviets had regained most of their territory. In the central and south central part of German-Soviet front, the Soviets had advanced into Rumania and had taken over the Ploesti oil fields. Allied bombing had crippled oil production but had not been 100 percent effective. When the Soviets captured Ploesti, almost all of Germany's natural crude oil supply was gone. However, they continued to produce some synthetic oil, but much of their industry was crippled by the lack of fuel.

By late August, 1944 Allied armies liberated Paris and moved eastward to the Rhine river. They had great success but discovered that the Germans were not yet beaten. In mid-winter the German armies on their western front embarked on a well-planned and well supported offensive against the Allied forces. At first the Germans made some advances but were not able to sustain their initial success.

As the weather warmed in the spring, the Allied forces drove into

Germany. On the front between the Soviet Union and Germany, Soviet forces moved onto German soil. As the battle moved into Germany, German resistance stiffened, but could not hold against the Soviet forces. 17. **Victory.** On the 25th of April, a significant historical event occurred, one of many that happened in the same short time period. Allied and Soviet forced met at the Elbe in central Germany. On the 30th of April Adolf Hitler committed suicide in a bunker in Berlin. Between the 1st of May and the 7th of May, the Germany surrender to the Allies became complete.

America and Britain were still at war with the Japanese. At the end of the war in Europe, the Soviet Union declared war on Japan. Japan surrendered on the 14th of August, 1945 after America dropped atomic bombs on Hiroshima and Nagasaki.

18. **Post-War Events.** As the war drew to an end, a meeting was held in San Francisco to develop a blueprint for a post-war international organization called the United Nations. This time the United States of America would be an active participant and at later time defeated former Axis powers would be active participants.

When the war in Europe ended, Soviet armies occupied many eastern European nations such as Poland, Latvia, Lithuania, Estonia, Bulgaria, Rumania, Hungary, Yugoslavia, Albania, and Czechoslovakia. The Soviets occupied part of Germany. The Soviets set up Communist governments in all of the aforementioned areas. The Soviet occupied area of Germany became East Germany, state separate from West Germany. West Germany became a democratic ally of the United States after World War II.

The Communist systems installed in Soviet occupied countries did not work very well. They were undemocratic and did not provide a standard of living equal to that of democratic and capitalist systems in western Europe. At the end of the 1980 and the beginning of the 1990s, the Communist regimes in eastern Europe and later in the Soviet Union were on the verge of economic collapse. In reaction to their economic difficulties they began to transform themselves into democratic and capitalistic societies.

Citations

Chapter 1
None

Chapter 2
2-1 http://www.gulf/coastautocrossers.com/history.html
2-2 http://www.ianmcinnis.com/backwards/main2.html

Chapter 3
None

Chapter 4
4-1 Martin Caiden, The Flying Fortress p.186
4-2 http://www.steinwachs.com/adventures/bombers/b-17.htm
4-3 http://www.memphis-belle.com/belle_story.com
4-4 http://www.valleyva.com32nd/32ndacts.html#X
4-5 http://www.daveswarbirds.comb-17/nose.htm

Chapter 5
None
Chapter 6
6-1 Belly Gunner by Carol Hipperson
6-2 Air Power Museum
6-3 http://www,cebudanderson.com/interviewparmer
6-4 http://www.303rdbga.com/crew-duties.html
6-5 http://www.303rdbga.com/crew-duties.html

Chapter 13
13-1 www.jg54greenhearts.com/eyewitne.html
13-2 www.jg54greenhearts.com/eyewitne.html
13-3 Theo Boiten and Martin Bowman, Battles With the Luftwaffe
13-4 http://stonebooks.com/archives/011118,shtml
13-5 http;//www.gustave-roosen, de/hamburg – chtm
13-6 http://www.429sqn.ca/flak.htm

13-7 http//www.ibiblio.org/hypenoir/AAF/USSBS/ETO –
Summary.html
13-8
http://guardian.co.uk/elsewhere/jornalist/story/0,7793,1068437,00.html
13-9 Earl R. Beck, Under the Bombs.

Chapter 14
14-1 http://www.cmstory.org/homefront/people/fergTranscript.htm
14-2
http://www.robins.af.mil/History/60%/20year%20history/PLOESTILR-
Swebb2..htm
14-3 http://www.google.com/webhp?source=navclienttie=UTF-
8&oe=UTF-8
14-4 http://www.com/bg/green.html
14-5 http://www.303bga.comh-facts.html
14-6 http://www.ww2guide.com/flak.shtml
14-7 http://www.en.wikipedia.org/wiki/List of the WW2
Luftwaffe#Messerschmidt

Chapter 15
15-1
http://www.mansfieldnewsjournal.com/news/stories/20040126/localnae
w/296023.html
15-2 http://www,461st.org/liberaider/first_fifty_years.htm
15-3 http://www. 91stbombgroup.com
15-4 data no longer available
15-5 http://www.b-26marauderarchive.org/CL1011.htm
15-6 http://www.afa.org/magazines/valor_print.html
15-7 Charles Watry and Duane Hall, Aerial Gunners-The Unknown Aces
of World War II
15-8 http://www. csd.uwo.ca/~pettypi/elevon/aces
15-9 http://www.acepilots.com/misc_hartman.htm
15-10 http:www.elknet.pl/acestory/hartman1.htm
15-11 http://www.usfighter.tripod.com/bong.htm
15-12 http://www.acepilots.com/usaaf_mto_aces.html
15-13 http://www.au.af.mil/au/goe/eagle.biss/85bios/Voll85.htm

Chapter 17
17-1 http://www.Erie Veterans.com/WWII Storie/Shorts_Robert/Shorts.html
17-2 http://www. b24net/stores/Keilman1.html
17-3 http://www.acepilots.com/usaaf_tusk_html
17-4 http://www.acepilots.complanes/P-47 thunderbolt.html
17-5 http://www. Arthur.com/index/military/htm#airspeed
17-6 http://www. ncsm.si.edu/research/aero/aircraft
17-7 http://www.Fock 190d.htm
17-8 http://www.chuckhawks.com/bestfighterplanes.htm
17-9 http://www. wwiitech.net/main/Britain/aircraft/hawkshurricaneindix.html
17-10 William Green, Famous Fighters of the Second World War

Appendix I
A-1 http://www.schoolhistory.org.uk/Franz Ferdinand.htm
A-2 http://www.firstworldwar.com/origins/causes.htm

Trip	Target
1	Vienna, Austria
2	Brod, Yugoslavia
3	Budapest, Hungary
4	Brasov, Rumania
5	Montpelier, France
6	Blechhammer, Germany
7	Pinzano, Italy
8	Budapest, Hungary
9	Ploesti, Rumania
10	Vienna, Austria
11	Memmingen, Germany
12	Turin, Italy
13	Wiener Neustadt, Austria
14	Brod, Yugoslavia
15	Port les Valence, France
16	Gyor, Hungary
17	Ploesti, Rumania
18	Savona, Italy
19	Beach 251, France
20	Ploesti, Rumania
21	Osweicem, Poland
22	Vienna, Austria
23	Pardubice, Czechoslovakia
24	Brno/Lisen, Czechoslovakia
25	Vienna, Austria
26	Vienna, Austria
27	Szolnok,Hungary
28	Novi Sad, Yugoslavia
29	Genoa, Italy
30	Athens, Greece
31	Szob, Hungary
32	Munich, Germany

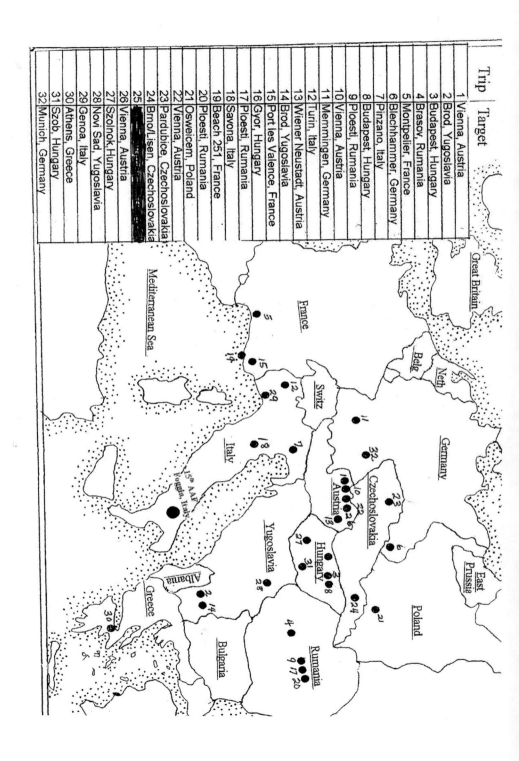

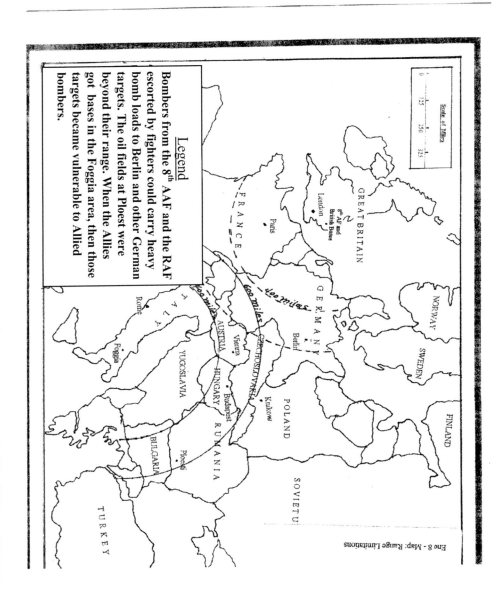

Legend

Bombers from the 8th AAF and the RAF escorted by fighters could carry heavy bomb loads to Berlin and other German targets. The oil fields at Ploesti were beyond their range. When the Allies got bases in the Foggia area, then those targets became vulnerable to Allied bombers.

Scale of Miles

0   125   250   325

GREAT BRITAIN

8th Air and
British Bases

London

FRANCE

Paris

NORWAY

SWEDEN

FINLAND

G E R M A N Y

Berlin

POLAND

Krakow

SOVIET U

I T A L Y

Rome

Foggia

AUSTRIA

Vienna

CZECHOSLOVAKIA

HUNGARY

Budapest

YUGOSLAVIA

R U M A N I A

BULGARIA

Ploesti

TURKEY

200 miles

400 miles

600 miles

BROTHER BOB'S MISSIONS

Date	Crew	Plane Number/ Name	Target	Comments
6/25/44	JMW	210851/Thunderbird	Sete, France	Early return – mission Did not count.
6/26/44	JMW	210851/Thunderbird	Vienna, Austria	
6/27/44	JMW	210851/Thunderbird	Brod, Yugoslavia	
6/30/44	JMW	232055	Budapest, Hungary	
7/04/44	JMW	232068/Heaven Can Wait	Brasov, Rumania	On this mission, the Plane;, "Thunderbird," Was shot down.
7/05/44	JMW	232068/Heaven Can Wait	Montpelier, France	
7/07/44	JMW	238201/Patches	Blechhammer, Ger.	Plane shown on book cover
7/13/44	JMW	232068/Heaven Can Wait	Pinzano, Italy	
7/14/44	JMW	297436/Vicious Vixen	Budapest, Hungary	
7/15/44	RDB	232032/Battlin Bobby	Ploesti, Rumania	
7/16/44	TSB	297570/Achtung	Vienna, Austria	
7/20/44	JMW	232055/Dinah Might	Memmingen,Ger.	
7/24/44	JMW	46286	Turin, Italy	
7/26/44	JMW	297436/Silver Meteor	Wiener-Neustadt, Austria	
7/30/44	JMW	297570/Achtung	Brod, Yugoslavia	
8/02/44	JMW	2102855/Weary Willie	Les Valence, France	
8/09/44	JMW	46182	Gyor, Hungary	
8/10/44	TSB	46286	Ploesti, Rumania	
8/12/44	JMW	297436/Silver Meteor	Savona, Italy	
8/15/44	JMW	297570/Achtung	Beach 251, France	Invasion of south France
8/18/44	JMW	2102855	Ploesti, Rumania	
8/20/44	REB	297570/Achtung	Osweicim, Poland	
8/23/44	HEB	232064	Vienna, Austria	
8/24/44	JMW	297436/Silver Meteor	Pardubice, Czech.	
8/25/44	HEB	232064	Brno-Lisen, Czech.	
8/27/44	LAD	46182	Blechhammer, Ger.	
8/28/44	WSB	46182	Vienna, Austria	
8/29/44	RHW	46182	Szolnok, Hungary	
8/30/44	HWM	232055	Novi Sad, Yugoslavia	
9/04/44	JMW	46435/ The Adventuress	Genoa, Italy	
9/15/44	JMW	46435/The Adventuress	Athens, Greece	
9/20/44	JMW	297733	Szob, Hungary	
10/04/44	CFS	46420	Munich, Germany	

Notes: 1. In the crew column, the crews were identified by their pilots initials. Bob's regular crew pilot was
Jay M. Weese. (JMW) Sometimes he was assigned to other crews; on his last time out he was on the crew of
Carlyle F. Strobel. (CFS)
2. Not every plane was named.
3. Bob made 33 trips, or sorties, on his way to accumulating 50 missions. Missions to Vienna and Ploesti certainly counted as double missions.

Comparison of Distances to Targets from 15th AAF Bases and 8th AAF Bases
(Distances are Approximations)

Important Axis Targets	Distance from 15th AAF Base	Distance from 8th AAF Base	Which AAF was Closest to the Target
Vienna, Austria	**500 miles**	**750 miles**	**15th by 250 miles**
Budapest, Hungary	440 miles	850 miles	15th by 410 miles
Weiner-Neustadt, Austria	460 miles	750 miles	15th by 290 miles
Vicenza, Italy	360 miles	630 miles	15th by 270 miles
Montpelier, France	600 miles	560 miles	15th by 40 miles
Zagreb, Yugoslavia	310 miles	350 miles	15th by 540 miles
Bologna, Italy	350 miles	700 miles	15th by 350 miles
Munich, Germany	510 miles	550 miles	15th by 40 miles
Pardubice, Czechoslovakia	600 miles	690 miles	
Ploesti, Rumania	**560 miles**	**1200 miles**	**15th by 640 miles**
Avignon, France	510 miles	520 miles	15th by 10 miles
Sete, France	460 miles	570 miles	15th by 110 miles
Novi Sad, Yugoslavia	330	1150 miles	15th by 820 miles
Frankfort, Germany	720 miles	330 miles	8th by 390 miles
Berlin, Germany	840 miles	510 miles	8th by 330 miles
Paris Airfield, France	850 miles	250 miles	8th by 600 miles
Calais, France	1250 miles	160 miles	8th by 1090 miles
Ascherleben, Germany	700 miles	290 miles	8th by 410 miles
Stuttgart, Germany	560 miles	410 miles	8th by 150 miles
Saarbrucken, Germany	700 miles	315 miles	8th by 385 miles
Caen, France	1150 miles	175 miles	8th by 975 miles
Memmingen, Germany	520 miles	500 miles	8th by 20 miles
Cologne, Germany	800 miles	280 miles	8th by 520 miles

Gallery of Fighters and Bombers

A. The B-17 in flight

D. P-51 Mustang

B. P-38 Lightning one of the best
American fighter planes

E. German Me 109 Fighter - Photo courtesy
Tom Stelzriede

The Ball Turret. This is a view of the ball turret seen from the side and slightly below. The ball could rotate to shoot downward if needed, or to shoot to rear, or in any direction except upwards. The two machine guns fired at the same time.

.

Sally-B on the West airfield side apron.

Both Photos by permission of Martin Claydon 23/04/04

The Sally-B is a flying museum plane in the United Kingdom

B-17 in flight - photo courtesy M. Stelzriede

Controls of B-17 (Stelzriede photo)

Two Views of the B-24 Bombers – The"**Liberators**"

Boeing B-17F-10-BO "Memphis Belle"
USAF Museum Photo Archives
Boeing B-17G "Flying Fortress"
USAF Museum Photo Archives

[1] The bottom photo shows a B-17 in flight. The top photo is the most famous of all B-17s, the Memphis Belle, on tour in the U.S. (Photos from USAF Museum Archives.)

15th AIR FORCE ORGANIZATIONAL CHART
AS OF OCTOBER 1944

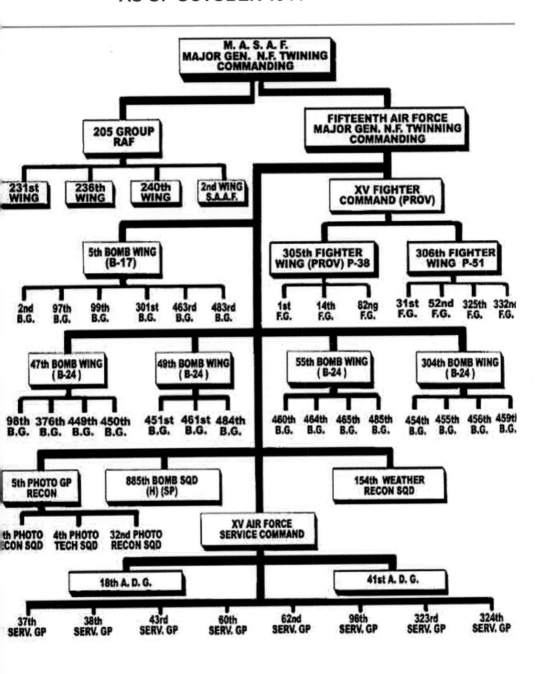